abnormal behavior

perspectives in conflict

Second Edition

Richard H. Price
University of Michigan

HOLT, RINEHART AND WINSTON
New York   Chicago   San Francisco   Dallas
Montreal   Toronto   London   Sydney

ACKNOWLEDGMENTS

Page 36: Photo by Max Halberstadt; courtesy W. E. Freud.

Pages 47–48, 118–119: From N. Cameron, *Personality development and psychopathology*. Boston: Houghton Mifflin, 1963. Copyright © 1963 by Houghton Mifflin Company.

Pages 53–54: From D. Shapiro, *Neurotic styles*. New York: Basic Books, 1965. Copyright © 1965 by Basic Books, Inc.

Page 79: Courtesy of Paul Meehl.

Page 94: Adapted from *Genetic theory and abnormal behavior* by D. Rosenthal. Copyright © 1970 by McGraw-Hill Inc. Used with permission.

Page 95: From *Madness and the brain* by Solomon Snyder. Copyright © 1974 by Solomon Snyder. Used with permission of McGraw-Hill Book Company.

Page 114: Courtesy of Harvard University News Office.

Page 127: From *Helplessness* by Martin E. P. Seligman. W. H. Freeman and Company. Copyright © 1975.

Page 148: Courtesy of Theodore R. Sarbin.

Page 157: Adapted from D. Miller and M. Schwartz, County Lunacy Commission Hearings. *Social Problems*, 1966, 14, 26–35. Copyright © 1966 by The Society for the Study of Social Problems.

Page 161: From "On being sane in insane places," by D. L. Rosenhan. *Science*, 179, 250–258, Jan. 19, 1973. Copyright 1973 by The American Association for the Advancement of Science.

Page 164: From D. Miller and W. H. Dawson, Effect of stigma on re-employment of ex-mental patients. *Mental Hygiene*, 1965, 49, 281–287. Copyright © 1965 by The National Association for Mental Health.

Page 185: By John T. Wood; courtesy of Carl Rogers.

Library of Congress Cataloging in Publication Data

Price, Richard H
  Abnormal behavior.

  Bibliography: p. 255
  Includes indexes.
  1. Psychology, Pathological. I. Title.
RC454.P67   1978   157   77–20504
ISBN 0–03–089964–8

pREfACE

The purpose of this book is to describe a number of different approaches to understanding abnormal behavior. I do not feel that it is possible to make a choice between these competing points of view at this early stage in the development of the field. Rather, I will argue that the advocates of these approaches *see essentially the same set of events from different perspectives.* Thus, my purpose has been to describe and critically examine each of these perspectives rather than to produce yet another polemic arguing for the superiority of some particular view.

I have found two things particularly striking in discussions of the relative merits of different approaches to understanding abnormal behavior. First, these discussions often lack the tentativeness and dispassionate treatment one might expect from behavioral scientists. I believe this is because the commitment to a particular point of view on the nature of abnormal behavior implies or even requires a commitment on the larger question of what it is that makes people human. This is a volatile issue on which even behavioral scientists hold strong opinions.

A second aspect is the degree to which the participants tend to talk past each other. It is common to see disagreements arising over such basic questions as what evidence is relevant or even what assumptions, if any, can be held in common. I think we can understand why advocates of different points of view are often unable to agree, even on basic assumptions, if we examine how they have come to view the problems as they have. I have argued that the views discussed have evolved as a result of a common process of thought. This process shapes our perceptions of events and has more in common with metaphor than it does with the more conventional "model." I have introduced a special meaning for the word "perspective" to emphasize the perceptual and organizing processes operating in these conflicting perspectives.

Both the emotional commitment and the disagreement over fundamental assumptions are hallmarks of what Thomas Kuhn has called the "paradigm clash" in his influential book *The Struc-*

ture of Scientific Revolutions. Paradigm clashes occur in the history of a scientific field when the prevailing view of the problem is challenged by one or more new conceptual schemes. I believe that the field of abnormal psychology is currently experiencing a scientific revolution ·of this kind. At this point we can only guess which, if any, of the perspectives I have discussed will survive the conflict and dominate in the future.

As I suggested at the outset, I have attempted to avoid producing yet another polemic in favor of one view over another, but it should be clear that I am not immune to the influences that I have just described. Writing this book has been an exciting and rewarding task. I only hope that I have been able to communicate some of that excitement to the reader.

Since publication of the first edition, a number of interesting changes in these perspectives has occurred. Even in the behavioral sciences this is a very brief period over which to examine changes in a field. Nevertheless, some of them are instructive. The learning perspective continues to gain advocates even while its emphasis has shifted inward in search of cognitive events that mediate observable behavior. The illness perspective continues to be under attack primarily for the use of medical approaches to the treatment of human problems in living. At the same time, paradoxically, more genetic and biochemical evidence for the origins of some forms of abnormal behavior is accumulating. Finally, the humanistic perspective seems to have been most profoundly affected by the cultural changes in America in the sixties. It is now preoccupied not just with self-actualization, but also with altered states of consciousness.

At the same time, there are things that have not changed since the writing of the first edition. No grand synthesis of views has occurred, nor do I believe it will occur for some time to come. The lack of tentativeness and the fervor of advocacy of various perspectives still remains.

In order to make the second edition more useful as a text, I have added several features. More clinical examples and empirical data have been included to illustrate aspects of each perspective. Tables, figures, and illustrations have also been added where they seemed appropriate. There are now suggested readings at the end of each chapter as well as "Projects for the Reader," which are intended to help bring each perspective to life and to relate it to the reader's own life experience. A glossary has been added for easier reference to key terms.

I want to thank Steven Lynn for his many helpful suggestions in the process of revising the book. His skill and sensitivity as a teacher are especially reflected in a number of the projects for the reader offered at the end of each chapter. I also wish to thank Andrew Crider and Richard Bootzin for their thoughtful reviews of the entire manuscript. Their criticisms were invariably fair and helpful.

Deborah Doty, Roger Williams, and Kathleen Nevils of Holt, Rinehart and Winston shared their enthusiasm and help at various stages of the project, for which I am very grateful.

As with the first edition, I owe the greatest debt to my wife Mary. Not only has she contributed her support and encouragement throughout this task, but her sound editorial judgment and critical skills have given this book whatever clarity of expression it may have.

Richard H. Price

Ann Arbor, Michigan
and
Barnard, Vermont
November 1977

CONTENTS

PART ONE

thinking
about
abnormal
behavior

iNTROduCTioN

PERSPECTIVES IN CONFLICT
SCIENCE AND SOCIETY
PLAN OF THE BOOK
"EMPTY YOUR CUP"

PERSPECTIVES IN CONFLICT

The interview is over. The patient, a balding, slight, thirty-six-year-old man, has answered questions about his early childhood, his hopes, his fears, and his current health and life situation. The experts seated around the table thank him for his patience and excuse him from the staffroom. A nurse leads him from the room. When he has left, the mood in the room changes. Before the experts seemed calm and detached as they asked the patient about his life. Now there is tension in the air. The Chief of Staff opens the discussion by asking for the opinions of the staff.

"It is clear that the man is still struggling with an unresolved Oedipal complex," offers one. "It is one of the most striking examples I have seen."

"Nonsense!" says another. "This man has a learning problem. His repeated loss of jobs is obviously the result of a long and consistent reinforcement history. I recommend that he be referred to our Life Skills Learning Program."

"You are both wrong," snaps a third expert. "This man is obviously a chronic borderline schizophrenic. His disease often produces this periodic pattern of job loss and disorientation."

These three experts all interview the same man and yet they see his problem in radically different ways. It is more than a disagreement about emphasis and detail. Each expert holds fundamentally different assumptions about the nature of abnormal behavior, and each one "sees" this patient through a different set of assumptions about its causes and treatment. The ideas each expert holds and their disagreement itself are the subjects of this book.

Despite the fact that the research literature concerned with the problem of abnormal behavior continues to increase at an enormous rate, no generally accepted view of the problem has yet emerged. In fact, the study of abnormal behavior appears to be undergoing what Kuhn (1962) has described as a "paradigm clash," in which a variety of fundamentally different viewpoints are competing for ascendency. Previously unquestioned assumptions are under attack from a variety of different sources. For example, Solomon Snyder (1975) can say with certainty, "Schizophrenia is a bad disease," while Thomas Szasz (1976) says with equal certainty that mental illness is a myth and that the only thing "wrong" with schizophrenics is their unconventional behavior.

The purpose of this book is to describe a number of different perspectives on abnormal behavior. It is probably not possible to make a choice between these competing points of view at this early stage in the development of the field. I will argue that these approaches see essentially the same set of events from different perspectives. Thus, I do not want to produce another polemic arguing for the superiority of some particular view. Instead, I have chosen to describe these perspectives and to attempt to illustrate how each point of view transforms the "data" of abnormal behavior when it is used to construe a set of events in the life of a single individual.

People hold strong opinions about these matters, and my account may have its own biases. Nevertheless, our discussion is being undertaken in the hope that a discussion of these different points of view will enable others concerned with the problem of abnormal behavior to make their own choices and commitments.

The competition among viewpoints is apparently not unique to the field of abnormal psychology. In fact, there is some reason to believe that it constitutes a distinct stage in the development of most or perhaps all scientific fields of inquiry. Kuhn (1962) argues that

> the early developmental stages of most sciences have been characterized by continual competition between a number of distinct views of nature, each partially derived from, and all roughly compatible with, the dictates of scientific observation and method. What differentiated these various schools was not one or another failure of method—they were all "scientific"—but what we shall come to call the incommensurable ways of seeing the world and practicing science in it (p. 4).

Kuhn's remarks anticipate some themes that will recur in our discussion. Not only is the number of competing points of view increasing in the field of abnormal behavior, but the concerns are not "theoretical" in the usual sense. Most points of contention are pretheoretical—that is, they involve fundamentally different ways of viewing abnormal behavior rather than controversies within a particular point of view.

There are a number of reasons for the development of competing viewpoints in this field. Several views have begun as an attack on the "mental illness" concept of abnormal behavior. Still other views have come about as a result of the increased emphasis upon interdisciplinary approaches to problems in the social and behavioral sciences. Even concerns about personal alienation and social disruption have played a role. Each of these influences has added its voice to the growing controversy and each has brought its own insights to bear on the problem.

SCIENCE AND SOCIETY

Understanding abnormal behavior is both a social and a scientific problem. In asserting this we do not wish to imply that it is always possible to distinguish between scientific and social influences upon current views. In fact, there is much evidence to the contrary. The demands of society and the needs of the scientist interact in complex ways which help to form the bases of our view. To cite only a single example, the current demands placed upon professionals for greater attention to current social conditions (Torrey, 1975) have served as an impetus for a concerted attack on perhaps the most firmly established current view of abnormal behavior, the "illness" or "disease" approach.

While it is true that social and scientific interests are inextricably intertwined in any attempt to understand the problem of abnormal behavior, this state of affairs has led to a number of problems. What passes for theory in the study of abnormal behavior is often mixed with large doses of ideology. Whether this is a beneficial effect is arguable. In any event, theory and ideology are often mistaken for one another, and it is sometimes unclear whether the intent of a particular viewpoint is descriptive or prescriptive.

Consider the following example. Gay liberation and other homosexual rights groups began a campaign in the late sixties and early seventies against the prevailing medical opinion that homosexuality was an illness. In December, 1973, the Board of Trustees of the American Psychiatric Association approved a change in its official manual of psychiatric disorders. Homosexuality, the Trustees voted, would no longer be considered a "psychiatric disorder." Was this a medical judgment or a political response? Did it have more to do with psychiatry or ideology?

Perhaps at this stage it is presumptuous of us to assert that social, political, and ideological considerations should be separated from the presumably more detached enterprise of examining these various perspectives on their own merit as conceptual systems. We may even find that it is not possible to do so. Nevertheless, for the purposes of our discussion the focus is on the perspectives themselves as ways of viewing the phenomena of abnormal behavior. Considerably less attention will be devoted to the social, political, and ideological problems and implications of these approaches. This latter problem is worthy of extended consideration and discussion in its own right, and even a cursory examination of the current professional literature in psychology and psychiatry would reveal that a lively debate is already underway (Denner & Price, 1973; Price & Denner, 1973; Torrey, 1975.)

PLAN OF THE BOOK

In Part One we ask how advocates of different perspectives on abnormal behavior have come to view the problem as they have. It is argued that various views have evolved as the result of a common process of thought. We want to look into the mind of the theorist and try to understand the process by which a particular view develops. This process has more in common with the use of metaphor than it does with the more conventional term "model." A special meaning for the term perspective is introduced to emphasize the influential perceptual and conceptual organizing processes operating in the conceptualization to be discussed.

Part Two discusses the psychoanalytic illness, learning, humanistic, and social perspectives. Each of these chapters is divided into two major sections; the first section describes the perspective and the second provides a critical discussion and elaboration of the perspective.

Part Three provides an overview of the perspectives and considers factors that may influence the future of abnormal psychology. A generalized case history also appears in Part Three. It is then rewritten from the point of view of each of the perspectives discussed in the book. We will use the generalized case history as part of our "raw data" for comparing case histories. The rewritten case histories will provide an illustration of how various perspectives on abnormal behavior mold and shape the raw data of abnormal behavior to fit their particular assumptions and basic metaphors.

Although a relatively large number of competing approaches to the problem of abnormal behavior now exist, I have made no attempt to discuss all of them. Instead, viewpoints which appear to be currently influential or show some promise of becoming influential have been selected.

"EMPTY YOUR CUP"

Before we begin, take a minute to think about this story.

> Nan-in, a nineteenth-century Zen Master, received a learned and famous university professor who had come to inquire about Zen. As Nan-in silently prepared tea, the professor expounded at length on his own philosophies and ideas. Nan-in quietly filled the professor's cup and kept right on pouring. Alarmed at the tea spilling all over, the professor exclaimed, "It's full! No more will go in!"
>
> "Like your cup," Nan-in said, "you are already full of your own opinions and speculations. How can I show you Zen unless you empty your cup?"

Like the university professor, each of us, whether we are aware of it or not, is already full of speculations and opinions about the nature of abnormal behavior. In the chapters that follow, it will be important for us to try to "empty our cups" in order to appreciate the unique contribution of each perspective we will examine.

how do we think about abnormal behavior?

models, metaphors, and perspectives

Rutherford's Discovery

For several years before that spring in 1911, Rutherford and his assistant Geiger had been shooting beams of alpha particles at a sheet of metal. In the Cavendish laboratory in Cambridge, England, Rutherford and other physicists were trying to penetrate the mystery of the atom.

> Rutherford experimented carefully and thought deeply. He did not rush to conclusions, but one day early in 1911, he walked into Geiger's office humming "Onward Christian Soldiers" as he did in moments of singular well-being or triumph. "I know what the atom looks like," he told the astounded Geiger.
> The atom Rutherford could "see" was made up of a tiny center, with a swarm of electrons wheeling around it at great distances. In one of the great feats of scientific imagination Rutherford visualized the atom as a miniature solar system. It was an imposing insight. No one before had suggested that the smallest unit of matter might reflect the architecture of the greatest (Moore, 1966, p. 37).

What goes on in the mind of the theorist that produces that flash of insight when the puzzle becomes clear? In the first chapter we noted that groups of scientists disagree about the fundamental nature of abnormal behavior. In this chapter we will try to look into the mind of the theorist to understand how theorists have arrived at the particular views they hold.

HOW THE THEORIST THINKS: "THEORY FINDING"

Let us try to look into the mind of the theorist. How do advocates of various perspectives actually go about arriving at a particular view of abnormal behavior? In addressing ourselves to this question we will suggest that the different views discussed in this book are reached by a similar process of thinking about the problem. These similarities exist regardless of the view that ultimately emerges. Thus our first task is to present an account of the thought processes of the scientists themselves.

But we are not going to discuss the process of formal theory construction. Indeed, most of the approaches are quite tentative and lacking in detail and do not yet warrant treatment at the level of formal theorizing. In fact, most writers appear to recognize how modest our beginnings actually are; generally they avoid the term "theory" in characterizing what it is they are doing, favoring instead such terms as "model" to describe their view of abnormal behavior.

In order to answer the questions we have posed, we must discuss the concepts of *model, metaphor,* and *perspective.* Each of these concepts involves a common process. In each case, a new, puzzling, or ambiguous situation or set of events is examined in terms of a more familiar concept. This process occurs before any formalized theory of abnormal behavior is possible. As Hanson puts it, "The issue is not theory-using, but theory-finding" (Hanson, 1965, p. 3).

There is another important feature of the use of models, metaphors, and perspectives that we will want to discuss. It is that the *very use* of a metaphoric approach to understanding puzzling events will affect our own way of thinking about the problem at hand. For example, we may find that having arrived at a particular formulation of a problem may make it hard for us to "shift gears" conceptually and take a fresh approach.

Models

The most popular term for describing the conceptualization of abnormal behavior is "model." Perhaps you have heard people refer to the "medical model" or the "learning model" of abnormal behavior. The term "model" has special appeal because of its scientific-sounding character. Perhaps its association with mathematical models has also added to its prestige, despite the fact that some authors (Mandler & Kessen, 1959) have argued that mathematical models are not models at all. In any case, it is fairly clear that most views of abnormal behavior are currently being characterized as models.

We shall examine briefly what is generally meant by this term, look at some examples of models, and discuss some of the functions which models seem to serve. Finally, we shall raise the question of whether the term model is an appropriate characterization of various conceptualizations of abnormal behavior.

The basic character of the model is that it is an analogy. In general, a model may be described as any conceptual analogue which is used to initiate empirical research (Lachman, 1960). When we are confronted with a set of events or a structure we do not understand, we try to give an account of the events or structure that relies upon analogy. Thus we may conceive of the brain *as if* it were a computer, or may think of the heart *as if* it were a pump. In each case we attempt to understand the puzzling events or structures that confront us by thinking of them as if they were other events or structures with which we are more familiar. Look at Table 2–1 for a summary of the use of models in scientific thinking.

TABLE 2–1   The Model in Scientific Thinking

BASIC CHARACTER OF MODELS	EXAMPLES OF A MODEL	FUNCTIONS OF MODELS
1. *Defintion*: A model is any conceptual analogue used to initiate empirical research 2. *Strategy of Models*: Using a set of events or structure to help think about a set of events we do not understand 3. *"As if" quality*: Treats one set of events "as if" it were another set	Thinks of the brain *"as if"* it were a computer (Familiar set of events or structure) Brain Computer "as if" (Unfamiliar set of events or structure)	1. *Aids in selecting events*: *Stimuli* "as if" *input, cortex* "as if" *storage, behavior* "as if" *output* 2. *Provides a mode of representation*: "The cortex is the 'storage component' of the brain" 3. *Aids in organizing events*: "Both behavior and computer output may be corrected via feedback loops"

Of course, we may use analogies to help us understand events that are more broadly conceived or problems that are less well defined than our examples of the heart or brain. For example, we may think of abnormal or deviant behavior as if it were an illness or disease. In using illness as a model, we are attempting to understand a set of events and behaviors which is puzzling to us (that is, abnormal behavior) by assuming that it is analogous to events we understand in more detail (that is, disease or illness).

Functions of Models in Scientific Thinking

Models as we have described them have several functions. First, models help us to *select* certain events as relevant to our inquiry and reject other events as irrelevant. Thus, if we are using an illness model of abnormal behavior, we will select certain behaviors and regard them as "symptoms." Other events will be regarded as irrelevant and will not be regarded as symptoms. For example, other people's reactions to symptoms will not be regarded as directly relevant. These events are usually considered beyond the scope of the illness model and will be ignored.

A second function of models is to supply us with a *mode of representation*. Thus, within the context of an illness model, certain behaviors or patterns of thought or belief may be regarded as "symptomatic." Similarly, certain biological states of individuals regarded as ill will be represented as "etiological" factors. Models help us label parts of the puzzle.

Finally, models aid us in *organizing* the events in question. They help us to specify the relations between events or aspects of the situation that have been selected and represented. For example, if we are using an illness model of abnormal behavior, factors identified as etiological will presumably stand in causal relation to symptoms.

Some Problems of Models

There are a number of difficulties in the use of models. An obvious one is that models invite generalization beyond the scope originally intended (Chapanis, 1961). When this happens models tend to lose their power to clarify the events in question. The very fact that models are merely analogies suggests this. It has been popular, for example, to think about the effects of LSD as a "model psychosis." The idea was that it might be possible to understand psychotic behavior or schizophrenia in particular as if it were an LSD trip. The temptation to generalize this model to other forms of deviant behavior is very great.

Furthermore, models are always incomplete representations. As a result, they seldom encompass all the events in the new or puzzling situation that we wish to have described and represented. This is both a strength and a weakness. Important events may be overlooked, but the simplicity of most models provides a conceptual clarity as well.

Finally, models may specify relations between events that hold or are accurate in the original concept but are not accurate in the new situation we wish to understand. This is an important limitation. We cannot know if our analogy is a good one unless we subject it to empirical test.

In spite of these difficulties we have seen that the model is regarded as the conceptual tool most appropriate to describe how we think about abnormal behavior. It is questionable whether this is the case. Models have one characteristic that most views of abnormal behavior do not exhibit: they are tentative; they have an "as if" character. Models are in the subjunctive mood, whereas most views of abnormal behavior tend to be much more prescriptive and literal (Boring, 1957). For example, we seldom say abnormal behavior *may be viewed as if* it were an illness. Instead, we say that abnormal behavior *is* mental illness. Thus, although the concept of model does share certain characteristics with the way in which various views of abnormal behavior are formulated, it is not an accurate description of how these views are first established and are then developed. Instead, we would argue that various views of abnormal behavior much more closely resemble metaphors than they do analogies.

Metaphors

As we have said, the term "model" has become popular as a way of describing how we come to make puzzling events comprehensible. Metaphor, on the other hand, more adequately describes the scientist's thought processes.

Most people think of metaphor as a literary device, an ornament in writing a poem or perhaps a short story. Because of this literary association that we have to the idea of metaphor, it seems somehow "unscientific." This bias may be yet another example of what C. P. Snow (1969) meant when he described the domain of the arts as "two cultures." But perhaps the process of discovery is not so different in science and art.

A metaphor is a form of speech in which a term is transferred directly from the object it ordinarily designates to an entirely new context. We are using a metaphor when we use the phrase, "the evening of life," or when we say, "All the world's a stage." The effect of metaphor on our thinking is powerful. It transforms our thinking about the object in a single stroke, calling up new associations and often helping us to see the object in new ways. As we will discover, scientists as well as poets often use metaphor in searching for new insights into the puzzling phenomena of abnormal behavior.

Some writers have discussed the concept of metaphor and its role in the emergence of new concepts. Cassirer (1946) has discussed what he calls the "radical metaphor," and some of his views have been elaborated and extended by Turbayne (1962), Schon (1963), and Mehrabian (1968). We will discuss the role of metaphor in the emergence of new concepts and attempt to examine how metaphors help to structure the new or strange.

Metaphoric Thinking in the Process of Discovery

When we refer to the concept of metaphor as a means of arriving at an understanding of phenomena we view metaphor as a *process of thought,* similar to the views of Schon (1963) and Cassirer (1946). This process of thought involves understanding new or puzzling events in terms of more familiar concepts. In this way, the function of metaphor is quite similar to that of models. But as we shall see, the concept of metaphor goes far beyond the idea of analogy or model. It has quite different effects on how we think about the problem of formulating a view of abnormal behavior—or of any problem for that matter. Table 2–2 summarizes some of the important points in the discussion to follow.

Schon (1963) describes the metaphoric process of thought as the "displacement of concepts," and identifies four phases. He makes it clear that these are not necessarily discrete events and may not follow each other in a fixed order. Instead, these phases may be thought of as different aspects of a complex process of thought.

The first phase is *transposition.* Transposition occurs when an old concept is shifted to a new situation and symbolic relations between the old situation and the new situation are first estab-

TABLE 2–2

BASIC CHARACTER OF METAPHORS IN SCIENTIFIC THINKING	EXAMPLES OF THE STAGES OF METAPHORIC THINKING	FUNCTIONS OF METAPHORS
1. *Definition:* The literal application of a concept to a new or unknown situation 2. *A process of thought* in which new or puzzling events are understood in terms of more familiar concepts 3. *Literal* not tentative; they assert that the new event is an instance of the older, more familiar concept	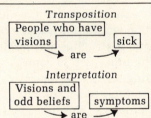 *Interpretation* *Correction* "Not all unconventional beliefs are symptoms; and beliefs and attitudes may qualify as symptoms" *Spelling out the metaphor* "Since people who have odd beliefs and visions are sick, they should be treated in a hospital"	As in the case of models, (1) *selects events;* (2) *provides a mode of representation;* and (3) *organizes events;* (4) *transforms both* structures (our ideas of visionaries and of sickness have been altered); (5) *Fixes our view of the new situation* (it is harder to think about visionaries as not being sick; (6) *Makes the new conceptualization seem real;* "we must discover a cure for mental illness"

lished. This is the making of the metaphor. For example, when we first identify odd and puzzling behavior in terms of illness we are transposing an old and familiar concept, that of illness, to a new situation. Transposition is not an all-or-none process, but instead involves a gradual transfer of clusters of concepts.

The second phase is *interpretation*. Interpretation involves assigning a term from the old and more familiar cluster of concepts to a specific aspect of the new situation. We may, for example, interpret a bizarre act or verbalization as a "symptom." Interpretation is distinguishable from transposition as a single "gesture" or act. Thus, when we transpose the concept of illness to the new situation of puzzling or odd behavior, we simultaneously transpose and interpret. Transposition and interpretation, then, are actually different aspects of the same act.

Once an old concept has been transposed and interpreted, it will not necessarily produce a good "fit." Both the new situation and the old concept require adjustment. For example, all the concepts that form the cluster of ideas we associate with "illness" may not apply in the new situation. As a result, they may be dropped in the application of the illness concept.

This leads us to the third phase described by Schon, *correction*. Correction is a two-way process. That is, the old concept is not simply corrected in terms of the new situation nor is the new situation corrected only in terms of the old concept. Instead, there is a process of mutual adaptation. As the old concept is elaborated and the new situation is structured in terms of the old concept, and as each modifies the other, we become less and less aware of the fact that we are using terms in a figurative sense only.

Schon calls the final phase in the displacement of concepts *spelling out the metaphor*. This phase involves examining areas of similarity and difference in the old concept and the new situation. At this point more elaboration of the metaphor occurs and a relatively complete description of the new situation is established in its terms.

Once the four phases of transposition, interpretation, correction, and spelling out the metaphor have occurred, abnormal behavior *is* illness. The metaphor, too, is itself transformed. At this point formal theorizing may begin. As we have seen, the scientist has done a great deal of thinking before he can undertake formal theorizing. In fact, much of the conceptual work is already finished before formal theory construction has begun. But the work of discovery is largely finished.

Functions of Metaphors in Scientific Thinking

From this description of the process of metaphor in scientific thought, we should be able to list certain functions that the metaphor serves. In describing these functions we wish to indicate not only the abstract functions of metaphor but also to show *how the use of metaphor affects our thinking* about the problem of abnormal behavior. This aspect of metaphor has been largely ignored; yet, as we shall see, it has a profound effect on the nature of the views we ultimately adopt.

The metaphor as a process of thought shares some of its functions with analogy. Both metaphor and analogy aid us in selecting events as relevant. Also, both metaphor and analogy provide us with a mode of representation of the events in question. Finally, both metaphor and analogy help us in organizing these events; that is, they help us to specify the relations between the events identified by the metaphor or analogy.

We may identify, however, at least three other functions that are unique to the metaphor as a process of thought. First, when we use metaphor the original concept we apply to the new situation *is itself transformed*. There is an interplay between the old concept and the new situation in a process of mutual adjustment to each other. Thus, in the case of metaphor, the original concept is transformed, and we may say that a "new" concept emerges. For example, when we assert that abnormal behavior *is* mental illness, the behaviors in question are viewed differently. They come to be viewed as manifestations of illness. But the concept of illness itself is transformed. We no longer think of illness as physical illness. We do not regard physical illness and mental illness as identical. This transformation of the original concept occurs as it adjusts itself to the new events to which it is applied. In the case of the analogy the original concept is not altered but remains essentially the same as it was before being applied to the new situation. For example, our concept of computer is not altered by its application in analogy to the brain. Thus we see that metaphor and analogy differ in that with the former, an interplay between the old concept and the new situation transforms the old concept and, in effect, produces a new concept which is both similar to and different from the original.

A second function unique to metaphor is that it *fixes our view of the situation in question*. Once our view of the metaphor is established, further inquiry into the meaning of the events in question tends to stop. We tend not to look for new ways of construing the events in question. Once we have established that the behavior in question is mental illness, we tend not to question this construction. In contrast, the tentativeness of analogy does not fix our view of the events as rigidly. Because analogy is in the subjunctive mood, we often continue to search for yet another analogy to describe the events in question.

A third unique function of the metaphor is that it *makes the new construction seem very real to us.* Once the events in question are identified by the metaphor and the process of the displacement of concepts is underway, the new construction begins to take on a reality of its own. Once the metaphor of mental illness is established, we do not doubt its reality. Similarly, the reality of symptoms as discrete entities is not questioned once the metaphor is established.

These three characteristics of metaphors have what we will call a *perceptual* aspect. This is the psychological effect of metaphor which we mentioned earlier. Once the metaphor is established and the displacement of concepts is underway we tend to *see* the events differently. Because of the unique functions of metaphor in transforming the original concept, making the events real, and fixing our view of the events, we now *see* abnormal behavior as mental illness.

Perspectives

There is a feature of metaphor as we have described it that is particularly striking. This is the *perceptual* effect of metaphor. Because adherents of differing views of abnormal behavior seem to experience the same events in radically different ways and because they tend to see the behaviors and events in question in terms of their own metaphor, we wish to emphasize the perceptual effects of metaphor. Therefore in order to characterize the way in which investigators think about the problem of abnormal behavior, it is appropriate to use the term *perspective.*

Concepts and their application to new situations have a Gestalt character. When we view a relatively ambiguous set of events, our view of those events tends to be structured in terms of the concepts we apply to those events. Our experience is structured by that concept.

Hanson (1965, p. 5) brings our point home forcibly when he poses the following situation:

Let us consider Johannes Kepler: imagine him on a hill watching the dawn. With him is Tycho Brahe. Kepler regarded the sun as fixed: it was the earth that moved. But Tycho followed Ptolemy and Aristotle in this much at least: the earth was fixed and all other celestial bodies moved around it. Do Kepler and Tycho see the same thing in the east at dawn?

Of course the answer to Hanson's question is no. Kepler and Tycho see the dawn in terms of their own conceptions of the nature of the universe. Similarly, we would argue that advocates of differing conceptions of abnormal behavior see the same events quite differently. *Their perspectives are structured by the metaphor they use to construe the events in question.* We tend to notice those aspects of the new situation that are identified in the displacement of the concept and not to notice those aspects that are not identified by the concept.

Learning How Perspectives Work

To clarify this idea we can use the example of an ambiguous figure. Once we look at an ambiguous figure (for example, Figure 2–1) as a vase, our experience of the ambiguous structure tends to conform with our concept. If we are told, on the other hand, that what we are looking at is a picture of two faces in profile, we may shift our experience as a result of the introduction of this

FIG. 2–1

new concept. It is interesting to note, however, that no matter how hard we try, we cannot experience the ambiguous figures in both ways at the same time. It is either a vase or it is two faces in profile. We cannot experience it as both simultaneously. But what has changed? Nothing physical or optical has changed. The process of metaphor has a similar effect on our construction of events. We come to "see" the events in terms of our concept, which becomes real for us and is very resistant to change.

A recent study by Chun and Sarbin (1970) illustrates nicely how metaphors may, although they begin as tentative formulations, take on a literal quality. The study presented experimental subjects with brief scientific reports. Both the titles and the contents were made to be either obscure or familiar. In each of the reports there were a number of statements containing "as if" qualifiers. Chun and Sarbin predicted that, in the cases in which either the title, the content, or both were obscure, the subjects would reproduce the stories with a higher frequency of "metaphor to myth transformations." That is, the carefully qualified "as if" statements would be transformed to literal statements in reproduction. The findings confirmed Chun and Sarbin's predictions both for immediate and delayed reproduction of the stories.

The views of abnormal behavior presented in this book share many of the characteristics of metaphor as we have described it. Most views of abnormal behavior at their current stage of development are attempts to structure ambiguous and puzzling events in terms of a fundamental concept or metaphor.

Why did we begin with a discussion of how scientists arrive at their views rather than just getting on with a discussion of one or another perspective? There are several answers. First, our discussion should help to characterize the stage that most thinking about abnormal behavior seems to have reached at this point. Second, our discussion should help us to arrive at some answers to two puzzling but related questions.

First, *why do advocates of different perspectives have such difficulty in communicating with one another?* Enthusiastic supporters of various perspectives have great difficulty going beyond polemics in their discussions. It is not hard to find evidence for this difficulty in communication. Often partisans of various views will say that a different view has "missed the point," or that their opponents are not addressing themselves to the "real" issues. A typical reaction to criticism of one's preferred position is to argue that the criticism fails to "explain" the phenomenon in question.

The remarks of Wiest (1967) in defending a behavioral point of view provides a case in point.

> Examination of criticisms by Breger and McGaugh, Chomsky, and others reveals that many of them contain errors of fact and interpretation, or stem from a confusion of observation and inference. *Providing pseudoexplanations by mere naming* is another phenomenon frequently found in mentalistic reformulations of behavior theory (p. 214, italics added).

Or note the opening remarks offered by Szasz (1961) in his attack on the concept of mental illness. "I submit that the traditional definition of psychiatry, which is still in vogue, places it alongside such things as alchemy and astrology, and commits it to the category of pseudo science" (p. 1).

These remarks suggest that even greater controversy rather than greater understanding is being generated by such discussions. This difficulty in communication is perplexing. But if one accepts the perceptual character of metaphor which we have described, it becomes clear that different advocates quite literally see the same problem differently. All of the advocates see the problem in terms of the central concepts of their own perspective. In constructing reality in their own way, they arrive at a view that is very resistant to competing viewpoints resulting from competing perspectives.

Second, *why is it so difficult to choose on an empirical basis between differing views?* The traditional means for solving scientific disputes involves making a differential prediction from competing theories or viewpoints. The predictions may then be tested by examining relevant evidence; the data serve to resolve the issue. This mode of resolution has seldom been used in attempts to choose between competing perspectives on abnormal behavior.

By now the answer to this question should be obvious. The same set of puzzling behaviors viewed from the two different perspectives may have little or no overlap in terms of the events which are considered by each perspective to be relevant. As a result differential predictions about the same events based on two different perspectives may be very difficult to formulate. The problem is a basic one: If two perspectives do not agree about what constitutes relevant data concerning the nature of abnormal behavior, settling the controversy by empirical methods is impossible.

A LOOK AHEAD

In examining a variety of perspectives on abnormal behavior we have several general goals in mind. First, we will present the basic assumptions, definitions, and language associated with each perspective. Second, we will show how each perspective "works" when we apply it to a set of events and behaviors.

But we will also need examples. As Kuhn (1962) suggests, new theories and concepts are never presented without a reference to a set of concrete phenomena.

> Scientists, it should already be clear, never learn concepts, laws, and theories in the abstract and by themselves. Instead, these intellectual tools are from the start encountered in a historically and pedagogically prior unit *that displays them with and through their applications.* A new theory is always announced together with applications to some concrete range of phenomena; *without them it would not be even a candidate for acceptance* (p. 46, italics added).

The traditional device for illustration is the case history, a document that has the advantage of being familiar to students of abnormal behavior. The ideal case history for our purposes should allow us *to examine the same events from each of the various perspectives we wish to discuss.* We could then observe how each perspective selects and construes the events described. This approach bears a great deal of resemblance to what Kelly (1963) has described as "constructive alternativism." He says, "We take the stand that there are always some alternative constructions available to choose among in dealing with the world" (p. 15).

A device that might allow us to view the same events from each perspective is what we call a *generalized case history.* It should make an attempt to describe events with theoretical neutrality and should be written as much as possible in everyday descriptive language. It should also have sufficient scope to allow for the selection of events by different perspectives and will therefore include more events than any single perspective would consider relevant.

In the last chapter you will find a generalized case history. It tells the story of Amy J. The story is told in a general form. After the generalized case history, Amy's story has been rewritten from the point of view of each of the perspectives we will learn about. You will have a chance to see each perspective in action as it selects, organizes, and interprets the events in Amy's life from its own point of view.

Suggested Reading

1. Hanson, N. R. *Patterns of Discovery.* New York: Cambridge University Press, 1965.
   Hanson offers a readable and insightful discussion of how he believes scientists develop their ideas.
2. Kuhn, T. S. *The Structure of Scientific Revolutions.* Chicago: University of Chicago Press, 1962.
   Thomas Kuhn's book has had a great impact on the social sciences. Although all of his examples are drawn from the physical sciences, many social scientists believe his account of "paradigm clash" fits their current situation.

LEARNING MORE
Projects for the Reader

1. One of the best ways for you to learn more about how analogies and metaphors shape your thinking is to apply an analogy to the concept of abnormal behavior. Consider the following sentence, "Abnormal behavior is just like a _____."

Now apply some analogies of your own by filling in the blank with a term of your own choosing. Or try a couple of these: (a) bad habit; (b) LSD trip; (c) high fever; (d) divinely inspired insight; (e) ignorance of proper rules of etiquette.

Try to spell out the analogy in each case. For example, if you are trying out the analogy, "abnormal behavior is just like a bad habit," what *other* ideas about abnormality does the analogy lead you to think about?

2. Once we have applied and tried to elaborate a particular analogy, some "cause" of abnormal behavior is almost immediately suggested to us. Try this sentence: "If abnormal behavior is really like a _____, then the cause(s) of abnormal behavior is (are) likely to be _____." Fill in the first blank with an analogy and see if you can "discover" the cause of abnormal behavior suggested in each case.

3. Not only are causes suggested by the application of an analogy, so are cures. In order to see how this works, try the following sentence: "If abnormal behavior is like a _____, then the most likely cure or the thing to be changed is _____." Fill in each analogy and see what "cures" are suggested to you.

PART TWO

THE PERSPECTIVES

3

tHE psyCHOANALYTIC pERSPECTIVE

THE DISCOVERY OF THE UNCONSCIOUS

It is Vienna just before the turn of the century. A young woman is lying on a couch in a hypnotic trance. Her eyes are closed and she is talking in a slightly slurred but intelligible voice. Two men sit nearby, listening intently. She is describing a bedroom in which her father lay dying. Her memory is vivid and details come easily. She recalls herself sitting all night by the bed and her feelings of anguish at her father's impending death. She is crying now as she recalls that painful night. During the night, she says, her legs fell asleep in an uncomfortable chair and she found it difficult to rise and walk.

Freud and Breuer look at each other incredulously. She could remember none of this before. Yet now, under the influence of hypnosis, she is able to recall the scene in great detail. Her current hysterical symptom, paralysis of the legs, seemed somehow tied to the traumatic night some time ago. Clearly, the "cathartic method" of recall under hypnosis is a powerful therapeutic tool, and this recollection represents a turning point in the woman's treatment.

But perhaps even more important, Freud and Breuer knew they had made a discovery. Before the hypnotic session the woman had no recollection of the scene she had just described in such detail. It was out of awareness, in the unconscious. And still, even while outside of conscious awareness, the memory seemed to play a role in the young woman's current paralysis. The dis-

covery of unconscious processes and their role in the determination of abnormal behavior was now established. Not long afterward, in 1893, Freud and Breuer published their groundbreaking
paper, *On the Psychical Mechanisms of the Hysterical Phenomena,*
and the psychoanalytic movement began.

THE PERSPECTIVE

There is little question that the psychoanalytic perspective developed by Sigmund Freud stands today as one of the most influential
approaches to the study of abnormal behavior. The intellectual
daring and breadth of Freud's theories place him in the first rank
of modern thinkers along with Einstein, Darwin, and Marx. His
writings, over nearly the entire first half of the twentieth century,
have radically altered the way Western people view themselves.

Recently both historians and psychoanalysts have begun to use
psychoanalytic concepts in writing historical biographies. These
writers find the ideas of psychoanalysis helpful in understanding
early formative experiences of historical figures. The writing of
"psychohistory," as practiced, for example, by Erik Erikson in his
biography of *Ghandi's Truth* (1969), has stimulated major intellectual movement in this direction.

The impact of Freud's thinking is not limited to professionals
or academics. His ideas and language have become part of our culture. A great many people today have at least a rudimentary idea
of Freud's fundamental concepts. Terms such as "Freudian slip,"
"ego," and "unconscious" are commonplace in our everyday language.

In addition, Freud's thinking has had an impact on art, medicine, literature, child-rearing practices, and the social sciences.
His insights have been used by social critics such as Herbert
Marcuse (1955, 1964) and by historians such as E. R. Dodds (1951,
1965). The influence of Freudian thinking on the social scientist
has recently been discussed in an excellent review by Hall and
Lindzey (1968, pp. 245–319).

Despite, or perhaps because of, the enormous impact of
Freud's thinking, the psychoanalytic perspective is now coming
under heavy attack. Both critics and leading psychoanalysts acknowledge the declining importance of psychoanalysis in psychiatric thinking. For example, Dr. Thomas Szasz has been quoted
(Leo, 1968) as saying, "Psychoanalysis is vanishing. It's as mori-
bund and irrelevant as the Liberal party in England." Similarly,

Dr. Judd Marmor has stated (Leo, 1968) that psychoanalysis is in danger of "receding into an unimportant side street" of psychiatry. Virulent attacks on psychoanalysis have come from a number of different quarters. An excellent example of such an attack is Andrew Salter's book *The Case Against Psychoanalysis* (1963).

Attack from other quarters has come from feminist writers and social critics. Germaine Greer has, for instance, been a leading critic of psychoanalytic theory. She and other feminist writers argue that Freud's generalizations concerning "penis envy" by female children are false and merely a product of Freud's ingrained assumptions regarding male supremacy.

Within the field of abnormal psychology Freud's thinking has had at least two effects. First, a variety of theorists have explicated and extended Freud's original thinking in their formulations concerning abnormal behavior. Two examples of such theorists are Fenichel, whose book *The Psychoanalytic Theory of Neurosis* (1945) is generally regarded as the single most authoritative account of a psychoanalytic view of neuroses, and Norman Cameron, who after a training analysis felt compelled to revise his views of abnormal behavior in the direction of psychoanalytic thinking. The result of this "conversion" is his text, *Personality Development and Psychopathology* (1963).

The psychoanalytic perspective has also had a heuristic impact of a different kind. Several proponents of newer perspectives on abnormal behavior have used Freud's ideas as a point of departure from which to launch their own competing ideas. We shall discuss this impact of Freud's thinking on other perspectives later in this chapter. Perhaps it is a tribute to Freud's influence that advocates of competing perspectives have found it necessary to attack his views in order to clarify and lend credence to their own.

Before beginning our discussion of the psychoanalytic perspective, a number of remarks are necessary. As Holzman (1970) has pointed out, psychoanalysis is not a single perspective but really a group of perspectives, focusing on three general areas. First, there is a group of ideas concerned with the nature of thinking and perception. Second, Freud formulated a series of propositions concerned with human development. And finally, a portion of Freud's thinking was devoted to the nature of psychopathology and its treatment. Together these assumptions are often referred to as the "metapsychology."

It is usually considered necessary for an adequate understanding of Freud's thinking to consider his work in historical perspective, since over the nearly fifty years of his work Freud's ideas underwent constant revision and evolution. But our description of the psychoanalytic perspective, while it will attempt a synthesis of his most important ideas concerning psychopathology, will be largely an ahistorical account. A number of excellent sources that examine the historical evolution of Freud's thinking are available. See, for example, Holzman's book *Psychoanalysis and Psychopathology* (1970). As a supplement to any historical analysis of Freud's thinking, an understanding of Freud the man is also helpful. For this purpose unquestionably the finest source is Ernest Jones' three-volume biography of Freud (1953, 1955, 1957).

Freud and the psychoanalytic movement is cast in still another light in the recently edited volume of letters exchanged by Freud and Jung. These two giants of psychoanalysis at first actively collaborated and finally parted enemies, unable to reconcile their theoretical and personal differences.

BOX 3-1
Language and Concepts of the Psychoanalytic Perspective

Unconscious The portion of the psychological structure of the individual where repressed or forgotten memories or desires reside. These memories or desires are not directly available to consciousness but can be made available through psychoanalysis or hypnosis.

Id The reservoir of instinctual drives in the psychological structure of the individual. It is the most primitive and most inaccessible structure of the personality.

Ego That part of the psychological structure which is usually described as the "self." It is the aspect of the personality that mediates between the needs of the id and reality.

Superego That structure of the personality which is concerned with ethical and moral feelings and attitudes. The superego is usually identified with the "conscience."

Pleasure principle In Freudian theory, the demand that an instinctual need be gratified at once. The principle that guides the id.

Reality principle Means by which ego balances the person's pursuit of gratification with the demands of external reality.

Neurotic anxiety Reaction when the ego is aroused by its perception of the possibility of being overwhelmed by the instincts of the id. Free-floating anxiety, phobia, and panic reactions are all forms of neurotic anxiety.

Defense mechanism A reaction designed to maintain the individual's feelings of adequacy and to reduce anxiety. Defense mechanisms operate at an unconscious level and tend to distort reality. Examples are denial, projection, reaction formation, regression, and repression.

Repression One of the fundamental defense mechanisms. Repression removes psychologically painful ideas from the individual's awareness. Dangerous desires or intolerable memories are kept out of consciousness by this mechanism as well.

Regression Retreat to an earlier stage of development in behavior to allow the id impulses expression at a level not possible at higher levels of development.

Basic Assumptions

The psychoanalytic perspective is based on a number of fundamental assumptions about human behavior, and we are going to begin our discussion with a number of them. Several writers, including Munroe (1955), Rapaport and Gill (1967), and Holzman (1970), have summarized these assumptions. A number of these may appear commonplace to us today, but it is important to realize that although some of these ideas were not original with Freud, he was the first to bring them together to bear on the problem of abnormal behavior.

Unconscious Psychological Processes

The hysterical paralysis of the young woman treated by Freud and Brewer is an example of the operation of unconscious processes. Slips of the tongue, sudden lapses of memory, and symbolic events in dreams are also thought to be due to *psychological processes operating outside our conscious awareness.*

The concept of unconscious psychological processes was not new with Freud. Herbert and Helmholtz, among others, had suggested the existence of psychological processes which occur without the awareness of the individual. But two sorts of data especially convinced Freud of the need for a concept like the unconscious. His observations concerning post-hypnotic phenomena and the failures of many neurotic patients to recall crucial events in their lives both convinced him that psychological processes often occurred in individuals without being available to their awareness.

In fact, Freud developed the ideas of *unconscious, preconscious,* and *conscious* mental activity as portrayed in Figure 3–1. Conscious mental activity refers to immediate experience, what

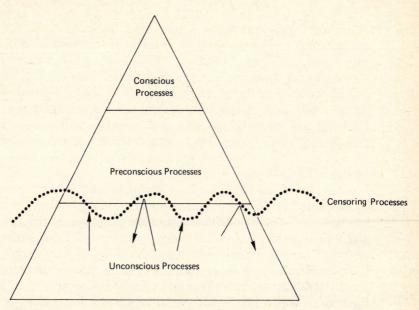

FIG. 3–1   Relationship between the unconscious, preconscious, and conscious domains of psychological life.

you are experiencing right now. Although this experience is most easily accessible, it also comprises the smallest amount of mental life.

The preconscious mental domain includes all those events, thoughts, ideas, and memories outside immediate awareness but which are available to you. Thus, although you remember a friend's telephone number or the color of a sweater, it is preconscious, and not always in your awareness. Finally, the largest domain of mental activity is the unconscious. The unconscious is a vast reservoir of childhood and current memories, fears, hopes, wishes, impulses, and thoughts that are seldom if ever available to one's consciousness. In fact Freud believed that these thoughts are kept out of awareness by a *censoring process* that protects the person from the threats of unacceptable unconscious wishes or threatening impulses.

Freud was aware that unconscious processes could only be inferred from observable psychological phenomena, and that the unconscious itself could never be directly observed. Futhermore, he believed that unconscious ideas were subject to distortion and unlike conscious ideas often lacked a logical relation to one another. Many of the apparently illogical events in dreams illustrate this quality.

Unlike previous writers who had invoked the concept of unconscious processes, Freud was inclined to give them a primary role as determinants of behavior. Other writers had suggested that although unconscious processes might exist, they were of secondary importance in the psychological life of the individual. Freud, on the other hand, perhaps because of his unique experiences with hypnosis and neurotic patients, was convinced that unconscious processes played a dominant role in determining behavior.

Behavior Is Purposive

For Freud, all behavior, both neurotic and normal, was seen as motivated or caused. Freud's causal statements about behavior attempted to describe both the present purposes of the behavior and its earlier determinants. Thus, symptoms did not simply appear but served a purpose. Often the purpose of symptoms as Freud saw them was to avoid painful memories or thoughts. His sensitivity and perceptiveness as a clinician allowed him to notice the way in which symptoms sometimes had a logic of their own.

Conflict of Motives

Freud believed people were continually struggling with conflicts within themselves. He saw these conflicts as occurring between opposing motives or drives. For example, he was particularly impressed with the fact that his patients often experienced conflicts between sexual drives and the constraints of reality. Once opposing drives were in conflict they seemed not to be openly expressed; nevertheless Freud saw the drives as remaining in force although blocked and out of awareness. Furthermore, the form that conflicts took within an individual changed as the person developed from childhood into adulthood. During development these conflicts became entirely internalized. Thus the conflicts which Freud's patients experienced were intrapsychic and existed totally within the individual.

Developmental Nature

As Holzman (1970) puts it, for every person the "past persists into the present." Thus, a psychoanalytic understanding of any behavior or symptom requires the tracing of its history. The behavior or symptom under consideration is understandable only in terms of the behavior or previous events from which it has developed. In addition, previous solutions or compromises of an intrapsychic conflict were thought to continue from the past into the present life of the individual. Some motives, aims, or drives may be "frozen" or *fixated* at infantile levels of development and may persist in their relatively undifferentiated form in the adult life of the individual. Freud believed that an understanding of such fixations is only possible when one looks at human behavior from a developmental point of view.

The Quantitative Aspects of Behavior

Freud assumed that drives or needs may differ in their intensity or quantity. The variations in the apparent intensity of suffering among his patients and the marked differences in their concern with themselves or the world around them led Freud to postulate his quantitative aspect of behavior. For Freud this was a crucial assumption since he regarded "abnormal" behavior as only quantitatively different from normal behavior. Thus, the distinction between what we call abnormal and normal behavior was a matter of degree, not kind.

Behavior as an Adaptation

Despite the fact that the psychoanalytic perspective is to a very large degree intrapsychic, Freud did not ignore the influence of the external environment on behavior. Instead, he argued that human behavior must be understood as a response to the demands placed on the person by both the physical and the social environment. This principle has been described by Rapaport and Gill (1967) as the *adaptative point of view*.

These basic principles or assumptions about human behavior lay the groundwork for the psychoanalytic perspective. They comprise Freud's most fundamental ideas about human nature. These themes will recur repeatedly as we examine the psychoanalytic perspective and its unique view of the character and genesis of abnormal behavior.

Stages of Psychosexual Development

The origins of adult fears, hopes, peculiarities, and virtues could be found in the early development of the child, according to the psychoanalytic view. Even before a child can speak or reason, it is engaged in a continual struggle to meet its own biological needs and to gain love and approval from its caretakers. These early struggles of life leave their marks on the character of the person and Freud believed they were of fundamental importance.

Consistent with his basic assumption concerning the importance of psychological development, Freud postulated a series of

Sigmund Freud on the Function of the Ego

"The constructive function [of the ego] consists in interposing between the demand made by an instinct and the action that satisfies it, an intellective activity which, after considering the present state of things and weighing up earlier experiences, endeavors . . . to calculate the consequences of the proposed line of conduct." (Freud, 1940, 1949)

developmental stages, usually called the psychosexual stages of development. The term "sexual" as it is used by Freud has a much broader meaning than the term usually connotes. It refers not only to the stimulation of the genital area but also of other erogenous zones. The principal erogenous zones were thought to be the mouth, the anus, and the genital organs.

Freud believed that the erogenous zones were important for the development of personality because they are the first sources of excitation with which the child must contend. In addition, actions that the child undertakes involving the erogenous zones may lead to parental censure. The child must deal with the resulting frustration and anxiety that may occur, and these initial modes of coping are of great importance in later development. Thus, the parents' concerns with the child's eating, elimination, and genital manipulation are assumed to have great impact on how the child comes to cope with problems later in life.

Freud differentiated three pregenital stages of development: the *oral stage*, the *anal stage*, and the *phallic stage*. Following the phallic stage, a period of 5 or 6 years (called the period of *latency*) occurs, when the dynamics of development are more or less stabilized. Following the latency period comes the final stage of development, the *genital stage*, during adolescence. Table 3–1 sketches

TABLE 3–1 Stages of Psychosexual Activity
in the Psychoanalytic Perspective

STAGE OF PSYCHOSEXUAL DEVELOPMENT	EROGENOUS ZONE	PROTOTYPICAL ACTIVITY	LATER PERSONALITY
Oral Stage (0–2 yrs.)	Mouth	Sucking; incorporation; biting	Oral-incorporative; "sucker"; aggressive; oral-sadistic
Anal Stage (2–3 yrs.)	Anal sphincter	Urge for elimination; strict toilet training rewarded	Anal-retentive or expulsive; productive; creative
Phallic (4–5 yrs.)	Genital organs	Masturbation; autoerotic activity; castration fear; penis envy	Oedipus complex; Electra complex; later relations with men and women

the major psychosexual stages and summarizes their most important features.

The Oral Stage

During the first year of life the predominant erogenous zone is the mouth. Children gratify their hunger through sucking and often incorporate objects into their mouths for the pleasurable tactile stimulation the objects provide. Later, as the children develop teeth, biting also becomes an important function in the oral stage. As Munroe (1955) points out, the Freudian perspective argues that most modes of relating to objects are derived from the oral stage of development.

The two basic modes of oral activity, incorporation and biting, may become "prototypes" for later character traits. Thus, the child who is fixated on an incorporative mode of development may later develop an "oral incorporative" personality. For example, this child may be gullible and therefore "swallow" almost anything he or she is told. On the other hand, if the child is fixated in the biting mode, oral aggression may become the dominant character trait. The child later may become a person who indulges in argumentativeness or verbal hostility. Since the child is almost entirely dependent on the mother for protection and sustenance, the oral stage of development also may have important effects on later adult feelings of dependency.

The Anal Stage

In the second and third year of development, the child begins to focus on the pressure upon the anal sphincter as a source of discomfort or as a source of erotic pleasure. The natural mode of relieving this discomfort is defecation. However, coincidentally toilet training is initiated by the parents. This usually represents the first instance in which the child must learn to regulate an instinctual impulse; consequently one of the important conflicts between the parents and child occurs.

As toilet training proceeds, the crucial developmental issue is the nature of the relationship between the parents and the child. If the parents are extremely strict and harsh in their methods, the child may hold back his feces and this mode of handling anal elimination becomes a prototype for later behavior. The child may develop a retentive character in later life, or on the other hand, he or she may, because of frustration and anger at repressive toilet training methods, develop what has been called an "anal expulsive" character organization, as an extension of having expelled the feces at inappropriate times during the anal stage. Freud also believed that if the parents praise the child for production of feces, the child will come to believe that this is an important activity and the product a valuable one. The effect of this mode of parental training in the character of the individual may become the basis for creativity or productivity.

The Phallic Stage

During the fourth and fifth years of the child's development, the genital organs become the principal source of satisfaction for the child. The child begins to engage in masturbation and autoerotic activity. The phallic stage is the stage in which the Oedipus complex develops. In general, the Oedipus complex involves the sexual attraction to the parent of the opposite sex and anger or hostility toward the parent of the same sex. Thus, the boy wishes to possess his mother and displace his father, whereas the girl wishes to possess her father and displace her mother. For Freud the Oedipus complex was a crucial determinant of later adult attitudes toward the opposite sex and toward people in authority.

In the case of the boy, he imagines that his father is a rival who may harm him for his desire of his mother. Since the genital organs are the major focus of this period, the child associates sensations from his genital organs with his affectionate feeling for his mother. He also fears that his father will remove the offending organs. This Freud described as "castration anxiety." Because of his fear of castration, the boy comes to repress his sexual desire for his mother and to identify with his father.

For the girl, the Oedipus complex has a somewhat different sequence of development. As she discovers that a boy possesses an exterior sexual organ while she possesses none, she holds her mother responsible for her castrated condition. Furthermore, she comes to view her father as a love object because he has the valued organ she wishes to have herself. She also is envious of her father and all other males because they have something she does not. This envy Freud called "penis envy." The Oedipus complex of the girl does not undergo repression as it did for the boy. Instead, it undergoes some slight modification during this period because of the realistic constraints against sexual relations with her father.

As we noted earlier, feminist writers have vigorously criticized psychoanalytic theory on this point. We will examine this argument in more detail in the commentary section of this chapter.

The Oedipus complex both for the boy and the girl during the fourth and fifth years of life were seen by Freud as major landmarks in the development of the child. Furthermore, as we have suggested, the resolution of the Oedipus complex and the modes of relationship that develop from it produce a variety of important modes of adaptation that persist in the later relationships of both males and females to members of their own and the opposite sex.

The Genital Stage

Following the period of latency there is a final active stage of psychosexual development in the child. This usually occurs during adolescence, when the narcissistic or self-oriented concerns of the pregenital stages are replaced to a large degree by realistic object choices in the real world. During the genital stage the child is transformed from a narcissistic self-oriented child into a socialized adult. The child becomes concerned with vocational choice, socialization, and peer relationships.

It should be noted, however, that the effects of the pregenital stages of development do not entirely disappear but remain "fused" with the later effects of the genital stage. According to psychoanalytic theory then, children praised for their "productions" on the toilet may transform this "productive" character trait into a more adult form and become perhaps writers or painters as adults. The final personality organization of the individual is not a product of the genital stage alone but of the residue of each of the stages of development as they persist in the adult character of the individual.

Psychological Structure

Recall for a moment our earlier discussion of models, metaphors, and perspectives in thinking about abnormal behavior. We noted that an important stage in the development of a perspective involved *elaboration* of the concept to fill in details and account for new facts or important clinical observations. Freud too was continuously elaborating his perspective and adding new concepts to capture and summarize his clinical observations. He soon found it necessary to elaborate his ideas about psychological structure in order to lay the groundwork for later speculation on the dynamics of thought and behavior.

The psychoanalytic perspective that Freud developed took on a much more explicit metaphorical character with the publication of "The Ego and the Id" (Freud, 1923, 1961, pp. 3–66). In this paper he laid the groundwork for a human psychological structure that delineated the three major provinces of the mind. For Freud, these three provinces were the major functional units of mental life. These units were called the *id,* the *ego,* and the *superego* and became the basic building blocks on which the dynamics of behavior were based. Later we shall examine the interaction among these three structures since their interaction is fundamental to the dynamics of behavior.

Table 3–2 summarizes the structural characteristics, functioning principles, and modes of operation of the id, ego and superego.

The Id

The id is the most primitive province of the personality structure. It contains the instincts (or, more accurately, drive) and is the source of human psychic energy. The function of the id is to discharge energy released in the organism either by internal or external stimulation and to keep the level of tension in the organism as low as possible. Thus the id seeks to gratify instinctual drives immediately and is said to operate according to the *pleasure principle.*

The id is the psychological representation of the biological substratum of human personality. It does not develop over time but remains unchanged and unaltered by external reality. For Freud the id is unorganized, "a chaos, a cauldron of seething excitement" (Freud, 1933, pp. 103–104).

The id may seek gratification and the discharge of tension directly through a motor reflex or through the primary process, which operates in the following way. If immediate gratification of

TABLE 3–2   Personality Structure according
to the Psychoanalytic Perspective

STRUCTURE	FUNCTIONING PRINCIPLE	MODE OF OPERATION
Id The instincts; source of psychic energy; biological substratum of personality	*Pleasure Principle* Seeks to gratify instinctual drives immediately	*Primary Process* Direct motor-discharge of energy or drive, e.g., dreams, wish fulfillment
Ego Developed from the id; reality-oriented; judging; executive	*Reality Principle* "Executive function," i.e., moderates demands of instinctual impulses and demands of external reality	*Secondary Process* Differentiates objective from subjective reality; relies on past experience; judges
Superego Developed from the ego; represents introjection of parental moral standards and values	*Moral Evaluation* Judges right and wrong, "good" and "bad"	*Conscience* Source of moral judgment *Ego Ideal* Image of person child would like to become

a wish or drive is impossible, then the memory traces of the
individual are activated and an image of the desired object may be
produced to gratify the need for tension reduction. This is known
as *wish fulfillment*. It is important to realize that the id does not
distinguish between the image of the object and the object itself.
It makes no distinction between objective reality and subjective
reality. Thus the primary process may produce hallucinations or
dreams in order to gratify id instincts or drives. For example, the
hungry sleeper may dream of food. The image of the food then
serves as the object of tension reduction for the id.

In order to survive in the harsh realities of man's external
environment, however, the id will not suffice. Thus a second
structure of mind develops from the id, and the basic function of
this structure is to deal with external reality.

The Ego

As the constraints of the external world impinge upon the
organism, a part of the id develops and becomes more differentiated. This new structure is called the ego. The role of the ego is
to pursue gratification but at the same time to take account of the

demands of external reality. Thus the ego is said to operate according to the *reality principle*.

The ego acts as a mediator between id impulses and reality. However, as Freud points out (1911, 1949, pp. 13–21), it does not actually displace id impulses but acts to assure the gratification of these impulses. For example, the ego may function to delay a short-term gratification only to assure a more enduring form of gratification that may occur at a later time. You may, for example, refuse a tempting dessert in favor of the long-term gratification of losing weight.

The mode of operation by which this "executive function" is carried out is called the *secondary process*. Unlike the primary process of the id, the secondary process differentiates between subjective and objective reality. The secondary process relies on past experience and the evaluation of this experience to make judgments about the most appropriate means of obtaining gratification. In order to carry out this task the ego must be a highly organized and differentiated structure. It is a structure in contact with both the conscious perceptions of the external world and the incessant demands of the id. The psychological functions of action, thought, memory, and perception are all used by the ego in order to evaluate the experience and to provide realistic gratification. Freud (1940, 1949) described the function of the ego in the following way:

> Its constructive function consists in interposing between the demand made by an instinct and the action that satisfies it, an intellective activity which, after considering the present state of things and weighing up earlier experiences, endeavors by means of experimental actions to calculate the consequences of the proposed line of conduct. In this way the ego comes to a decision whether the attempt to obtain satisfaction is to be carried out or postponed or whether it may not be necessary for the demand of the instinct to be altogether suppressed as being dangerous (p. 110).

Thus we see that the ego functions to maintain the organism in the face of "three harsh masters," (a) the id's demands of total fulfillment of biological impulses, (b) the persistent demands of external reality, and (c) the injunctions of the superego.

The Superego

Freud also wished to have a way of representing the domain of moral values in human behavior. For this purpose he postulated the superego as an additional portion of the personality structure.

Just as the ego develops out of a portion of the id, so the superego develops from a portion of the ego. As children grow they are influenced by their parents through reward and punishment. In this way they learn their values from their parents, and as the children identify themselves with their parents, they internalize or *introject* these values.

Thus a portion of the ego, the superego, comes to evaluate acts according to moral standards and the children learn to judge themselves using these standards. They come to react with shame or pride when evaluating their own actions.

The superego is usually identified with the idea of *conscience*. In addition, however, a second system is associated with the superego, that of the *ego ideal*. The ego ideal is a composite of the values the children have learned. The ego ideal becomes important for growing children as an image of the sort of person they should strive to become. Usually parents are the source of this ego ideal in children and become the person with whom they identify. But later, particularly in adolescence, children may come to identify with other figures as the ego ideal.

Both the ego ideal and the conscience aspects of the superego play a crucial role in the socialization of children. The dictates and values of society are transmitted through the parents to the children, and the parents become the first representations of the society with which children must ultimately cope.

We have noted that the three provinces of mind we have just described were offered by Freud originally as organizational principles to give order and form to the enormous complexity of human behavior. But from their initially tentative nature in his earlier writing these structures began to take on a life and a reality of their own. That is, they became less tentatively offered hypotheses, and treated like real entities. That is, they became *reified*.

We noted in the chapter on models, metaphors, and perspectives that one of the functions of metaphorical constructions is to make the new construction seem very real to us. So it is with these three metaphorical structures of personality. The id, the ego, and the superego may have originally been only convenient concepts to organize the data of man's behavior, but they soon came to be viewed as real entities. Later psychoanalytic writers and Freud himself tended to reify the concepts of id, ego, and superego, and they were thus assured a permanent place in the psychoanalytic perspective.

We can see that these three structures represent potentially conflicting motives and goals for the individual. Although the ego may attempt to mediate these conflicts, situations in the life of the individual will continually arise in which conflict is inevitable. It should be somewhat clearer to the reader at this point why Freud posited the existence of intrapsychic life. Next, we shall discuss the nature of this conflict and its relationship to anxiety.

Anxiety and Conflict

Think about the last time you were approaching a particularly difficult exam or other anxiety-producing event. Focus on your feelings and reactions. Did you feel "butterflies" in your stomach? Did your hand perspire? Was it difficult to sleep? Most people have a characteristic pattern of responses to anxiety-provoking situations. But nevertheless, anxiety is a nearly universal experience. Freud recognized the pervasiveness and importance of anxiety in his formulations.

Anxiety plays a role not only in the understanding of abnormal behavior but also in the normal development of the personality. In one of his best-known works, *The Problem of Anxiety* (1926), Freud described anxiety as an unpleasant feeling which is associated with the excitation of the autonomic nervous system.

For Freud the birth trauma is the prototypical anxiety experience. The neonate experiences intense stimulation for the first time at birth. Children's first exposure to the world produces an "emergency reaction" in their physiological systems. This mobilization of the physiological system is an adaptive reaction, but anxiety is far from a pleasant experience, and the developing organism attempts to devise ways of reducing or removing anxiety.

Anxiety functions as a signal to the ego, and, as we shall see, the ego may institute measures to deal with the anxiety. Thus, anxiety also serves the function of alerting the person to the presence of existing or potential, internal or external threats.

Freud differentiated three types of anxiety: (1) reality or objective anxiety, (2) neurotic anxiety, and (3) moral anxiety. In all three types, the ego is threatened with being overwhelmed by internal or external forces. In addition, with each of these three types of anxiety ego mechanisms are instituted that come into conflict with external or internal forces. Reality, neurotic, and moral anxiety do not differ in quality. All three forms of anxiety are experienced as fear by the ego, but, as we shall see, they do differ in the source of threat.

Reality Anxiety

Do you remember your reaction when you had a close call when crossing a dangerous intersection? That feeling is what Freud called *reality anxiety.*

Reality anxiety is an unpleasant emotional experience resulting from the perception of danger or threat from the external environment. Reality anxiety may be learned through experience. For example, we learn the realistic fears associated with touching a hot object through experience. Or, reality anxiety may be a reflex reaction such as the organism's reaction to sudden physical stimulation, loud noises, or pain.

It is the ego that experiences the threat of reality anxiety. As the organism develops and accumulates experience, the ego learns methods of coping with reality anxiety by avoiding the threatening situation or feeling.

Figure 3–2 is a diagrammatic portrayal of reality anxiety. This diagram suggests that the coping mechanisms of the ego and the forces of the external threat come into conflict, producing reality anxiety. It should also be noted that the ego learns to feel reality anxiety not only in the actual physical presence of danger but also in the expectation of danger or threat from the external world.

Neurotic Anxiety

The ego is threatened not only by external forces but by internal forces as well. The second major type of anxiety postulated by Freud is *neurotic anxiety.* In the case of neurotic anxiety the ego is aroused by its perception of the possibility of being overwhelmed by the instincts of the id.

Again the basic paradigm is one of conflict. In this case the conflict exists between the incessant instinctual demands of the id for some object (object cathexis) and the attempts of the ego to

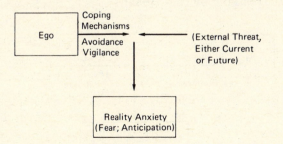

FIG. 3–2   Development of reality anxiety.

counteract the object cathexis, thus protecting itself from being overwhelmed (anti-cathexis). Figure 3–3 shows the nature of the id-ego conflict and the resulting neurotic anxiety.

Neurotic anxiety is a danger signal to the ego that the instinctual demands of the id are striving for expression and that the ego is struggling to avoid being overwhelmed, seized, and made helpless. It may also be the result of a past history of punishment for or frustration of the expression of libidinal drives.

Neurotic anxiety may be expressed clinically in at least three different ways, as free-floating anxiety, phobia, or panic reaction. In the case of free-floating anxiety the person appears always to be apprehensive or fearful that something dreadful will happen to him or her. If one hasn't experienced this kind of anxiety, it is hard to appreciate. The most characteristic experience is of constant but apparently causeless and meaningless alarm. Often this free-floating anxiety will attach itself to almost any convenient environmental event and the person will attribute his fear to that event. As Hall (1954) says, "We might better say that he is afraid of his own id. What he is actually afraid of is that the id which is constantly exerting pressure upon the ego will seize control of the ego and reduce it to a state of helplessness" (p. 65).

The person experiencing phobic anxiety is one for whom neurotic anxiety is manifested as an intense irrational fear. The fear is irrational in that it is out of proportion to the actual physical danger presented by the feared object. For example, an individual experiencing phobic anxiety may experience it as an intense terror of high places, crowds, or snakes. The object of the fear in phobic anxiety is thought to be a symbolic representation of a temptation to instinctual gratification. Thus, behind the phobic fear there is actually a primitive wish of the id for the object or something which the object may represent. An example of a phobic fear is the following offered by Hall (1954):

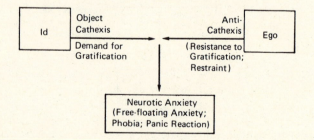

FIG. 3–3 Development of neurotic anxiety.

A young woman was deathly afraid of touching anything made of rubber. She did not know why she had this fear; she only knew that she had had it as long as she could remember. Analysis brought out the following facts. When she was a little girl, her father had brought home two balloons, one for her and one for her younger sister. In a fit of temper, she broke her sister's balloon, for which she was severely punished by her father. Moreover, she had to give her sister her balloon. Upon further analysis, it was learned that she had been very jealous of her younger sister, so much so that she had secretly wished that her sister might die and leave her the sole object of her father's devotion. The breaking of her sister's balloon signified a destructive act against her sister. The ensuing punishment and her own guilt feeling became associated with the rubber balloon. Whenever she came into contact with rubber, the old fear of the wish to destroy her sister made her shrink away (pp. 65–66).

Yet another example of phobic anxiety is the famous case of "Little Hans."

The most famous case of zoophobia is also the first one ever to be studied dynamically, the case of Little Hans. This boy of five years refused to go out into the street because he was afraid of horses, actually feared being bitten by them. In the course of therapy it turned out that the horses symbolized the hated and feared aspect of his father. The little patient harbored hostile aggression against his only male rival for his mother's love, but at the same time he also loved his father dearly.

Reduced to its simplest terms the phobic solution was about as follows. The love this boy bore his mother was repressed, it disappeared. The love for his father was retained, while the hatred for him was displaced on the horses. This had the added advantage that the horses could easily be avoided, whereas his father could not. In the usual role reversal of fantasies and dreams, the boy expected primitive retaliation from his father for the primitive hostility he himself felt. This expectation likewise was displaced. It became the regressive oral fear that the horses would bite him.

The whole displacement in the case of Little Hans was made by certain other partial identities. (a) The father had often played "horsie" with Hans; (b) the horses' bridles reminded Hans fearfully of his father's dark moustache; (c) therapy also brought out his wishes that his father might fall and hurt himself, as the boy had seen horses fall, and as his playmate with whom he also played "horsie" had fallen and hurt himself. As a result of therapy this patient recovered from his phobia. It is interesting that, years later when Hans chanced upon the account of his illness and its treatment, all memory of the once vivid phobia had been completely repressed. Some of the incidental comments about his parents made him wonder if he could have been this famous little patient, and led him to visit Freud where he found out that he was (Cameron, 1963, pp. 294–295).

A third form which neurotic anxiety may take is that of panic reaction. The panic reaction is characterized by the sudden appearance of intense, debilitating fear for no apparent reason. Usually the individual experiencing a panic reaction is at a loss to explain it.

A college student reported to the health services in a state of severe agitation. He stated that for no apparent reason, in the middle of breakfast, a feeling of intense fear seemed to sweep over him. His breathing became rapid and shallow, and his heartbeat seemed irregular and very fast. He was unable to explain the experience and could not think of any recent or impending life event that might account for the panic. The reaction gradually subsided over a period of several days.

Panic reactions may also be associated with sudden, impulsive antisocial behavior. In this case the panic reaction is a reaction to the discharge or breaking through of id impulses. The behavior is an attempt to rid the person of painful anxiety by doing that which the id demands.

Despite the fact that id-ego conflicts often result in "neurotic" anxiety, we should realize that normal individuals also experience neurotic anxiety. Neurotic anxieties are not the sole possession of the clinically diagnosed neurotic individual. Here Freud's quantitative principle is again being invoked. The difference between the "neurotic" and normal individual is the degree to which the person's life is controlled by the anxiety.

Finally, in the case of neurotic anxiety we should recognize that the conflict is genuinely *intrapsychic*. That is, the conflict exists between two of the major provinces of the personality. Intrapsychic conflicts are difficult for the individual to identify or cope with since they exist within the person. Because neurotic anxieties are exclusively intrapsychic, they are not as easily handled by escape or avoidance as is the case with many types of reality anxiety. Further, neurotic symptoms are always a consequence of neurotic rather than other types of anxiety.

Moral Anxiety

The third major form of anxiety which Freud differentiated was moral anxiety. Moral anxiety is the result of a conflict between id impulses and the superego or conscience. The individual experiencing moral anxiety often will feel intense shame or guilt. The diagrammatic paradigm for moral anxiety is shown in Figure 3–4. We can see that when an instinctual object choice of the id seeks expression in the form of an act or even in the form of the thought of an act, the superego or conscience is threatened. Thus the superego, the internalized agent of parental authority, will block the id impulse. Although the id impulse is blocked, the conflict remains in force. The product of that conflict is moral anxiety, often, as we have said, in the form of shame or guilt. For example, the id may express an instinctual sexual impulse or object cathexis toward some sexually attractive person. The superego, however, may react to this impulse as wrong or immoral, producing an anti-cathexis.

A nineteen-year-old man reported feelings of intense anxiety after his first sexual experience. The young man was persuaded by some friends to visit a house of prostitution in a nearby town. Although he had sexual relations with one of the prostitutes that night while slightly intoxicated, the next morning his recollection of the night's events produced a severe anxiety attack. In this case, it appears that the superego was temporarily overwhelmed, but the intrapsychic conflict was renewed with resulting moral anxiety the next day.

Our brief review of the three types of anxiety Freud described should make it clear that anxiety is a result of the conflict between the various provinces of the personality. Conflict inevitably results in anxiety experienced by the ego. Anxiety is a danger signal indicating to the ego either that it is being threatened by some event in the external world or that the id is seeking expression and is being blocked by either an ego or superego anti-cathexis.

Our discussion of the various forms of anxiety should leave

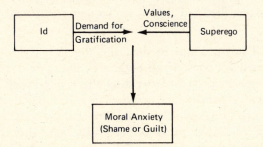

FIG. 3–4   Development of moral anxiety.

us with some appreciation of how the various provinces of the personality interact with one another dynamically. As we proceed through our discussion of defenses and their relation to conflict and anxiety, the fundamental structural metaphor of the psychoanalytic perspective and its dynamics will become clearer.

The Defense Mechanisms

A sudden eating binge, forgetting the name of someone you know well, resorting to numerous naps, constant use of excuses each could be evidence that *defense mechanisms* are in operation. Defense mechanisms are; according to the psychoanalytic perspective, the way that the ego copes with the problem of painful anxiety.

Freud suggested that the ego may engage either in realistic problem solving (as is often the case in dealing with reality anxiety), or it may resort to irrational methods which distort or deny reality. These irrational methods of dealing with anxiety were grouped under the general classification of defense mechanisms.

Freud, earlier in his thinking (1894, 1962, pp. 43–61), used the term "defense" purely to refer to attempts by the person to protect the self from dangerous instinctual demands through repression. However, as his thinking progressed and as his clinical experience became more extensive, Freud decided to use the concept of defense in a much more general way. Thus, in his monograph, *The Problem of Anxiety,* he wrote:

> I now think that it confers a distinct advantage to readopt the old concept of defense if in doing so it is laid down that this shall be the general designation for all techniques of which the ego makes use in the conflict which could potentially lead to neurosis, while repression is the term reserved for one particular method of defense, one which because of the direction that our investigations took was the first with which we became acquainted (Freud, 1936, p. 144).

We will not attempt to describe the defense mechanism in detail, nor will we provide an extensive list. Our description will serve only the purpose of providing the reader with the general idea of the nature of defense mechanisms. In the course of our discussion certain things will become apparent, namely, that defense mechanisms are operations of the ego, and that the defense mechanisms will exhibit two features in common: (a) the denial or distortion of reality, and (b) operation at an unconscious level.

Repression

Repression is the mechanism by which dangerous instinctual impulses derived from the id and in conflict with the ego or superego are dismissed from consciousness. These instinctual choices, when they are kept from consciousness, are unable to evoke anxiety. Repression may operate in a number of different ways. It may distort what we see or hear, thus protecting the ego from the perception of objects it may regard as dangerous, or it may operate on the memory. Memories that have been associated with traumatic experiences or which remind us of threatening events may be repressed and simply made unavailable to awareness. In either case, the purpose of repression is to deal with moral, neurotic, or reality anxiety by removing from consciousness the internal or external threat to the ego.

As an example, recall that in the case of "Little Hans" the memory of his once-vivid phobia of horses had been completely repressed. Only a chance remark about his parents in the case history led him to discover that he was the subject of one of Freud's most famous cases.

Although repression is actually accomplished by the ego in order to remove threatening id impulses from our awareness, it may be initiated by the superego. Thus a wish that appears wrong to the superego and is derived from the id may be repressed (removed from consciousness) by the ego, yet the initiator of the repression is the superego.

Many psychoanalytic thinkers believe that a number of psychosomatic disturbances, such as ulcers, asthma, and arthritis can stem in part from repression. Although the anxiety-provoking id impulse may be kept out of awareness, it may express itself through some physiological system such as the musculature, the pulmonary system, or the digestive system rather than exclusively through neurotic symptoms. Furthermore, repressed ideas or impulses, although they remain out of awareness, may continue to develop in the unconscious.

Reaction Formation

In some cases the ego will deal with an instinctual demand by the expression of its opposite. Thus feelings of hate and anger may be transformed into exaggerated expressions of love. Similarly, intense sexual impulses may be transformed into extreme feelings of disgust at the thought of sexual contact. The mechanism by which an instinctual impulse is hidden from awareness by its opposite is usually called reaction formation. One of the cardinal characteristics of reaction formation is its exaggeration. That is, we can distinguish between a real impulse and a reaction formation in that the reaction formation is considerably more extreme than we might expect. The individual "protests too much" and the id impulse is kept out of awareness by the strong development of an impulse in the opposite direction. However, in many cases the direct expression of the id impulse and the reaction formation may exist side by side in the personality of an individual. For example, he may appear to love and hate the same object or he may appear to desire sexual contact and at the same time be repulsed by it.

A fairly typical example of reaction formation is given by Cameron (1963). The subject here was deeply resentful of the attentions of her parents to her younger brother.

> After Billy was born everything got worse. He was clearly the favorite of her father no less than her mother. All through the rest of her childhood she felt herself compared unfavorably with him. At first she used to say to her father, "Put him down! Take your own baby!" She remembered brooding over this preference for her brother, feeling terribly jealous of him and resentful toward her parents.
>
> In time, however, Sally gave up expressing hatred toward Billy. She adopted instead a protective attitude toward him of tender loving care. This change was a product of *reaction formation*. The hate was still there not far from the surface; for whenever Billy teased her, she responded with violent temper outbursts (p. 389).

Projection

Another mechanism by which id impulses may be denied is to attribute them to some object or person in the external world. Thus, the individual who experiences sexual impulses toward another but who cannot tolerate this feeling will project the impulses onto the other person. Instead of saying "I love him," he may say, "he loves me." When the ego resorts to projection, it is as if neurotic anxiety is transformed into "objective" anxiety. That is, it places the object of threat in the external world. This is not surprising if we understand that developmentally the individual has learned that it is much easier to cope with threats in the external world than it is to cope with threats from the id. Moreover, projection may do a good deal more than simply remove anxiety. It provides the individual with an opportunity to express real feelings, but now these feelings are projected onto an external object. For example, the individual who hates another may say "she hates me" (the projected impulse) and therefore "I hate her." The original impulse is allowed expression by its external provocation.

An example of the development of projective defense is offered by Shapiro (1965).

A very intelligent thirty-three-year-old college professor, stiff and self-conscious but also quite ambitious and sometimes rather arrogant, had always been sensitive to any rebuff or slight to his dignity, to being "forced" or ordered to do anything arbitrarily, or otherwise treated, as it seemed to him, like a "kid." In this instance, he had recently taken a new job with a different institution and had become interested, although ashamed to admit it, in impressing an important senior professor, obviously with the hope of becoming a protégé of his and probably also with the idea of ultimately outstripping him. At any rate, he was initially quite impressed with this man, and, consequently, he was quite nervous in his presence and concerned with what the older man might think of him. Sometimes, he was concerned that he might be thought "weak," while, at other times, too self-aggrandizing. He watched for signs of both reactions.

So far this intensification of defensive tension, including the intensified sense of vulnerability and defensive concern, may still be regarded as preprojective. However, it soon became clear that this defensive tension and intensified sense of vulnerability was gradually giving rise to an intensification of rigidity and an increasingly antagonistic defensive stiffening. Thus, he not only watched for signs of rebuff or disapproval, but also increasingly anticipated them and, accordingly, braced himself with each hesitant overture. He remembered now that he despised fawning yes-men, and, therefore, he now approached the older man only in a determinedly dignified and equalitarian way.

In the course of some weeks, apparently marked mostly by indifference on the side of the older man, this defensive stiffening progressed further. He watched the older man closely now, no longer with concern, but with suspicion. He angrily seized on some quite ambiguous evidence of disparaging slights and arbitrary commanding attitudes on the senior man's part. He would not "take it," and he frequently became not merely equalitarian, but defensively arrogant in the relationship. Thus, he refused "menial" department assignments. Once angry and suspicious, he began to watch the colleague, in the way such people do, like a small boy playing cops and robbers around an unconcerned father, only with more intensity and seriousness, interpreting each movement according to the game—now he is pretending not to notice me, now he is getting ready to shoot, and so on. From this angry, suspicious, and, by now, defensively quite haughty view, he discovered clues that showed him that he had been right; the older man resented his independence, wanted only a mediocre yes-man in the department, and was trying to reduce him to that status. He declared that the situation between them had come to a "contest of wills" (pp. 90–91).

Denial

Denial is a relatively primitive defense mechanism, often observed in children. Typically, denial is used when the conflict is between an id impulse and some reality frustration in the external world. When circumstances of reality frustrate an impulse, denial acts in such a way as to deny the existence of the realistic situation that confronts the person.

Denial should not be confused with repression. In the case of repression, the conflict is between id impulses and either the ego or the superego, but in the case of denial, the conflict is between id impulses and realistic circumstances in the external world.

Regression

Once an individual has reached a certain stage of development, if he is threatened by id impulses, he may retreat to an earlier stage of development in his behavior. This retreat is called regression. Regression allows the expression of id impulses in a way that would not be possible at higher levels of development and is yet another way of dealing with the instinctual impulses of the id.

Kisker (1964) offers the following clinical example of regression.

Ora J. is a seventeen-year-old high school girl who was admitted to the psychiatric hospital as a result of an episode in which she seemed suddenly to regress to her early childhood. She sat on the floor and played with her younger sister's dolls, and appeared not to recognize any of her other brothers and sisters. The difficulty began approximately eight weeks earlier when the patient received her report card at school. Her grades were not high enough for her to obtain a college scholarship, and she became extremely upset. She withdrew from her family and friends, did not want to go to school, and spent most of her time sleeping (p. 293).

Psychoanalysts interpret a wide variety of different behaviors as regressive, particularly when they appear in adults. Hall (1954) includes among them the tendency to talk baby talk, destroy property, masturbate, have temper tantrums, dress like a child, fight, and even the tendency to take naps.

When Is Behavior Abnormal?

Our discussion of the stages of psychosexual development, anxiety, conflict, and defense gives us a reasonably clear idea of the psychoanalytic view of the genesis of abnormal behavior, but it does not answer the question of when behavior is considered abnormal. When does a defense become "pathological"? Freud readily acknowledged that anxiety and defenses are a part of every person's psychological life and, indeed, in *The Psychopathology of Everyday Life* (1901, 1960) he suggests and illustrates this explicitly.

But when does a defense become a symptom? When does a particular behavior become neurotic? Does the presence of conflict or defense or anxiety indicate that a person is abnormal? Freud's answer is derived from the quantitative metapsychological point of view we discussed earlier. Munroe (1955) describes his position:

> Freud repeatedly emphasized the idea that the trends and conflicts he discovered were not the specific "cause" of neurosis. Neurosis results from the *quantitative distribution of energies,* not from the mere existence of conflict. . . . Pathology develops as one or another aspect of the problem becomes quantitatively unmanageable by the techniques that the personality has established (p. 281).

Behavior is pathological when it becomes unmanageable and interferes with the day-to-day functioning of the individual. The implication is clear that the criterion for deciding when a given behavior is or is not abnormal is fundamentally quantitative.

In making this point, we should not overlook a related idea concerning the function of pathology which qualifies the quantitative view. Freud also held that symptoms may function as *adaptive* mechanisms, that is, represent ways of dealing with conflict and the resulting anxiety. Thus, although a symptom may be adaptive in that it "copes" with underlying conflict, it may also—if the quantitative distribution of energies is intense enough—interfere with the daily functioning of the individual and be abnormal or pathological.

Thus, from the psychoanalytic perspective, a defense is seen as "adaptive" when it deals with psychic energies and conflicts.

It is considered abnormal only when it comes to interfere with the daily life of the individual.

Summary

The psychoanalytic perspective makes a number of assumptions about human nature and behavior. It posits the existence of unconscious psychological processes, the idea that behavior is motivated, that drives or motives may conflict with each other, that behavior is a result of development, that the perspective has a quantitative aspect, and that humans are adapting organisms.

From the psychoanalytic point of view, everyone goes through a series of dynamically differentiated stages of psychosexual development: the anal, the oral, the phallic, and the genital stages. Each of these stages represents a different period of interaction between the child and the socializing forces (principally the parents) that impinge upon him or her, and leaves its residue in the final adult character of the individual.

Freud described the adult personality as consisting of three basic structures: the id, which is the reservoir of instinctual impulses; the ego, which deals with external reality; and the superego, which is the conscience of the individual. The motives associated with each of these psychological structures inevitably come into conflict, and one product of this conflict is anxiety. In order to deal with the anxiety, defense mechanisms arise that operate at an unconscious level and deny or distort reality. Everyone uses defense mechanisms to deal with anxiety generated by the conflict of drives. By themselves, the existence of defenses does not constitute the crucial criterion of abnormal behavior. Instead, behavior is considered abnormal from a psychoanalytic point of view only when it begins to interfere in an individual's effective functioning.

COMMENTARY

Now we have sketched the principal assumptions and concepts of the psychoanalytic perspective. There is little question that Freud was a brilliant observer of human behavior and was able to capture his observations with creative conceptions that form the basis of the perspective. But, as we noted, psychoanalysis has always drawn strong responses both from critics and supporters.

In the sections to follow we will survey some of the main criticisms of the psychoanalytic perspective.

Sources of criticism come from very different quarters. First, we will examine psychoanalysis as a scientific theory. *Do Freud's concepts meet the requirements of a scientific theory?* Philosophers of science have argued this point a great deal, and we will briefly examine their arguments. Second, we will examine some *clinical and research evidence* offered in support of psychoanalytic concepts. Third, we will examine the *views of prominent critics of Freud's ideas* with particular emphasis on the effects of Freudian doctrine on the socialization of the child.

Is Psychoanalysis a Scientific Theory?

Criteria for a Scientific Theory

One of the most frequent charges made against psychoanalysis is that it is a vague, speculative, and loosely formulated set of ideas and opinions rather than a scientific theory. Despite the frequency with which these charges are made, critics seldom describe explicit criteria against which the scientific merit of psychoanalysis can be assessed. One author, however, has offered such criteria. Nagel (1959) describes three basic requirements he believes any theory must satisfy if it is to be capable of empirical validation.

1. *Theoretical assumptions must produce "if–then" statements.* It must be possible to identify explicit consequences that will arise from the assumptions made by the theory. This is necessary in order to judge the meaning of any empirical data for the assumption we are examining. Nagel argues that unless a theory meets this basic requirement it has no definite content, and the validity of the assumption can be decided only by "privileged authority or arbitrary caprice" (p. 40).

In the field of physiology, for example, a theoretical concept like "activation" has "if–then" properties. Physiologists can say *if* a person is in a state of physiological activation, *then* his or her palms will sweat, his or her heart rate will increase, and other changes will predictably occur. Thus, the concept of activation has predictable, explicit consequences.

Nagel (1959) offers an example of the inability of psychoanalytic theory to meet this requirement. In doing so he examines several of Freud's theoretical assumptions as they are described by Hartmann (1959).

Dr. Hartmann has stated for us the four classes of assumptions that constitute metapsychology; and among the energic principles he mentions the following two: "the drives (in particular 'sexuality' and 'aggression') are the main sources of energy in the mental apparatus"; and, secondly, "the regulation of energies in the mental apparatus follows the pleasure principle ('the tendency to immediate discharge'), the reality principle (i.e., 'considerations of reality') derived from it under the influence of ego-development, and a tendency to keep the level of excitation constant, or at a minimum." Now is it really possible to deduce from these assumptions, even when they are conjoined with the remaining ones, any determinate conclusions in the familiar sense of "deduce"? For example, can one conclude anything even as to the general conditions under which the sexual drive will discharge its "energy," rather than (to use Freud's own locution) combine with the aggressive drive to form a "compromise" or have its "level of excitation" raised because of "considerations of reality"? (Nagel, 1959, pp. 40–41).

2. *The concepts in the theory should be operationally defined.* Nagel suggests that even if many or most theoretical assumptions are not explicitly defined by empirical procedures, at least some of them must be given definite and unambiguous specifications in terms of some rules of procedure. Often these rules of procedure are called *coordinating definitions* or *operational definitions*. Thus, the concept of "anxiety" can be defined operationally by a score on a questionnaire, or achievement motivation could be operationally defined in terms of the number of hours spent on one's job. Nagel finds the attempts by psychoanalysts to provide operational definitions for their concepts to be wanting as well. For example, he notes that the operational referents of id, ego, and superego are extremely vague, as are the attempts to specify the interrelations among them.

3. *Theoretical concepts must specify when they do not apply in a particular case.* Nagel offers a third requirement that theories must meet in order to qualify as scientific. This third requirement is related to the second. A theory must not only be capable of confirmation, but also must be capable of being disconfirmed. Thus a theory cannot be formulated in such a way as to be able to be manipulated in order to fit the evidence at hand, no matter what the evidence might be.

This is a difficult idea to grasp at first. Concepts have to be formulated so that we know *when* they apply and when they don't. If we don't know this, the concepts are of little use.

Sidney Hook (1959) regards the criterion of disconfirmability as extremely important in deciding whether a theory is scientific or not. Hook describes a question he posed to a group of psychoanalysts and that he feels speaks to the question of disconfirmability for Freudian theory.

> It was in order to pinpoint the discussion on the possibility of falsifying one of the central doctrines of psychoanalysis that I asked psychoanalysts present to describe what kind of evidence they were prepared to accept which would lead them to declare in any specific case that a child did not have an Oedipus complex. . . .
>
> In asking this question I was *not* assuming that an Oedipus complex can be seen or touched or directly observed any more than intelligence can be seen or touched or directly observed. I was not even assuming that it was observable. All I was asking for was the evidence on the basis of which one could legitimately deny its presence. This is not a tricky question but one often asked to specify the meaning of terms, the statements that contain them, and the conditions under which the statements are warranted. For example, we hear that someone is "intelligent" or "friendly." Many types of behavior can be cited as evidence for the presence of "intelligence" or "friendliness." But unless we are also told what we would have to observe to conclude that an individual is *not* intelligent or friendly, the terms could be applied to anyone in all situations (pp. 214–215).

It was not surprising that Hook could not find any psychoanalysts who were able to provide him with adequate evidence which would lead them to conclude that the Oedipus complex did not exist in a particular case. In fact, there is little question that the psychoanalytic perspective has great difficulty in meeting this requirement described by Nagel and Hook for status as a scientific theory.

The requirements we have described are widely accepted ways of judging the qualifications of a particular set of ideas for status as a scientific theory. They are not idiosyncratic or unduly rigid, but we may ask whether psychoanalysis or any of the other perspectives we discuss in this book could qualify as a scientific theory using such criteria. The answer is that it is unlikely.

Perspectives are by their very nature metaphors which are prescientific and pretheoretical in nature. That is, they represent fundamental reorganizations of data based on a set of often vaguely defined concepts. Perspectives are conceptual tools that scientists may use when they begin to examine phenomena and

before they engage in the painstaking task of making their definitions explicit, attempting predictions based on their assumptions,
and specifying the rules of evidence and the data on which their
theory may be tested.

Clinical Evidence

The psychoanalytic interview and the clinical data derived
from it have been used as both a source of psychoanalytic hypotheses and a source of data for the validation of those hypotheses. As we might anticipate from the preceding discussion, a number of difficulties arise when one uses clinical evidence from the
psychoanalytic interview as a means of validating the assumptions
of the psychoanalytic perspective. We shall examine some of
Nagel's (1959) criticisms of the use of evidence drawn from
clinical interviews.

In the psychoanalytic interview the analyst seeks to discover
the cause of the patient's present condition. Generally speaking,
he assumes that the patient's difficulties are a result of internal
conflicts which have in turn been produced by repressed wishes.
The principal technique the analyst uses is to interpret the free
associations of the patient. The question is, what are the difficulties inherent in the psychoanalytic interview which render questionable the evidence the analyst takes as appropriate to validate
his or her hypotheses?

1. *Lack of standardized and public observation.* In the psychoanalytic interview the analyst is presumably a passive observer
of the "free" association of the patient. How free these associations actually are, of course, is questionable. It is certainly likely
that associative material produced by the patient is often directed
and influenced in subtle ways by the therapist.

Furthermore, no matter how objective the therapist tries to
be, the material of the analytic interview is private. Thus the
analyst is the sole reporter of the nature of his interventions or
the lack of them as they occur in the consulting room. The validation of hypotheses and the pursuit of objectivity can only be
achieved through independent examination of publicly accessible
information by independent observers. Unforunately, this is seldom the case in the presentation of clinical evidence. Regardless
of how much the analyst strives for standardized and objective
observations, we cannot know anything about the usefulness of
the evidence presented from clinical interviews unless this evidence is available to public scrutiny.

2. *Coherence is not enough.* Psychoanalysts often argue that

an interpretation is likely to be valid if it is consistent with all the other material disclosed by the patient. Thus the coherence of the psychoanalyst's interpretation becomes the criterion for the acceptance of its validity. We may ask, is the interpretation coherent with all information or only with selected portions of it? If, as is likely, it is coherent or consistent only with selected portions of the material, we must ask how these portions have been selected. Unfortunately, such information is seldom available.

In addition, it is possible that alternative interpretation of a very different kind might be offered on the basis of other selections of the material which are equally "coherent." This problem calls into question the usefulness of coherence as a criterion for validating analytic propositions in the clinical interview.

3. *"Predictable reactions."* Another argument often offered by psychoanalysts is that the analyst may choose between alternative interpretations on the basis of whether the patient states that the interpretation has given him "insight" into his difficulties. Often the analyst attributes insight to the patient when the interpretation elicits the sudden recollection of past experiences that the patient previously could not remember. But why should the patient's assertions that he now "understands" the nature of his difficulties be taken as competent evidence that the interpretation the analyst offered is correct?

Another "predictable" reaction which analysts often take as evidence for the validity of their interpretation is symptom change. When an interpretation is followed by a symptom change, the analyst may attribute the change in the patient's behavior to the interpretation. This is acceptable only if it can be shown that the interpretation and only the interpretation—rather than some other aspect of the interview situation or the patient's life—produced the change in symptom. Naturally this is virtually impossible in the relatively uncontrolled circumstances of the clinical interview. Thus, use of the criterion of symptom change as an index of interpretative validity may be questioned.

4. *Retrospective reports as evidence.* The psychoanalyst may argue that different neurotic syndromes are the result of different types of childhood experiences. As we pointed out in our discussion of the psychosexual stages of development, the regularities that are observed in the current patterns of the patient's neurotic behavior may elicit interpretation concerning previous childhood events in his or her life.

But, we may ask, are these relationships between particular symptom patterns and the patient's *allegations* of childhood ex-

periences, or between the symptom patterns and actual experience? Of course, it is virtually impossible to collect evidence on
this point. The systematic biases and distortions in the patient's
reports of his or her past experiences are now almost universally
recognized as important sources of error in the use of retrospective
information. Besides, we may still ask, because some event (real or
imagined) occurred in childhood, must it necessarily lead to the
production of a particular symptom pattern? How do we know
that there are not many other people with similar childhood experiences who have never developed the predicted symptom
patterns?

Nagel (1959) clarifies this point when he says:

> Thus, the fact that many men who have certain kinds of traumatic
> experiences in childhood develop into neurotic adults does not
> establish a causal relation between the two, if there is about the
> same proportion of men who undergo similar childhood experi-
> ences but develop into reasonably normal adults. In short, data
> must be analyzed so as to make possible comparisons on the basis
> of some *control* group, if they are to constitute cogent evidence for
> a causal inference. The introduction of such controls is the *mini-*
> *mum* requirement for reliable interpretation and use of empirical
> data (p. 53).

The lack of standardized and public observation procedures,
the questionable use of the coherence criterion, the capricious
use of interpretation, and the uncritical acceptance of postulated
relationships between developmental experiences and current
behavior all pose problems for the use of clinical evidence for the
validation of psychoanalytic hypotheses. Thus we may conclude
that psychoanalytic interpretation of therapeutic events clearly is
not the appropriate source of evidence for the validation of psychoanalytic hypotheses. However, as Levy (1963) points out, this
does not mean that interpretation itself is an illegitimate enterprise, or that interpretation does not have predictable effects upon
the patient-therapist relationship and the subsequent behavior of
the patient. In an original and thorough examination of the process
of psychological interpretation, Levy (1963) has described some of
these effects and has offered a theory of interpretation in psychotherapy.

Research Evidence

The tone of the preceding sections might suggest that few attempts have been made to provide empirical evidence for psycho-

analytic propositions. Just the opposite is true; one indication of the impact of psychoanalysis has been the large volume of research it has stimulated. For example, the work of Sears, Maccoby, and Levin (1957) on patterns of child rearing, Sarnoff and Corwin (1959) on castration anxiety, and Blum and Miller (1952) on the oral character were all stimulated to a large degree by psychoanalytic thinking. A recent brief review of experimental work on psychoanalytic propositions has been offered by Hilgard (1968, pp. 37–45).

We will examine here two different lines of research that use very different methods. The first, on perceptual defense, uses controlled laboratory techniques and has today nearly run its course. It does, however, provide us with an example of how a psychoanalytic hypothesis was translated into operational terms and tested. The second line of research concerns the genesis of symptoms in the psychiatric interview setting. Unlike the research on perceptual defense, this line of research is relatively recent and represents a new departure in the testing of psychoanalytic propositions. Although a review of both these research programs is instructive, it is not intended to provide a comprehensive discussion of research in this area.

1. *Perceptual Defense: Repression or Suppression?* We have noted that defense mechanisms such as repression or denial are hypothesized to involve the perceptual distortion of threatening material. Thus it is not surprising that researchers have attempted to study the effects of potentially ego-threatening material on perceptual processes. We will briefly examine some of this research since it provides an excellent example of experimental attempts to test psychoanalytic hypotheses and since it represents a line of research which, although now relatively inactive, was at one point the subject of considerable controversy in the field.

An example of early work in this area is a study conducted by McGinnies (1949). He studied the perceptual recognition threshold and galvanic skin response (GSR) of persons when they were exposed to brief visual presentations of both "taboo" and neutral words. Essentially, the perceptual recognition threshold reflects the amount of time required for an individual to recognize a word presented for a very short time. The galvanic skin response is a measure of autonomic activity and is therefore presumed to be an indication of the relative level of anxiety experienced by an individual.

McGinnies found that higher recognition thresholds were obtained for taboo words than for neutral words. Furthermore, he found higher galvanic skin responses on the prerecognition trials (the trials before the subject correctly identified the word) for taboo words than for neutral words. He interpreted the recognition threshold result as evidence for an active inhibition of conscious detection of taboo words. The GSR findings were interpreted as "unconscious" detection of threatening material and a manifestation of anxiety associated with the presentation of the taboo words.

However, shortly thereafter, Howes and Solomon (1950) attacked this research on two grounds. The first basis on which the McGinnies research was attacked is summarized by Eriksen (1963).

> Consider the typical undergraduate brought into the experimental situation by a professor. The subject is exposed to fragmentary perception through tachistoscopic exposure. Let us assume that the word "house" is projected and the subject sees what looks like a medium-length word with an "H" at the beginning and what looks like an "S" toward the end. Let us say that he tried to think of some word that will fit these partial cues and comes up with "house." The next word exposed is "whore." He may pick up a fragmentary perception of something resembling a "W" and maybe an "H" and he guesses "whom." On the next occurrence of this stimulus word he actually says to himself, "My God, that looks like whore, but it couldn't be. The professor wouldn't show a word like that." And so he waits for a longer duration before hazarding a guess, or overtly he says "whom" again. Of course, one would expect a very sizeable GSR to accompany this rather startling subjective experience. On the subsequent exposure he is not going to risk saying "whore" and being incorrect. After all, what would the experimenter think of somebody who would say a word like that when it really wasn't the word that was being shown? This possibility of deliberate response suppression is sufficient to account not only for the longer durations required for recognition of the "taboo words" but also for the greater GSRs accompanying the prerecognition response to these words (p. 38).

The second basis on which Howes and Solomon (1950) criticized McGinnies' experiment was that the "taboo" and neutral words differed in their familiarity, and thus the nontaboo words were relatively easier to recognize than were the taboo words. Both of these criticisms led investigators to remain skeptical about the phenomenon of perceptual defense.

However, Eriksen (1963) pointed out that most experiments on perceptual defense had failed to meet two conditions necessary for the demonstration of perceptual defense. These conditions were (1) that independent operations must exist to show that the stimulus which was expected to produce perceptual defense is in fact anxiety-producing for the particular subject, and (2) that independent criteria were required to demonstrate that the subject does in fact use avoidance defenses rather than other possible defensive reactions in the situation. In a series of ingenious and carefully designed experiments Eriksen (1951a, 1951b, 1952) did meet these criteria and demonstrated that it is in fact true that higher recognition thresholds can be obtained for emotionally threatening words.

However, Eriksen does not explain the perceptual defense demonstrated in recognition experiments as a process by which the unconscious detection of threatening material leads to repression, as analytic supporters of the hypothesis might suggest. Instead, he points out that we must distinguish between perceptual processes and the responses from which they are inferred. He suggests further that the perceptual defense studies (including his own) have only demonstrated the effect of threatening words on the observer's responses. Eriksen (1963) suggests that taboo words have been punished more than nontaboo words in the experience of most people, and therefore "we are in a position to account for perceptual defense effects in terms of nothing more mysterious than the empirically established effects of punishment on the probability of occurrence of responses" (p. 54).

This line of research provides an example of how competing explanations from another perspective—in this case the learning perspective—have supplanted earlier psychoanalytic hypotheses. It also demonstrates how advances in methodology, in particular the distinction between perceptual processes and the responses from which they are inferred, have clarified the general problem of the relation between perception and personality (Price, 1966).

2. *Searching for the Cause of Symptoms.* Although a number of lines of research based on psychoanalytic views have ceased to be productive, new lines of research are being developed which have psychoanalytic assumptions as important features of their conceptual base.

One notable example is the work of Luborsky and his colleagues (Luborsky, 1964, 1967, pp. 175–217; 1970), who are interested in the formation of symptoms by patients during the psychoanalytic hour. He notes that one of the problems of previous research on symptom formation is that the research is retrospective. That is, patients describe symptoms after they have appeared and

then discuss the circumstances surrounding the symptom formation. As we noted earlier, evidence of this kind, because of the
possibility of systematic distortion, is of limited value in understanding the genesis of the symptom.

Thus Luborsky and his colleagues have developed a method
of finding crucial points in the psychoanalytic hour when symptoms occur and then examining the context of thoughts which
surround the symptom formation. They call their method the
symptom-context method.

The symptom-context method has been used to test a specific
hypothesis offered by Freud (1926b, 1953). The hypothesis states
that the neurotic symptom is an attempted solution to a situation
or event that the person evaluates as being dangerous and in the
face of which he experiences feelings of helplessness. An example
Luborsky (1970) offers should help clarify this hypothesis.

> For example, each time Mr. H, the patient to be described, had a
> memory dysfunction (momentary forgetting), it was preceded by a
> trend of associations which brought him to recall a situation he
> evaluated as dangerous: his impulse to feel affection or sexuality
> for a girl. Our method should tell us whether the patient's language
> in treatment would regularly reveal specific verbal contents cor-
> responding to the "latent meanings" of the symptom, as specified
> in Freud's hypotheses, and whether the specific contents appear
> more frequently before a symptom than at other times. No one
> knows, furthermore, whether all symptoms would have similar
> psychological preconditions, or whether some, such as headache,
> palpitation, or other physical symptoms, would have fewer of them
> than the psychological one, such as obsessional thoughts about
> being killed in an auto accident (p. 661).

As the above example suggests, Luborsky sees momentary
forgetting as a prime example of symptom formation. He examined the verbal productions of 19 patients during a total of 2079
psychoanalytic sessions. Fifteen of the 19 patients produced at
least one example of momentary forgetting. The total number of
instances of momentary forgetting was 69, a surprisingly low
figure. The 550 words preceding and the 550 words following each
instance of momentary forgetting were examined and compared to
control passages that did not include instances of momentary forgetting. These passages were rated for the degree of cognitive
disturbance they reflected and the type of thematic material that
preceded and followed the instance of momentary forgetting.

Luborsky and his colleagues found a gradual increase in the

amount of cognitive disturbance before the forgetting and then a gradual disappearance shortly after the instance of forgetting. They also found a significant increase in the number of direct references to the therapist in the time immediately preceding the momentary forgetting. These references were ones which were judged to be threatening to the patient, and Luborsky believes that they may reflect an increasing and immediate involvement in those aspects of the therapeutic relationship that are of particular significance to the patient.

These investigators have extended their symptom-content method to examine other symptoms including stomach pain, migraine headaches, and petit mal epilepsy. Among their general findings were: (1) they found consistent differences within a given patient between control passages and passages that contained instances of a symptom; (2) they found that thematic differences between symptom and control passages tended to be more similar within than between patients; (3) they found that the thematic material they found for somatic symptoms differed from that for instances of forgetting. For example, the theme of helplessness was central for the occurrence of somatic symptoms. Luborsky sees this as a confirmation of Freud's hypothesis concerning the genesis of neurotic symptomatology.

This is an interesting new line of research and, as the author points out, it is a method more appropriate for generating hypotheses than for testing them. Despite this caveat, we may ask about the relative importance of the phenomenon that Luborsky and his colleagues are investigating, especially in light of the fact that only 69 instances of symptom formation were found in over two thousand psychoanalytic sessions. We might wonder, too, how many instances of the appropriate thematic content (for example, "feelings of helplessness") occur *without* the occurrence of the predicted somatic symptoms. Luborsky offers no evidence on this crucial point.

The symptom-context method used by Luborsky remains essentially retrospective despite the fact that it is relatively free of the usual distortions of retrospective report. A study using prospective methods would seek to identify antecedent thematic material and examine the probability of symptom occurrence. Knowing how likely a symptom is to occur, given the appropriate thematic content, is as important as knowing the likelihood of the occurrence of the predicted thematic content when the symptom has occurred. Nevertheless, the work of Luborsky and his colleagues represents a new direction in research drawn from the psychoanalytic perspective and one that ultimately may yield support for certain psychoanalytic hypotheses.

Critical Views

O. H. Mowrer: Neurotics Are Undersocialized, Not Oversocialized
O. H. Mowrer, intellectual renegade, original thinker, and single-minded critic of psychoanalysis (Mowrer, 1961, 1964a, 1964b, 1966a, 1966b) has provided us with one of the most vigorous criticisms of the psychoanalytic perspective. The underlying premise of his criticisms is his belief that neurotics are *not* "oversocialized" with oppressive superegos as Freud would suggest. Just the opposite is true. Mowrer believes that neurotics have not been trained strictly enough in childhood to be responsible for their own actions. Any anxiety they display is actually fear of having their own misdeeds discovered.
1. *The dynamics of neurosis.* In outlining his conception of the dynamics of neurosis, Mowrer directly opposes himself to the traditional Freudian viewpoint. The Freudian version of the dynamics of neurosis as Mowrer views it is described in Figure 3–5.
We can see that in this scheme the superego is enlarged and appears stronger than other structures in the system. Mowrer indicates that this is consonant with the Freudian assumption that the superego is disproportionately strong because of socializing influ-

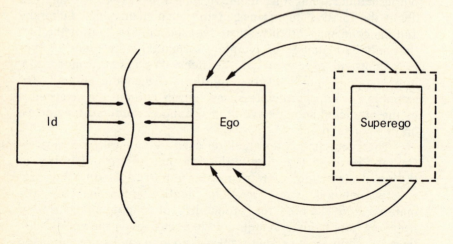

FIG. 3–5 Freudian view of the dynamics of neurosis. (Redrawn from O. H. Mowrer, Abnormal reactions or actions? (An autobiographical answer.) In J. A. Vernon (Ed.), *Introduction to psychology: A self-selection textbook.* Dubuque, Iowa: Wm. Brown, 1966. Reproduced by permission.)

ences on the individual. The curved arrows in the diagram suggest that the superego takes over the ego functions of the individual. In this situation, the ego is forced to reject the instinctual demands of the id. As a result, a barrier is constructed between the ego and the id. Repression now occurs (as represented by the barrier) as the motives and instincts of the id are held back. In this scheme, the neurosis is due to anxiety. The anxiety, in turn, is a response to the danger which the ego senses from the possibility of being overwhelmed by id impulses.

Mowrer offers a revised version of this system. His revision employs the same elements as the original Freudian version, but the arrangement of these elements has been cleverly changed. The revised system is shown in Figure 3–6.

In this figure the ego is taken over by the id rather than the superego. In this scheme, it is the superego which is repressed. The voice of conscience is being stifled. Anxiety now is assumed to be a result of guilty knowledge; or to use Mowrer's picturesque phrase, anxiety is a result of "the unheeded railings and anger of conscience" (Mowrer, 1966b, p. 31).

What are the implications of each of these two schemes? Mowrer argues that his modified scheme accounts adequately and more completely for the appearance of certain clinically observed symptoms. Of particular interest are the frequently observed clinical symptoms of "withdrawal." Withdrawal is assumed to have relatively mild manifestations in neurotics such as stage-fright or shyness. In psychotics, however, withdrawal is both more

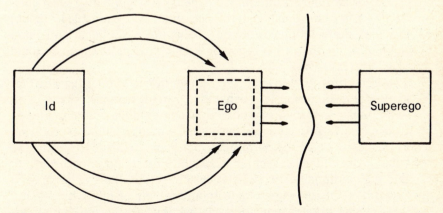

FIG. 3–6 Mowrer's view of the dynamics of neurosis. (Redrawn from O. H. Mowrer, Abnormal reactions or actions? (An autobiographical answer.) In J. A. Vernon (Ed.), *Introduction to psychology: A self-selection textbook.* Dubuque, Iowa: Wm. Brown, 1966. Reproduced by permission.)

severe and more pervasive. The symptoms of withdrawal in cases of psychosis include a generalized fear of other people, seclusiveness, and mutism. If Freud's idea of a strongly overdeveloped superego were in fact correct, then both neurotics and psychotics should be "well-integrated socially" (Mowrer, 1966b, p. 30). This conclusion follows, Mowrer suggests, because it is assumed within the Freudian scheme that it is the superego which is directing the individual's actions.

But, Mowrer argues, the "clinical facts" favor his version of the dynamics of neurosis. If the individual is cut off or isolated from the superego, then it follows that he or she will also be cut off from the society which represents the values of the superego. Thus, the clinical symptom of withdrawal and accompanying feelings of alienation are a result of concealed misdeeds, or "sins." The concealed misdeeds result in guilt, and the feelings of guilt then lead the individual to "withdraw" from social contacts.

Mowrer's scheme differs from the Freudian scheme in both the direction and the content of repression. The Freudian scheme argues that the id is repressed by the ego, which has in turn been taken over by the superego. Mowrer's scheme, on the other hand, argues that the id is repressed by the ego, which has in turn itself been taken over by the id.

We can see from this that Mowrer has opposed his own view of the dynamics of neurosis to that of the Freudian version using the same dynamic mechanisms and the same structure of personality.

3. *Symptoms as attempts to deal with guilt over past misdeeds.* Mowrer's most general accounts (Mowrer, 1965, 1966b) consider the relationship among behavior, symptoms, and emotions. As in many of his arguments he contrasts the conventional view with his own.

According to Mowrer the conventional view suggests that irrational or inappropriate behavior by other persons results in an individual's abnormal emotions; he then exhibits symptoms as in Figure 3–7. In this view, an individual's own behavior is not seen as "causal," or as a determining factor in the disorder. Only the behavior of others is seen as "causal." Furthermore, according to this conventional view, whatever the person does is seen as a "symptom" of some deep underlying problem or difficulty. Within this scheme little responsibility is ascribed to the individual. Instead, all responsibility for the abnormal behavior of the individual is attributed to the irrational and inappropriate behavior of others.

The moral perspective suggests a very different view, shown

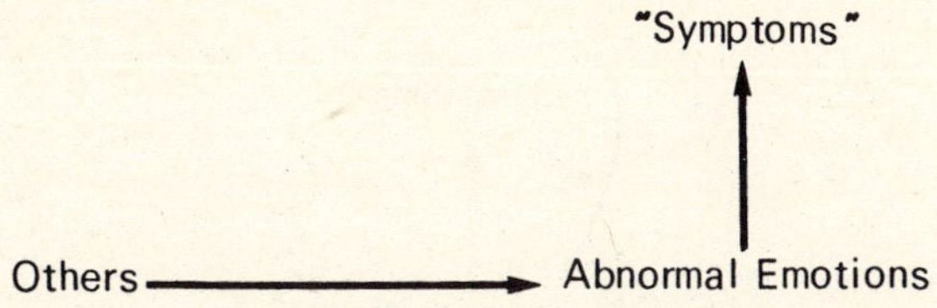

"Symptoms"

Others ————————————→ Abnormal Emotions

FIG. 3–7 Conventional view of the relation among emotions, symptoms, and the behavior of others. (Redrawn from O. H. Mowrer, Abnormal reactions or actions? (An autobiographical answer.) In J. A. Vernon (Ed.), *Introduction to psychology: A self-selection textbook.* Dubuque, Iowa: Wm. Brown, 1966. Reproduced by permission.)

in Figure 3–8. Here the deviant lifestyle of the individual *is* the abnormal behavior. As the brackets in the diagram suggest, this deviant or sinful behavior is often concealed from others. Because the individual is engaging in behavior which is contrary to society's norms, he experiences quite *normal* emotions, such as real guilt, feelings of inferiority, and anxiety.

Symptoms occur as a further result of these normal emotions. According to this view, the individual's own bad or "sinful" behavior is seen as the principal determinant of the difficulties. Furthermore, symptoms result from emotional discomfort (normal emotion) which the individual deserves because of some sinful or deviant act that he or she has performed. Finally, the individual's own conduct and responsibility are considered to be primary rather than secondary.

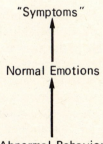

"Symptoms"

Normal Emotions

(Abnormal Behavior)

FIG. 3–8 Mowrer's view of the relation among abnormal behavior, symptoms, and emotions. (Redrawn from O. H. Mowrer, Abnormal reactions or actions? (An autobiographical answer.) In J. A. Vernon (Ed.), *Introduction to psychology: A Self-selection textbook.* Dubuque, Iowa: Wm. Brown, 1966. Reproduced by permission.)

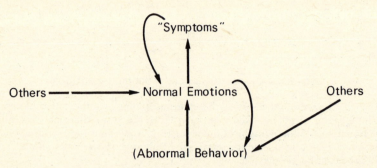

FIG. 3–9 Relation among abnormal behavior, symptoms, emotions, and the behavior of others. (Redrawn from O. H. Mowrer, Abnormal reactions or actions? (An autobiographical answer.) In J. A. Vernon (Ed.), *Introduction to psychology: A self-selection textbook.* Dubuque, Iowa: Wm. Brown, 1966. Reproduced by permission.)

Figure 3–9 brings together the assumptions we have just discussed and provides an even more complete picture of Mowrer's view of the relation among abnormal behavior, emotions, and symptoms. The symptoms that an individual displays are assumed to be an attempt at "self-cure." That is, they represent attempts to deal with the emotion the person is experiencing. Naturally, Mowrer argues, symptomatic behavior is an attempt to relieve the individual's discomfort, although it will not be successful. Symptomatic attempts at self-cure of emotional discomfort will fail because it is incorrectly assumed that the emotions themselves are the center of the problem.

The only effective therapeutic intervention that is possible involves the efforts of other individuals to actually change the abnormal behavior which is the true cause of the problem. That is, efforts by others must be directed to change the individual's wrongdoing and sinful behavior. This involves both openly confessing one's guilt and also expiation.

Thus, for Mowrer, the basic problem is misconduct on the part of the individual. The misconduct results in guilt and other quite normal emotions which in turn lead to ineffective symptomatic attempts to relieve the emotional discomfort. It is noteworthy that in this scheme abnormal behavior and symptoms are not synonymous. Instead, abnormal behavior is misconduct, while symptoms are attempts at self-cure which eventually result from the misconduct.

Psychoanalysis and Sex-Role Stereotypes

As we mentioned in the introduction to this chapter, the psycho-analytic view of psychosexual development has come under vigorous attack in recent years. Both male and female feminists have criticized the Freudian view on a number of different grounds. Let us begin to catalogue some of these criticisms.

Bernard (1972) has documented the changing role of marriage and the family in our society. These larger social changes have stimulated renewed questioning about women as the primary source of parenting, and male domination as patriarchy in the home. Bem and Bem (1971) have noted that sex-role stereotypes reflect our hidden ideology about sex roles, in part reinforced by tradi-tional psychoanalytic thought. Although Freud's speculations about appropriate behavior for female and male children are culture-bound, increased documentation of cultural differences in sex-role socialization is now available (Seward & Williamson, 1970). All of these influences have been important in focusing our awareness on the limited generalizability of some of Freud's con-cepts such as "penis envy" or "castration anxiety."

At least three specific lines of criticism of Freudian ideas about sex-role differences have developed. First, psychoanalytic thinking about sex-role development itself is now being questioned. For example, Stoller (1974) has noted that Freud believed that genital psychosexual maturity was more difficult for women be-cause their first attachment was to their mother (nonheterosexual), while the first attachment for men was a heterosexual one (with mother). Stoller notes that children at that early age do not dis-criminate gender differences in any case and that this idea is of dubious merit.

Second, increasing dissatisfaction with male psychotherapists among women (Rice & Rice, 1973) has most frequently focused on psychoanalytically trained clinicians. Apparently, many women feel that psychoanalytic theory and treatment are not relevant to their problems and world view.

Finally, Freud's ideas about the female's sexuality have re-cently been severely criticized (Sherfey, 1972). Psychoanalytic doctrine has considered orgasms resulting from clitoral stimulation to be "immature" and to reflect penis envy and rebellion against the woman's "inferior" sexual equipment. More mature orgasmic experiences, Freud believed, were the result of vaginal stimula-tion. Recent empirical research by Masters and Johnson renders this interpretation dubious at best.

Although there are writers who retain some sympathy for dynamic formulations of the psychology of women (Bardwick, 1972), in general Freud and psychoanalysis have sustained a theoretical battering at the hands of recent critics. The criticism we have outlined should remind us that perspectives often have ideological underpinnings, whether we are aware of them or not.

Summary

We have seen that psychoanalysis, as judged by contemporary standards, fails to meet the criteria necessary for status as a scientific theory. In particular, many of the propositions of psychoanalysis fail to meet the basic criterion of disconfirmability. However, few if any of the perspectives discussed in this book would meet such rigorous standards. Perhaps psychoanalysis is best viewed as a perspective or group of related metaphors which are essentially pretheoretical in nature.

In addition, clinical evidence offered to support the psychoanalytic view has been criticized on a number of grounds. Several lines of research, including that on the issue of perceptual defense, have either failed to support the psychoanalytic view or have substantially modified earlier conceptions. Nevertheless, new approaches such as that of Luborsky and his colleagues continue to evolve; these hold promise that solid empirical evidence will emerge on some psychoanalytic hypotheses.

We have examined Mowrer's theoretical critique of the psychoanalytic formulation of neurosis. In his view, neurotics do not suffer from an overly severe superego but just the opposite—they suffer from being cut off from the superego.

From a cultural point of view, feminists have been among the severest critics of the perspective. Disagreements with Freud's ideas about psychosexual development, the usefulness of psychoanalytic therapy, and female sexuality are all issues in dispute.

In the last analysis we must agree with Holzman (1970) that psychoanalysis represents an influential view of human nature and of human beings themselves.

It is more than the conception of multiple determined factors and behavior, or the idea of unconscious processes that continuously influence our experience. . . . [We feel that] psychopathology is to be regarded not as a thing that plunders the person but as an expression of [human] struggles with love and hate, life and death (Holzman, 1970, p. 177).

Suggested Reading

1. Fisher, S., & Greenberg, R. P. *The Scientific Credibility of Freud's Theories and Therapy*. New York: Basic Books, 1976.
   This review of research testing psychoanalytic propositions and hypotheses on dreams, anxiety, homosexuality, and the results of psychoanalytic treatment is a valuable sourcebook and guide to empirical research in the dynamic tradition.
2. Hall, C. S. *A Primer of Freudian Psychology*. New York: New American Library, 1954.
   Hall's discussion of Freudian theory is still one of the clearest and most carefully written of any secondary source. This account can be read in a relatively short period of time and yet will provide the reader with an excellent overview.
3. Holzman, P. S. *Psychoanalysis and Psychopathology*. New York: McGraw-Hill, 1970.
   Holzman's book is a somewhat more scholarly and selective account of psychoanalytic theory, particularly that aspect bearing on the question of abnormal behavior. An excellent source.
4. Munroe, R. *Schools of Psychoanalytic Thought*. New York: Holt, Rinehart and Winston, 1955.
   This is a much broader discussion of Freud and the Freudians. It includes not just the thinking of Freud, but of Jung, Adler, and others.
5. Salter, A. *The Case Against Psychoanalysis*. New York: Citadel, 1963.
   Salter mounts a vigorous attack on psychoanalytic thinking and its implications for our treatment of human disturbance. Clearly a polemic, but worth examining for a strong critical point of view.

LEARNING MORE
Projects for the Reader

There are many ways to learn more about the psychoanalytic perspective. One way of learning is to apply these concepts to your own experience. The exercises and projects listed below are designed to help you experience and reflect on the phenomena that Freud found so fascinating. The exercises are designed so that you can do them yourself or your instructor may want to use one or more of them as the basis for class discussion.

1. Try keeping a dream diary. Keep a pad and pencil beside your bed and the moment you awake, try to record your dreams from the previous night. Be sure to record your dreams immediately, or the memory will quickly fade. After a week or so you will find it easier to recall your dreams and record them in detail. After a week or so read over your diary. Do you detect common themes? Can you find evidence of primary process thinking? Wish fulfillment? Do you recognize themes or events that relate to events in your life right now?

2. List 10 things that make you anxious. What sort of anxiety do they seem to reflect: reality anxiety? neurotic anxiety? moral anxiety? Can you speculate about the conflicts that might underlie them?

3. Choose a character from a well-known book you have read. Discuss or speculate on his or her psychosexual development. Do you see any events that might have produced a fixation? Are there themes in the character's early relationships with his or her parents that seem to be reflected in behavior later in life?

4. Write the word "angry" at the top of a piece of paper. Now list from top to bottom, as many associations as you can. Try to fill up the page. Now look at the first and last word you have written. What relationships seem to exist between them? How do they relate to your present life experience?

5. One way to look at the defense mechanism or projection is to examine your own "pet peeves" about other people. List three "pet peeves." How do they relate to some of your own personal characteristics?

6. Think of one of your guiltiest secrets. How do you think other people (family, close friends) would react if they learned about your secrets? Are any of your own actions motivated by a desire to conceal these misdeeds, as Mowrer would suggest?

4

tHe illNess peRspective

The State of the Art

This is the opinion of a respected scientist and scholar about the problem of mental illness.

There are also more positive reasons for wanting to know all there is to be known about mental illness. Perhaps one of the most exciting aspects is the progress that modern science is now making toward understanding the nature of severe mental illness. There now exist valuable drugs which alleviate the symptoms of schizophrenia. Other drugs are known which can provoke symptoms closely mimicking those of schizophrenia. By knowing how the antischizophrenic drugs act in the brain to alleviate psychotic symptoms and by knowing how other drugs produce mental disturbances akin to schizophrenia, we may be coming close to an understanding of what is askew in the brains of schizophrenics. Not only is schizophrenia a real disease or group of diseases, but it may be possible in the not-too-distant future to understand its fundamental base just as clearly as we can identify the causative organism in bacterial pneumonia (Snyder, 1975, p. 8).

Now listen to this conversation.

Yossarian looked at him soberly and tried another approach. "Is Orr crazy?"

"He surely is," Doc Daneeka said.

"Can you ground him?"

"I sure can. But first he has to ask me to. That's part of the rule."

"Then why doesn't he ask you to?"

"Because he's crazy," Doc Daneeka said. "He has to be crazy to keep flying combat missions after all the close calls he's had. Sure I can ground Orr. But first he has to ask me to."

"That's all he has to do to be grounded?"

"That's all. Let him ask me."

"And then you can ground him?" Yossarian asked.

"No. Then I can't ground him."

"You mean there's a catch?"

"Sure there's a catch," Doc Daneeka replied. "Catch-22. Anyone who wants to get out of combat duty isn't really crazy."

There was only one catch and that was Catch-22, which specified that a concern for one's own safety in the face of dangers that were real and immediate was the process of a rational mind. Orr was crazy and could be grounded. All he had to do was ask; and as soon as he did, he would no longer be crazy and would have to fly more missions. Orr would be crazy to fly more missions and sane if he didn't but if he was sane he had to fly them. If he flew them he was crazy and he didn't have to; but if he didn't want to he was sane and had to. Yossarian was moved very deeply by the absolute simplicity of this clause of Catch-22 and let out a respectful whistle.

"That's some catch, that Catch-22," he observed.

"It's the best there is," Doc Daneeka agreed (Heller, 1961).

For some it seems only a matter of time before medical science scores a victory over mental illness. For others, mental illness is a fiction, one of the "Catch-22's" of society. In this chapter we will learn more about both of these conflicting viewpoints.

THE PERSPECTIVE

The illness perspective is unquestionably the most widely held view of abnormal behavior. In discussing abnormal behavior, we use the language and concepts of physical medicine as a matter of course. Seldom, however, do we consider the source of these concepts. As Maher (1966) puts it,

Paul Meehl on Schizophrenia

"I consider that there are such things as disease entities in functional psychiatry, and I do not think that Kraepelin was as mistaken as some of my psychological contemporaries seem to think. It is my belief, for example, that there is a disease schizophrenia, fundamentally of an organic nature, and probably of largely constitutional etiology." (Meehl, 1966, p. 9)

Society currently uses the model of physical illness as a basis for the terms and concepts to be applied to deviant behavior. Such behavior is termed *pathological* and is classified on the basis of *symptoms*, classification being called *diagnosis*. Processes designed to change behavior are called *therapies* and are applied to patients in mental *hospitals*. If the deviant behavior ceases, the patient is described as *cured* (pp. 21-22).

Similarly, our major social and governmental institutions concerned with the problem of abnormal behavior identify themselves in ways which suggest that they are concerned with the problem of health and illness (e.g. National Institute of Mental Health, Mental Health Administration). Some authors (Cumming & Cumming, 1957; Schroder & Ehrlich, 1968; Schwartz, 1957) have distinguished between the public's view of abnormal behavior, which is more concerned with the violation of social norms, and the psychiatric view held by mental health professionals. Nevertheless, many professionals and the public at large retain the idea that deviant behavior is mental illness.

Milton and Wahler (1969) illustrate this point nicely by quoting from pamphlets designed to educate the public about abnormal behavior:

The most important thing for your patient's chances of recovery and for your own peace of mind is to realize that mental illnesses are illnesses like any others (Stern, 1957).

If everyone would just realize that mental illness is no different from any other prolonged disease and that a heart attack victim differs only from a mental victim in the localization of the affliction, the psychiatrist-therapist's job would be greatly simplified (Mind over Matter, 1962).

While the signs of a neurosis frequently first appear in the late teens or early adult life, the disease may have a background in events of early infancy (The Mind, 1954).

People with either mental or emotional illness need help from a medical specialist, just the same as people with pneumonia, or ptomaine (Some Things You Should Know about Mental and Emotional Illness).

At least 50 percent of all the millions of medical and surgical cases treated by private doctors and hospitals have a mental illness complication (Facts about Mental Illness, 1963, p. 8).

It should be made very clear that these assertions about

abnormal behavior refer to the *functional disorders;* that is, dis-ordered behavior which does not have known physiological or organic correlates. Even the harshest critics of the illness perspec-tive do not argue against the proposition that general paresis or Korsakoff's syndrome is an illness. Rather, the disputed territory involves those disorders which have not yet been shown to have etiologies.

The "Medical Model" Controversy

Dynamic and Organic "Medical Models"
    Recently a great deal more has been written in criticism of the medical or illness perspective on abnormal behavior than has been written in support of it. The so-called medical model is under attack from a number of different quarters (Sarbin, 1967; Szasz, 1961; Ullmann & Krasner, 1965).
    Critics of the illness perspective often confuse several differ-ent but important issues. Sarason and Ganzer (1968) suggest that there are actually several different models which have been called the "medical model." For example, Ullmann and Krasner (1965) have included two distinguishably different approaches to abnor-mal behavior under this rubric. These two points of view are: (1) a formulation of abnormal behavior which assumes that the deter-minants are organic, and (2) approaches to abnormal behavior which assume that the determinants are psychodynamic.
    Sarason and Ganzer (1968) suggest that these two versions of the medical or illness perspective should be distinguished from one another.

> Current dynamic formulations of maladaptive behavior are not necessarily based on the assumption of physical pathology and are therefore not strictly medical. It is inappropriate to criticize psycho-logical approaches to deviant behavior as invalid because they are based on a medical model when the only basic similarities they bear to medicine are the assumption of underlying cause and some borrowed terminology (e.g., symptom, prognosis) (p. 507).

    We agree with Sarason and Ganzer on this point. In our description of the illness perspective, we will restrict our discus-sion to formulations that are fundamentally organic or physi-ological in what they assume about the determinants of abnormal behavior.
    The confusion between organic and psychodynamic formu-

lations may be partly a result of the fact that medical professionals and particularly psychiatrists may advocate both dynamic
and organic approaches. However, this fact in itself should not
constitute grounds for treating both the dynamic and the organic
approach to abnormal behavior as parts of the same model or
perspective.

There is one real similarity between the psychodynamic and
the organic approaches, however, which should not be ignored.
Wolfer (1969) calls it the "symptom-underlying-illness paradigm."
According to Wolfer, the symptom-underlying-illness paradigm
assumes that the determinants of abnormal behavior are agents
or processes residing in the organism. The abnormal behavior is
thought to be symptomatic of the underlying illness. According
to this view, symptoms will remain until the underlying cause is
discovered and corrected.

Science and Ideology

Sarason and Ganzer (1968) make a second distinction well
worth mentioning. On the one hand, there is the question of which
professional groups should be responsible for the management
and care of those designated as mentally ill. This is in part a
professional and value issue in the domain of institutional
psychiatry.

Current professional practices have raised the political and
ideological consciousness of women (Chesler, 1972), minority
groups (Grier & Cobb, 1968), criminologists (Kittrie, 1973), and
others. The treatment of people designated as "mental patients"
(Price & Denner, 1973) and the role of the mental health professions in the community are being critically reexamined (Denner
& Price, 1973) as a consequence.

On the other hand, there is a scientific and intellectual issue
that has been discussed much less. This involves the question of
the suitability of the illness perspective as a theoretical framework and classification scheme. It is the intellectual issue that we
will consider for the most part in the discussion that follows.
However, it is not always possible in practice to separate value
issues from intellectual issues. For example, in one sense, the
issues are related, as Wolfer (1969) points out: "Acceptance of
this model may have provided some tacit justification for insti-
tutionalized medical control of the training and delivery of therapeutic services" (p. 607).

But the distinction between intellectual and value issues
is still a useful one, even if it can be made only in principle. It

should allow us to examine the intellectual issues (the assertion that abnormal behavior is mental illness), while, on the issue of value, still recognize that the illness perspective has profound social and professional implications which deserve separate and detailed treatment in their own right.

The Beginnings of the Illness Perspective

The illness perspective is so much a part of our current thinking that we might forget to ask "where did it all begin?"

Although Hippocrates (460–377 B.C.) certainly may be credited with one of the earliest discussions of abnormal behavior as a product of illness, it was probably Johann Weyer (1515–1588) who made the first modern use of the illness perspective. In 1563, Weyer declared that most individuals accused of and punished for their practices of witchcraft were actually mentally ill.

Weyer may have been one of the earliest spokesmen for the illness perspective, but it was Philippe Pinel who was instrumental in popularizing this view. As chief physician in the Bicêtre in Paris in 1792, Pinel was responsible for the removal of chains and other restraints that had been routinely used to control the behavior of deviant individuals. Pinel's desire for humanitarian reform in the treatment of deviant individuals led him to the conclusion that these were sick people who deserved all the consideration that sick people require.

With Kraepelin's comprehensive, descriptive work in the nineteenth century, the illness perspective began to be elaborated, drawing increasingly upon the concepts of physical medicine. Diefendorf (1921) quotes Kraepelin as saying that:

> Judging from our experience in internal medicine, it is a fair assumption that similar disease processes will produce identical symptom pictures, identical pathological anatomy, and identical etiology. If, therefore, we possessed a comprehensive knowledge of any one of these three fields—pathological anatomy, symptomatology, or etiology—we would at once have a uniform and standard classification of mental diseases. A similar comprehensive knowledge of either of the two fields would give not only just as uniform and standard classifications, but all these classifications would exactly coincide. Cases of mental disease originating in the same cause must also present the same symptoms and the same pathological findings (p. 200).

Kraepelin is quite clearly adapting the concepts of physical medicine to the problems of deviant behavior. Despite the fact that his formulation is now considered entirely too naïve and simplistic to account for the observed findings, it was a statement based on the belief that deviant behavior could be understood in precisely the same way as other organic illnesses. As Sarason and Ganzer (1968) point out:

> The system represented the first cohesive classification of diseases and is credited with being among the first comprehensive medical models of deviant behavior. It was a true medical analogy in the strict sense: the etiology was organic (a central nervous system disease or disorder), and the prognosis was believed definite. From a Kraepelinian standpoint, it was necessary to describe and classify as accurately as possible a given set of symptoms in order that appropriate therapy might be applied (p. 508).

Thus, by the end of the nineteenth and the beginning of the twentieth centuries, the illness perspective had developed considerably. No longer merely a slogan used in the name of humanitarian reform, it had become a fully elaborated metaphor embodying specific assumptions about the nature of abnormal behavior which served as a conceptual framework for psychiatry.

The Illness Perspective Today

Key Concepts
Today the illness perspective occupies a central position in psychiatric thinking. As we have suggested in the introduction to this chapter, many of the concepts and much of the language of the illness perspective are used so frequently in the discussion of abnormal behavior that we often forget the origin of these terms in physical medicine. Let us examine briefly some of the basic concepts of the illness perspective as they are given in Box 4-1.

Perhaps an example would help us to see how these concepts are used. Consider the case of *schizophrenia*. This category is a group of *disorders* with a *syndrome* characterized by disturbances in thinking, mood, and behavior. The specific *symptoms* include misinterpretation of reality, delusions, hallucinations, and disturbances in the ability to form concepts. Schizophrenic disorders appear in both *acute* (brief, severe) episodes and in lifelong *chronic* forms. *Prognosis* can vary substantially with good prognosis for some acute forms. *Etiology* is unknown, but some forms seem to involve genetic abnormalities, although how these genetic mechanisms operate is unknown. *Treatment* most frequently in-

BOX 4-1
Language and Concepts of the Illness Perspective

Symptom A physical or behavioral manifestation of illness.

Syndrome Patterns or constellations of symptoms that are typical of a disorder.

Disorder One or more syndromes with common etiological factors.

Acute disorder Disorder with a sudden onset and of short duration. Acute disorders are usually considered reversible.

Chronic disorder Disorder that is longlasting and tends to be irreversible.

Disease Disorder characterized by symptoms, either mental or bodily, that indicate mental or physical dysfunction.

Nosology The classification of diseases.

Diagnosis The determination of the nature of a disease or abnormality based on symptoms displayed.

Etiology Causation; the systematic study of the causes of disorders.

Precipitating cause A cause of psychological disorder that serves as a "trigger" for the disorder. A precipitating life event could be a sudden loss of a loved one, a disaster, a major failure in one's life, or a sudden physiological change.

Predisposing cause An event or condition that occurs long before any abnormal behavior is observed, yet may predispose a person to later difficulties.

Specific etiology That causal condition which is necessary but not sufficient for an illness to occur; it does not by itself produce the illness.

Therapy The application of various treatment techniques either to affect symptoms or to affect etiological factors.

Prognosis Statement concerning the likely course and outcome of a disorder.

volves brief hospitalizations and administration of tranquilizing drugs. *Diagnosis* is usually based on a judgment that thinking processes are severely disturbed.

Current Structure

These definitions may aid us in our understanding of the illness perspective, but we should also have at least a rudimentary understanding of the relations between these concepts.

Figure 4–1 shows the relationships among etiological factors, symptoms, syndromes, and disorders. It also shows the points

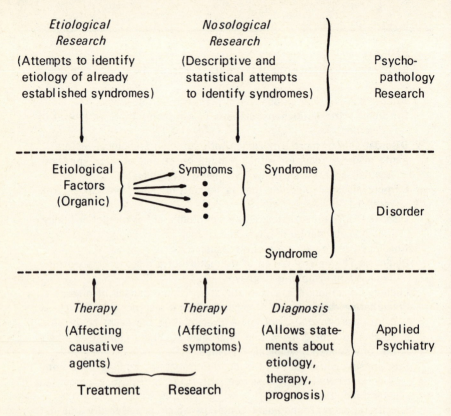

FIG. 4–1 Current structure of the illness perspective.

at which diagnosis or therapy may occur in relation to the disorder. The role of research activities is also shown, both in terms of attempts to identify syndromes from the examination of symptom clusters (nosological research) and attempts to discover the etiology of syndromes that have already been described (etiological research).

Examples of *etiological research* include studies of brain chemistry, genetic inheritance, and stress. Currently the area of *nosological research* is becoming more sophisticated and is using mathematical models and computer methods to improve classification systems (Blashfield, 1976) currently in use. For the most part, *treatment research* has focused on the effects of various drugs, including stimulants, antidepressants, and tranquilizers, on symptoms of depression, schizophrenia, and neurosis.

Three Types of Disease
So far we have discussed the illness perspective and described some key concepts, but we have not defined the concept of illness or *disease.*

There actually is more than one way to think about diseases. Buss (1966) points out that there are at least three generally accepted kinds of disease in medicine. The first of these is called a *traumatic disease.* This is a disease that is produced by some external or environmental event or agent. Serious physical damage due to external stress, such as poisoning, or perhaps a skull fracture, is an example of a traumatic disease. A second major type of disease in medicine is the *infectious disease.* In infectious diseases, a microorganism such as a virus attacks the body through a particular organ or system of organs. Probably the most famous infectious disease in psychiatry is general paresis, a behavior disorder associated with syphilis of the brain.

Infectious or traumatic diseases do not provide the best concepts for understanding abnormal behavior as illness. The third type of disease, the *systemic disease,* probably provides the best and most interesting concept. In the systemic disease, some organ or organ system breaks down or fails to function properly, primarily because it already possesses some inherited defect or weakness. Thus, the organ or organ system is *predisposed* to break down, and may do so if it is subjected to prolonged stress. It should be noted that this idea, though very simple, takes into account both external environmental stresses and the physiology of the organism as it is shaped by heredity.

Classifications and Diagnosis

Purposes of Classification
Classification as an activity is not confined to medical scientists and psychiatrists. Astronomers, chemists, zoologists, plumbers, detectives, and accountants are classifying events or objects every day. In fact, we are, all of us, classifying objects and events in our world all the time. In the field of abnormal psychology and particularly in the context of the illness perspective, classification has always played an important role. Consider the purposes of classification as described by Blashfield and Draguns (1975).

1. *A basis for communication.* One way to view a classification system in the field of abnormal psychology is to think of it as a dictionary of terms that allows us to discuss a person

or a disorder as a member of a large class. In doing so, we are communicating information about that individual in a kind of shorthand. When a psychiatrist says that an individual is a "reactive depressive," he or she is using an abbreviation to imply a much larger range of features.

2. *A key to the scientific literature.* Classification assumes that the name of a disorder is the key to scientific information describing it. By looking at the literature discussing "manic-depressive psychosis," we ought to be able to find information on its description, what is known about its causes, and perhaps how people have tried to treat it.

3. *A means of description.* Both clinical practitioners and research scientists want to be able to describe the characteristics of the people whose behavior they study. If the classification system we are using categorizes individuals so that the groupings are fairly homogeneous, then the name of the group will provide a fairly accurate summary of the important characteristics of the person, at least insofar as abnormal behavior is concerned.

4. *Prediction.* Once we have classified an individual, it should be possible to predict (1) what the causes of the disorder are likely to be, (2) how that individual will respond to treatment, and finally, (3) the probable course of the disorder. As we noted earlier, in the context of the illness perspective, a very large portion of the efforts of scientists are devoted to discovering the relationships between particular types of abnormal behavior and possible causes, effects of treatment, or the relationship between a particular type of abnormal behavior and its future outcomes.

5. *Scientific theory building.* A category in a classification scheme can become a concept in a theory about abnormal behavior. For example, the classification "schizophrenia" has long served as the reference point for a set of ideas about people who are thought to share certain characteristics. Schizophrenia is an *idea* shared by scientists. It is not a theory, but a scientific concept used to summarize a set of characteristics of people's behavior.

Diagnosis and the DSM

Diagnosis is of great importance in the illness perspective. Putting patients into diagnostic categories serves at least three functions. First, treatment decisions are most often based upon diagnosis. For example, a patient who is diagnosed as depressed is likely to receive electroconvulsive therapy or antidepressant drugs, while a patient diagnosed as schizophrenic is more likely to receive tranquilizing drugs as the major form of treatment. Second, identifying the syndrome a patient displays is usually thought to be a necessary prerequisite for the discovery of causal factors or etiology of the illness. As Cattell (1940) puts it, "nosology necessarily precedes etiology." Similarly, Marzolf (1945) indicates that the "establishment of syndromes is preliminary to the discovery of etiologies." Third, diagnosis of illness provides the diagnostician with information concerning the prognosis—the probable course and outcome of the illness.

Typically, in diagnosis the patient is examined to determine the syndrome or symptom cluster which he or she has developed. The syndrome identified in the examination is then taken as an indication of the disorder from which the patient suffers. Eysenck (1960a) notes the similarity between diagnostic practice in psychopathology and physical medicine when he says:

> Traditionally, classification in the field of abnormal psychology has been by means of specific diseases or syndromes; we speak of hysteria, or schizophrenia, or manic-depressive psychosis in much the same way as we speak of tuberculosis, or neurosyphilis, or cancer (p. 1).

The diagnostic examination involves a number of different procedures. The patient may undergo a series of laboratory tests to assess his or her current physiological status. In addition, psychological tests may be administered. Finally, the patient will often be given a mental status interview to evaluate his or her affect, memory, judgment and orientation, and insight into the nature of his illness. The diagnostician combines and evaluates all of this information and uses it as the basis for the final diagnostic decision.

In medicine, as Eysenck (1960a) suggests, diagnosis may be made in terms of the agent that is designated the "cause" of the disease or on the basis of the symptom syndrome which is regarded as characteristic of the disease; in some cases both types of information may be presented at the same time. In psychiatry, diagnosis is almost never based upon causal factors since they are seldom known. Thus the diagnosis of abnormal behavior is done almost exclusively on the basis of symptoms or syndromes.

In the United States the standard reference for diagnosis is the *Diagnostic and Statistical Manual of Mental Disorders* (DSM II) (1968). Interestingly, in the Foreword to the second edition of the Manual, Gruenberg (1968, pp. vii–x) states that this revision has been constructed to conform closely with the International Classification of Diseases. Gruenberg indicates that "the rapid integration of psychiatry also helped to create a need to have psychiatric nomenclature and classification closely integrated with those of other medical practioners" (p. vii).

The intention of those producing the official nosology of the American Psychiatric Association was to retain an explicitly medical orientation. This most recent revision of the nomenclature (DSM II) contains the ten major diagnostic subgroupings shown in Table 4-1.

This revision is a product of compromise, as Kramer (1968) points out. Variations in the orientation of consultants with differing points of view have been reconciled by finding a middle ground acceptable to all those involved in the task rather than by recourse to empirical methods.

Although considerable skepticism has been voiced recently concerning the effectiveness of diagnostic practice, Meehl (1966) remains convinced of its usefulness:

> The fundamental argument for the utility of formal diagnosis can be put either causally or statistically, but it amounts to the same kind of thing one would say in defending formal diagnosis in organic medicine. One holds that there is a sufficient amount of aetiological and prognostic homogeneity among patients belonging to a given diagnostic group, so that the assignment of a patient to this group has probability implications which it is clinically unsound to ignore (p. 9).

Meehl's language is certainly more sophisticated and more

TABLE 4-1   Major Categories in the Diagnostic and Statistical
Manual of Mental Disorders (American
Psychiatric Association, 1968).

   I. Mental Retardation
  II. Organic Brain Syndromes
 III. Psychoses Not Attributed to Physical Conditions Listed Previously
  IV. Neuroses
   V. Personality Disorders and Certain Other Nonpsychotic Mental Disorders
  VI. Psychophysiological Disorders
 VII. Special Symptoms
VIII. Transient Situational Disturbances
  IX. Behavior Disorders of Childhood and Adolescence
   X. Conditions without Manifest Psychiatric Disorder and Nonspecific Conditions

cautious than Kraepelin's remarks quoted earlier, but we can see certain similarities in their views.

Diagnosis, then, plays a vital role in the identification of symptom syndromes, whether the problem is in organic medicine or abnormal behavior. Furthermore, once the patient is identified as a member of a particular nosological group, it is assumed that we can make inferences about etiology and statements about prognosis. Such statements are possible because members of the same nosological group are assumed to be suffering from the same illness.

Insane People or Insane Places?

Psychiatric diagnosis has been severely criticized on a variety of grounds. The reliability of diagnostic judgments, their power to stigmatize the person so labeled, and other criticisms have been levelled at diagnostic practice. One of the most dramatic and fascinating studies offered in support of these criticisms has been done by Rosenhan (1973). Rosenhan asked the question, "Can the sane be distinguished from the insane?" and decided to do a study that he thought would help him find out.

He began with a group of friends and collaborators including three psychologists, a psychiatrist, a pediatrician, a painter, and a homemaker. These people were asked by Rosenhan to become "pseudo-patients." That is, they were each to report to a mental hospital and to request admission.

The only "symptom" they were allowed to report to the examining physicians during the intake interview was that they heard voices sounding "empty, hollow, thudding." The pseudo-patients also falsified their names and their work, but otherwise presented themselves as they really were. All of these individuals were admitted to the hospital upon reporting their initial symptom, even though the symptom had never been recorded in the psychiatric literature as an indicator of severe psychiatric disorder. Furthermore, each of these people was diagnosed, with one exception, as suffering from schizophrenia. All were later discharged, most of them with a diagnosis of "schizophrenia in remission." Rosenhan believes that the results of his experiment dramatically demonstrate that it is not possible to distinguish those of us who are "insane" from those of us who are "sane."

Later in the commentary section of this chapter we shall see that there is great disagreement about what Rosenhan's study did or did not demonstrate. However, one thing is clear. His study and the reactions it evoked indicate that differences of opinion about the value of diagnosis and, indeed, about the value of the illness perspective itself are emotional and run deep.

Etiology: The Search for the Causes of Mental Illness

One accompaniment of the illness perspective on abnormal behavior is what Maher (1966) calls the "organic orientation." Once one assumes that deviant or abnormal behavior is a consequence of illness, then it follows that research into organic causes will be undertaken as a matter of course.

We should not find it surprising that considerable effort has been devoted to biochemical (Kety, 1959) and genetic (Kallman, 1953; Rosenthal, 1970) research with various diagnostic groups. The goal of such investigations is to identify organic factors that may have etiological significance for particular syndromes.

As we have suggested, Kraepelin's original notions of etiology are considered today to be much too simplistic to account for our observations concerning the nature of abnormal behavior. However, the illness perspective still retains a strong set of assumptions about the determinants of abnormal behavior.

Types of Causal Factors in Mental Illness

Although it is assumed that organic factors play an important role in mental illness, medical scientists tend to think about different *classes* of causes. For example, some causal factors are described as *predisposing causal factors*. These are events or conditions that occur long before any abnormal behavior is observed and yet may predispose the individual to later difficulties. Predisposing causes can be a consequence of previous experiences or some genetic and physiological events or both. The important point is that they pave the way for later psychopathology. A second major type of cause is the *precipitating causal factor*. This is an event that serves as a "trigger" for the disorder. A precipitating life event could be a sudden loss of a loved one, a disaster, a major failure in one's life, or a sudden physiological change. The ingestion of LSD, for example, can sometimes precipitate severe reactions in individuals who are predisposed to react in that manner. Finally, a third type of cause of condition is the *maintaining cause*. Maintaining causal factors are those that serve to reinforce abnormal behavior and thus maintain it over time. For example, poor conditions in a mental hospital could maintain a person's withdrawal and depression for a considerable period of time.

It may be difficult at times to decide whether a particular event or condition served as a predisposing event, a precipitating event, or both. The advantage of classifying causal events in this way, however, is that one can construct a picture of the causal process underlying abnormal behavior that is more complex and therefore likely to capture the complexity of the actual causal process.

Genetic Evidence

The idea that abnormal behavior may have a biological basis has naturally led to studies attempting to establish a genetic basis for various disorders (Rosenthal, 1970).

Some of the most convincing evidence exists in the case of schizophrenia. Using the *twin method* investigators have studied identical (monozygotic) and fraternal (dizygotic) twins. The logic of the approach is straightforward. Identical twins have essentially identical genes. Fraternal twins are no more similar genetically than other siblings. Therefore, if you locate an individual twin that is schizophrenic, examine the cotwin. If the genetic hypothesis is correct, identical twins will more likely display *concordance* (both be schizophrenic) than will fraternal twins. Table 4-2 shows the results of a number of such studies.

Notice that the concordance rate for monozygotic (identical) twins is generally much greater than that for dizygotic (fraternal) twins. This suggests that there may be a genetic component in schizophrenia but, of course, tells us nothing about how the genetic mechanism works.

Although the twin method has been criticized, other methods comparing children of schizophrenic mothers and normal mothers separated from their mothers at birth (Rosenthal, 1970) have also supported the genetic hypothesis. Thus, for schizophrenia at least, there is evidence of a biological basis for the disorder.

Brain Chemistry: Evidence from Drug Treatment

Another line of evidence for a biological basis of abnormal behavior comes from research on the effects of drugs on schizophrenics (Snyder, 1975).

Snyder argues that a particular class of drugs called *phenothiazines* have *specific* effects on the brain chemistry of schizophrenics. This is evidence, he feels, that it is not merely the general tranquilizing quality of the drug in operation but something in the brain chemistry of schizophrenics that is amiss in

TABLE 4-2 Concordance Rates in the Major Twin Studies of Schizophrenia
(Adapted from Rosenthal, 1970, p. 119)

STUDY	SOURCE	MZ TWINS MONOZYGOTIC		DZ TWINS DIZYGOTIC	
		Number of Pairs	Percent Concordant	Number of Pairs	Percent Concordant
Luxenburger, 1928a, 1934	Germany	17–27	33–76.5	48	2.1.
Rosanoff et al., 1934–1935	United States and Canada	41	61.0	101	10.0
Essen-Möller, 1941	Sweden	7–11	14–71	24	8.3–17
Kallmann, 1946	New York	174	69–86.2	517	10–14.5
Slater, 1953	England	37	65–74.7	115	11.3–14.4
Inouye, 1961	Japan	55	36–60	17	6–12
Tienari, 1963, 1968	Finland	16	0–6	21	4.8
Gottesman and Shields, 1966	England	24	41.7	33	9.1
Kringlen, 1967	Norway	55	25–38	172	8–10
Fischer, 1968	Denmark	16	19–56	34	6–15
Hoffer et al.	United States veterans	80	15.5	145	4.4

the first place and that is uniquely affected by phenothiazines.

Look at Table 4-3. Here the effects of phenothiazines on schizophrenics from numerous studies are summarized. Fundamental symptoms (believed basic to schizophrenics) are most affected, accessory symptoms (not basic to schizophrenia) are next most affected, and other nonschizophrenic symptoms are not markedly affected. Thus, the effects of tranquilizers on brain chemistry are offered as possible evidence for the biochemical basis of schizophrenia.

The Concept of Specific Etiology

We have briefly examined some genetic evidence and some speculation about the biochemistry of one form of abnormal behavior, schizophrenia. We can now look at some speculations about how chemical and genetic causal assumptions are combined to produce a hypothetical causal chain in the case of schizophrenia.

In his now-famous paper describing his theory of schizophrenia, Meehl (1962) describes one such set of causal assumptions. Drawing directly upon nonpsychiatric medicine he suggests that we consider the concept of *specific etiology*. Briefly, this

TABLE 4–3 Analysis of Symptom Sensitivity to
Phenothiazines (From Snyder, 1974)

BLEULER'S CLASSIFICATION OF SCHIZOPHRENIC SYMPTOMS	RESPONSE TO TREATMENT
Fundamental	
Thought disorder	+ + +
Blunted affect-indifference	+ +
Withdrawal-retardation	+ +
Autistic behavior-mannerisms	+ +
Accessory	
Hallucinations	+ +
Paranoid ideation	+
Grandiosity	+
Hostility-belligerence	+
Resistiveness-uncooperativeness	+
Nonschizophrenic	
Anxiety-tension-agitation	0
Guilt-depression	0
Disorientation	0
Somatization	0

concept refers to that causal condition which is necessary but not sufficient for the illness to occur. Thus, the causal factor which is designated as the specific etiology must be present for the illness to occur but this causal factor may not by itself produce the illness.

Meehl uses the analogy of a "color psychosis" to illustrate the concept of specific etiology. He points out that the specific etiology of color blindness is known to involve a mutated gene on the X chromosome. If an individual who possessed this specific etiology and who therefore was color-blind grew up in a society which was entirely oriented around making fine color discriminations, he might develop a "color psychosis." Cultural and social factors would inevitably play a role in the development of his illness. Nevertheless, if we ask, "what is basically the matter with the patient?" the answer must be, according to Meehl, that the mutated gene on the X chromosome is the specific etiology of the "color psychosis."

Meehl is careful to point out, however, that when the concept of specific etiology is applied to a disorder such as schizophrenia, a number of misunderstandings may arise. In particular, he points to five misunderstandings concerning the concept of specific etiology: (1) the presence of the etiological factor does not necessarily produce the clinically observed disorder; (2) the form and content of the clinically observed disorder is not necessarily understandable or derivable from the specific etiology alone; (3) the course of the disorder is not treatable only by procedures which are directed against the specific etiology itself; (4) people who share the specific etiology will not necessarily have the same or closely similar histories and symptoms; and (5) the largest source of variance in symptoms is not necessarily the specific etiology.

These disclaimers make it clear that the notion of specific etiology does not imply a simple cause-effect relationship between etiological factors and symptoms. In fact there may be more links in the causal chain between the specific etiology and the symptom ultimately displayed by the patient.

One important reason that different symptom patterns may arise with the same specific etiology is that some of the behavior displayed by the patient may be compensatory in nature. That is, two patients with the same specific etiology or organic defect may behave quite differently in response to that defect. One patient may respond with lethargy and withdrawal while the other might engage in a series of energetic attempts to overcome the difficulty. The result, of course, will be two quite different symptom pictures associated with the same specific etiological factor.

Summary

We have seen that the illness perspective views abnormal behavior as the product of disease or illness. The discipline of physical medicine provides the principal source of concepts for the perspective. Thus mental illness is manifested by symptoms that are grouped into syndromes and have an organic etiology. Furthermore, various nosological entities or diseases are assumed to have similar prognoses. Among the various types of diseases, traumatic, infectious, and systemic, it is the systemic concept of disease that is the most promising conception of abnormal behavior. The determinants of abnormal or symptomatic behavior are presumed to be either (1) the organic etiology itself, (2) compensatory reactions to the basic organic defect, or (3) some combination of these. In any case, the organic etiology plays the crucial role in understanding the illness.

We have also seen that there is a growing body of evidence that some forms of abnormal behavior, for example, schizophrenia, may have a genetic and biochemical basis.

The displacement of these concepts from physical medicine to the problem of abnormal behavior and the resulting mutual adaptation of events is apparent in several ways. First, abnormal behavior is often assumed to be the product of illness even when there is no known organic etiology that would properly qualify the disorder as a disease. Second, the concept of illness is significantly broadened in its application to deviant behavior. Behavior patterns such as psychopathy, or even homosexuality, are sometimes considered illnesses, thus significantly extending what is meant by the term "illness." Both the original concepts from physical medicine and the phenomena to which they are applied are changed and restructured in the process.

COMMENTARY

Mental Illness: Myth or Disease?

The controversy over the usefulness of the concept of mental illness is one of the best known and most heated debates to have taken place recently in the field of abnormal psychology. At this point we should remind ourselves that the controversy we are about to describe revolves around the status of the functional disorders. Both critics and defenders of the illness perspective are concerned with the question of whether or not deviant behavior for which there is no known physiological correlate should be seen as disease. Unquestionably the single most vocal leader of the "anti-mental illness" movement is Thomas Szasz (1960, 1967, 1976). Although a psychiatrist himself, Szasz has been one of the profession's severest critics.

Mental Illness as Myth

Szasz begins his attack by asserting that mental illness is a myth. He argues that most behavior deviations may be more usefully thought of simply as problems in living. Problems in living were historically conceived first in terms of demonology and possession. Then, with the advent of humanitarian reform, problems in living were viewed as the products of medical disease and called mental illness. At the time, this shift in perspective constituted a sweeping conceptual revolution and marked a great step forward in the humane treatment of deviant individuals. Today, however, the concept of mental illness has outlasted its usefulness.

Szasz is convinced that the concept of mental illness cannot withstand logical scrutiny. For example, he argues that although mental illness is a medical term it is defined not by medical but by social criteria. More specifically, the defining criteria of mental illness tend to be ethical, psychosocial, and legal. And if this were not inconsistent enough, we use social criteria to define this medical term "mental illness," and at the same time we assume that medical actions will correct the disorder. Thus the mental illness concept is subject to the double inconsistency of being a medical term defined by nonmedical criteria but nevertheless treated by medical means.

We have suggested that the illness perspective implies an organic orientation to possible causal factors in abnormal behavior. Szasz (1960) is in essential agreement with this point and notes that

> "Mental illnesses" are thus regarded as basically no different than all other diseases (that is, of the body). The only difference, in this view, between mental and bodily diseases is that the former, affecting the brain, manifest themselves by means of mental symptoms; whereas the latter, affecting other organ systems (for exam-

ple, the skin, liver, etc.), manifest themselves by means of symptoms referrable to those parts of the body (p. 113).

In Szasz's view, this set of assumptions contains two fundamental errors. First, if an illness is the result of neurological defects, then it is in fact a disease of the nervous system, and not a problem in living. As such, it should be described as a neurological disease, and not as "mental illness."

The second error is epistemological and involves a fundamental dualism between physical and mental events. Physical symptoms are a manifestation of physical disturbances, whereas mental symptoms refer to the way in which patients communicate about themselves and others, and the world around them. Thus the dualism implied in the term mental illness is a confusion of anatomical and social contexts.

From this point of view, the phenomena to which we refer when we use the term mental illnesses are actually communications which express unacceptable ideas often framed in an unusual idiom. In addition, these communications are judged within a value context. Both the values of the patient and those of the examining physician are involved in the use of the concept of mental illness.

Furthermore, Szasz argues, the responsibilities both of the patient and of the psychiatrist are obscured when problems in living are seen as products of mental illness. In particular, the patients are relieved of responsibility for their actions when they are able to view their behavior as mental illness, a condition over which they have no control. Similarly, the psychiatrists by implication are absolved of their responsibility to take action on the behavior of the individual who has problems in living, since they view the behavior as mental illness for which there is no known cure.

Szasz (1960) summarizes his argument in the following way:

> Our adversaries are not demons, witches, fate, or mental illness. We have no enemy whom we can fight, exorcise, or dispel by "cure." What we do have are problems in living—whether these be biological, economic, political, or sociopsychological. In this essay I was concerned only with problems belonging in this last mentioned category, and within this group mainly with those pertaining to moral values. The field to which modern psychiatry addresses itself is that, and I made no effort to encompass it all. My argument was limited to the proposition that mental illness is

a myth, whose function it is to distinguish and thus render more palatable a bitter pill of moral conflict in human relations (p. 118).

Personality Disorder as Disease

Szasz's criticisms of the mental illness concept have not gone unchallenged. Ausubel (1961) has examined Szasz's argument and concludes that the assertion that mental illness is a myth is based upon four "unsubstantiated and logically untenable propositions" (p. 70).

Ausubel begins by questioning Szasz's argument that only symptoms from demonstrable physical lesions are legitimately considered as manifestations of disease, and therefore that mental symptoms not involving physical lesions may not qualify as examples of illness. Ausubel points out that the somatic view of illness supports the idea that anatomic or physiological integrity has no effect upon behavior in a general fashion. He goes on to point out that even if we accept Szasz's notion that brain pathology does not account for personality disorders, we still do not have to accept the idea that a disease must have physical symptoms in order to qualify as such.

> Adoption of such a criterion would be arbitrary and inconsistent both with medical and lay connotations of the term "disease," which in current usage is generally regarded as including any marked deviation, physical, mental, or behavioral, from normally desirable standards of structural and functional integrity (p. 71).

The second of Szasz's propositions with which Ausubel takes issue is the dichotomy between mental and physical symptoms. He argues that this distinction is not as clear-cut as Szasz would suggest. Nearly all symptoms of bodily disease involve some subjective judgment, either on the part of the examining physician or on the part of the patient. For example, pain may be a response to real physical damage, but it is a subjective state as well. Similarly, almost all patients will react psychologically to physical illness, thus requiring subjective decisions by the examining physician. Even if it were possible to distinguish between mental and physical symptoms, Ausubel suggests that this does not mean that physical treatment is unwarranted for mental symptoms.

Another of Szasz's arguments with which Ausubel disagrees is that mental symptoms are simply problems in living and therefore cannot be regarded as a result of some pathological condition. It is possible, Ausubel points out, that a particular symptom may be a reflection of problems in living *and* a manifestation of disease.

It is quite true, as Szasz points out, that "human relations are inherently fraught with difficulties" (p. 117), and that most people manage to cope with such difficulties without becoming mentally ill. But conceding this fact hardly precludes the possibility that some individuals, either because of the magnitude of the stress involved, or because of genetically or environmentally induced susceptibility to ordinary degrees of stress, respond to the problems of living with behavior that is either seriously distorted or sufficiently unadaptive to prevent normal interpersonal relations and vocational functioning. The latter outcome—gross deviation from a designated range of desirable behavioral variability—conforms to the generally understood meaning of mental illness (p. 72).

Finally, Ausubel questions the proposition that personality disorders are a product of moral conflict and ethical choice. While he admits that Szasz may be correct in saying that the mental health profession has underemphasized the ethical and moral bases of human behavior, Ausubel feels that it is usually possible to distinguish between ordinary cases of immoral behavior and mental illness.

The Szasz-Ausubel exchange provides us with an opportunity to consider the usefulness of the disease concept as a way of characterizing abnormal behavior. The basic issue confronting us here involves the question of what we mean by "disease" in a general sense, and what we mean by disease when we refer specifically to abnormal behavior. Szasz wishes to eliminate the idea of "mental illness" with its automatic assumption that all behavioral deviations are the result of brain disease. Ausubel, on the other hand, regards disease, mental or otherwise, as "any marked deviation, physical, mental, or behavioral, from normally desirable standards of structural and functional integrity."

Neither of these definitions is entirely satisfactory. Ausubel's definition of disease is so broad and inclusive that it is difficult to imagine any difficulty that an individual might encounter which would not qualify as a "disease" or as "mental illness." Also, this definition is so general that it begs the question of what we mean when we use the terms. Furthermore, since any deviation from "normally desirable standards" can qualify as disease, the possibility exists that even the "ordinary cases of immorality" which he wishes to distinguish from personality disorders could also be legitimately described as examples of disease. Thus, Ausubel's definition of disease has been stripped of much of the explanatory power it might have had by its extreme generality.

Szasz would argue that physiological diseases have known

organic etiologies, whereas mental illness is a misuse of medical terminology to characterize human problems in living which are essentially ethical, legal, or social in nature. This is a useful distinction and we will return to it later in our discussion.

Social Impact of the Illness Perspective

We have indicated that the illness perspective is unquestionably the dominant public perspective for understanding abnormal behavior. A number of writers have been concerned recently about the social impact of the illness perspective. Do individuals whose behavior is considered abnormal benefit from being called mentally ill? Or, on the other hand, does this designation derogate and stigmatize them? An exchange between Ellis (1967) and Sarbin (1967) provides an excellent review of this problem and the arguments on both sides.

After reviewing literature which suggests that people labeled as mentally ill may suffer social discrimination (Davidson, 1958; Menninger, 1965), self-denigration, and interference with their treatment, Ellis (1967), nevertheless remains convinced that at least some people should be so labeled. He believes that the term mental illness can be used as a sort of shorthand for more elaborate operational definitions and in this way can be appropriately applied to certain individuals without necessarily having negative consequences.

> Thus, instead of saying, "He is mentally ill," we could say, "He is a human being who at the present time is behaving in a self-defeating and/or needlessly antisocial manner and who will most probably continue to do so in the future, and, although he is partially creating or causing (and in this case is responsible for) his aberrant behavior, he is still not to be condemned for creating it but is to be helped to overcome it." This second statement is more precise, accurate, and helpful than the first one, but it is often impractical to spell it out in this detail. It is, therefore, legitimate to use the first statement, "He is mentally ill," as long as we clearly understand that it means the longer version (p. 445).

Sarbin (1967) strongly disagrees with this argument and suggests that Ellis is guilty of accepting the premise which he has set out to prove. He feels that Ellis' arguments

> represent not so much a lack of attention to the rules of evidence . . . as the acceptance of an entrenched and unwarranted belief

that operates as a major premise. When operative, the premise may be stated: The label "mental illness" reliably denotes certain forms of conduct that are discriminable from forms of conduct that may be reliably denoted as "not mentally ill" (p. 447).

Sarbin argues that retaining the mental illness label leads Ellis and others so disposed to accept a number of tacit but fundamentally wrong assumptions concerning the nature of people so labeled. Not only are these assumptions incorrect or misleading, but they tend to restrict our descriptions of the conduct we are trying to understand. That is, once the conduct called mental illness has been identified as such, we view the person displaying that conduct quite differently. Finally, Sarbin would argue that once our perceptions of the individual have been restricted, alternative actions toward that person have been restricted as well. When we see the person as mentally ill, we behave toward him or her in highly predictable ways. For example, since the person is mentally ill we may incorrectly conclude that he or she requires hospitalization for the illness.

Sarbin's conclusions flow from a linguistic and historical analysis of the concepts of "illness" and "mind." Illness, according to Sarbin, was first used as a metaphor and later transformed into a myth by dropping the qualifying "as if," as in, "he acts *as if* he were ill."

"Illness," as in mental illness, is an illicit transformation of a metaphorical concept to a literal one. To save unfortunate people from being labeled witches, it was humane to treat persons who exhibited misconduct of certain kinds as if they were ill. The Galenic model facilitated the eliding of the hypothetical phrase, the "as if," and the concept of illness was thus deformed to include events that did not meet the original conjunctive criteria for illness. A second transformation assured the validity of the Galenic model. The mystifying behaviors could be treated as if they were symptoms equivalent to somatic symptoms. By dropping the "as if" modifier, observed behavior could be interpreted as symptomatic of underlying internal pathology (p. 449).

It is not only illness that is reified in the dual metaphor "mental illness." Mental states are also seen as real, palpable objects.

Thus mental states—the objects of interest and study for the diagnostician of "mental illness"—were postulated to fill gaps in early knowledge. Through historical and linguistic processes, the construct was reified. Contemporary users of the mental illness concept are guilty of illicitly shifting from metaphor to myth. Instead of maintaining the metaphorical rhetoric "it is as if there were states of mind," and "it is as if some 'states of mind' could be characterized as sickness," the contemporary mentalist conducts much of his work as if he believes that minds are "real" entities and that, like bodies, they can be sick or healthy (p. 450).

These linguistic and historical developments in the case of the mental illness label have led us to regard people who carry that label as different from those who do not. According to Sarbin's argument, however, there is no set of behaviors which can reliably distinguish those people we regard as mentally ill from those we do not.

From Sarbin's point of view, the solution lies in omitting the label "mental illness" from our vocabulary, since there is no evidence that societal problems can be ameliorated by diagnosing deviant individuals as "ill." In place of the mental illness metaphor Sarbin suggests that we refer to "the transformation of social identity." This term captures the antecedent and concurrent events associated with becoming a *norm violator* (Sarbin, 1967).

Sarbin's views are similar to those of advocates of the *social perspective* (see Chapter 6). He points up the idea that mental illness is not just a logical error, but also has real social impact. It is viewed as a label that stigmatizes the person and *changes the way we view and react to that person.*

Evidence for Social Impact

But is there any evidence that the illness perspective really has an impact on the lives of people labeled as "mentally ill" as Sarbin claims? Price and Denner (1973) have collected a wide range of studies that suggest that there is indeed evidence of the social impact of the illness perspective. Price and Denner have traced the social processes through which a person goes, beginning at the point when a relative or friend notices something "peculiar" about the person, through initial contact with police, psychiatrists, the courts, through mental hospitalization, and finally release back into the community. At each point along the social path to the hospital, it is the *presumption by other people that the person is mentally ill* that shapes their behavior toward that person.

The presumption of mental illness affects referral to psychiatrists or police (Bittner, 1967), the results of mental competence hearings in court (Wenger & Fletcher, 1969), decisions regarding hospitalization (Mendel & Rapport, 1969), medical decisions and diagnosis (Temerlin, 1968), and treatment itself (Zeitlyn, 1969). Thus, it appears correct to assume that the presumption of illness does affect both professional and nonprofessional perceptions and behavior toward the person labeled mentally ill.

The study conducted by Rosenhan in which pseudopatients were hospitalized because of a single complaint has been offered as evidence of the fallibility of the current diagnostic system based on the illness perspective. However, defenders of medical diagnosis (e.g., Spitzer, 1975) have argued that Rosenhan's logic is "in remission" and that his study does not illuminate the real problems in current diagnostic practice.

Perhaps the best indication that perspectives are in conflict here comes from the "Letters to the Editor" section of *Science* magazine after the publication of Rosenhan's article. Consider these reactions, for example.

> The attack on psychiatric nomenclature as some kind of pernicious "labeling" comes very close to a denial that any mental disorders characterized by objectively ascertainable symptoms, behaviors, and tests altogether exist. In the not so distant past, "tuberculosis" and "syphilis" were words shunned by polite society. Fortunately, this did not deter physicians and researchers diagnosing and treating these conditions (*Science*, vol. 180, p. 364).

> I am deeply concerned about the state and fate of psychiatric care in this country. I am also deeply concerned about the destructive potential of such pseudo-studies as the one under discussion. Appearing in *Science*, it can only be productive of unwarranted fear and mistrust in those who need psychiatric help, and make the work of those who are trying to deliver and teach about quality care that much harder (*Science*, vol. 180, p. 358).

Scientific Impact of the Illness Perspective

We have just noted that the presumption of mental illness can have adverse effects on people labeled as "mentally ill." Thus the metaphor can have real social impact. But what about the scientists themselves? What are some of the effects of the illness perspective on the questions scientists ask and the research they do in the field of abnormal psychology?

Usefulness of the Organic Assumption

Although some of the original assumptions Kraepelin made

in elaborating the illness perspective are now thought to lack empirical support, Kraepelin still has advocates. Among the most forthright of these is Meehl, whose work we have already mentioned. In a paper entitled "Some Ruminations on the Validation of Clinical Procedures" (1966), Meehl makes his position quite clear regarding Kraepelin's assumptions and the concept of schizophrenia as a disease.

> I consider that there are such things as disease entities in functional psychiatry, and I do not think that Kraepelin was as mistaken as some of my psychological contemporaries seem to think. It is my belief, for example, that there is a *disease* schizophrenia, fundamentally of an organic nature, and probably of largely constitutional aetiology. I would explain the viability of the Kraepelian nomenclature by the hypothesis that there is a considerable amount of truth contained in the system; and that, therefore, the practical implications associated with these labels are still sufficiently great, especially when compared with the predictive power of competing concepts, that even the most anti-nosological clinician finds himself worrying about whether a patient whom he has been treating as an obsessional character "is really a schizophrenic" (p. 9).

Several things are worth noting about Meehl's formulation. He appears to mean by disease something quite similar to what we have outlined in our description of the illness perspective. It is interesting to note that his position is a clear-cut example of the displacement of concepts: the concept of disease is applied to a new and puzzling situation, that is, schizophrenia, applied not by analogy but as a literal statement.

Meehl appears to believe that calling schizophrenia a disease has scientific utility. Specifically, he believes that the use of the disease concept will yield superior *predictions* concerning future behavior than will alternative concepts. Although he does not elaborate what he means by this, we may infer reasoning similar to the following:

1. GIVEN A CLUSTER of symptoms or syndrome diagnosed as schizophrenia,
2. AND GIVEN that the disease entity schizophrenia has certain reliable properties,
3. WE MAY PREDICT:
   a. the specific etiology of the disorder when discovered will be organic and perhaps genetic.
   b. the outcome of the disorder in terms of prognosis.

Of course, such a set of statements has clear-cut empirical implications. The utility of asserting that schizophrenia is a disease can be judged by the degree to which these predictions can be empirically verified.

We have noted that genetic and biochemical evidence for an organic basis for *some* disorders is accumulating with convincing regularity (Rosenthal, 1970; Snyder, 1975) in recent years.

Mythmaking?

Perhaps the single most outstanding issue raised by our commentary is the question of whether mental illness should be viewed as myth or disease. Both Sarbin and Szasz strongly suggest that the idea of mental illness is essentially mythical in nature, a label without reliably observable behavorial referents. Ellis and Meehl, on the other hand, believe there is a substantive, real thing called mental illness which results in ineffective social behavior and which can be studied scientifically like any other disease.

It is unlikely that any reconciliation of these views would please all of these authors. Yet we may be able to integrate their views in a way that is consistent with our position, namely, that approaches to psychopathology are essentially metaphors which serve to provide the psychopathologist with a way of viewing human behavior.

In another connection, Sarbin suggests there is a common tendency to transform metaphors to myths. By myth he means "a literal statement, unsupported by empirical evidence, used as a guide to action" (Sarbin, 1968, p. 414). Given the current state of knowledge concerning most forms of abnormal behavior, the assertion that abnormal behavior is mental illness certainly seems to qualify as a myth as Sarbin describes it.

There is a real danger in concepts that have attained the status of myth. They may lose the tentativeness of scientific hypotheses and become, instead, dogmatically espoused guides to action. We would suggest that, in this sense at least, Sarbin and Szasz are justified in attacking the concept of mental illness.

There is also the danger of overgeneralization in the illness perspective. Torrey (1975) puts it well when he says,

One of the results, then, of the medical approach to mental "disease" is that everybody ends up qualifying as mentally "ill." The spectre of mental "disease" haunts us and becomes "the nation's number one public health problem." It is even more prevalent than hemorrhoids (p. 55).

On the other hand, we have also suggested earlier that metaphors, whether they have become myths or not, have other important functions. To review briefly, the metaphor aids us in selecting events as relevant, provides a mode of representation of the events in question, and allows us to specify the relations between events. These are important functions that lay the groundwork for systematic inquiry.

We would suggest that when Meehl says that there are disease entities in functional psychiatry, he is in effect proposing a systematic framework and mode of attack on the problem of abnormal behavior. In general, treating one set of events (abnormal behavior) as if they were another set of events (disease) is just such a proposal. This proposal has as one of its products a set of testable hypotheses concerning the events in question. For example, to assert that "schizophrenia is a disease" implies that there are discoverable organic etiological factors involved. Similar hypotheses have invited and will continue to invite empirical test. The future of the illness perspective will depend upon the outcome of these tests.

Summary

The lines of argument are clearly drawn. The controversy over the usefulness of the illness perspective centers on the question of whether abnormal behavior may be legitimately considered a disease or not. Szasz has asserted that mental illness is not a disease but a myth and that behaviors now classified as mental illnesses are more usefully considered to be simply problems in living. Such a designation would, according to Szasz, serve to emphasize the fact that most abnormal behavior involves moral and ethical conflict. Ausubel and others have criticized Szasz's argument on a number of grounds and have asserted that a particular symptom may be both a problem in living and a manifestation of disease. But we noted that Ausubel defines disease so broadly that he weakens the potential persuasiveness of his argument considerably.

The term "mental illness" is not strictly analogous to the concept of physiological disease. It is interesting to note that this may in part reflect the fact that metaphors tend to undergo a process of mutual adaptation when they are taken from one field of inquiry and applied to a new and puzzling problem. The original meaning of the concept of disease has, it appears, been altered in its application to the problem of abnormal behavior.

We have also considered the social impact of the concept of mental illness. Some psychologists suggest that we may use the term mental illness as a kind of shorthand to designate certain persons as being in need of psychological help without necessarily producing negative social consequences for the person so labeled. Sarbin, on the other hand, has provided a linguistic and historical analysis of the concept of mental illness and suggests that it functions as a reified metaphor. That is, mental illness is a metaphor which is now uncritically accepted as a real, palpable entity. Sarbin goes on to assert that we cannot identify a set of behaviors which reliably distinguishes those people who are mentally ill from those people who are not.

The scientific usefulness of the illness perspective will depend heavily on whether it is used as a source of testable hypotheses or merely accepted as an established fact. If it is taken as a broad assumption suggesting a series of conceptually related and testable hypotheses, then there remains at least the possibility of empirical test of the assumption. If, on the other hand, it is taken uncritically as a dogmatically espoused guide to action, then it is likely to impede both scientific and social progress.

Suggested Reading

1. Rosenthal, D. *Genetic Theory and Abnormal Behavior*. New York: McGraw-Hill, 1970.
   This thorough and thoughtful book reviews the existing research evidence for genetic involvement in a range of forms of abnormal behavior. Chapters on research methods and theoretical issues are also very well done.
2. Snyder, S. H. *Madness and the Brain*. New York: McGraw-Hill, 1974.
   This scholarly yet readable book describes our present knowledge about drugs, brain chemistry, and schizophrenia. A researcher convinced that schizophrenia is a disease, Snyder makes a detailed and impressive case.
3. Szasz, T. *Schizophrenia: The Sacred Symbol of Psychiatry*. New York: Basic Books, 1976.
   This is the latest in a series of books attacking the concept of mental illness, the mental health professions, and institutional psychiatry in particular. Szasz spearheaded the most recent attack on the illness model fifteen years ago and is still worth careful attention.

4. Torrey, E. F. *The Death of Psychiatry*. New York: Penguin Books, 1974.

Like Szasz, Torrey is an outspoken critic of the illness perspective and the institution of psychiatry and is a psychiatrist himself. This book also offers an alternative to the illness perspective based on educational rather than medical assumptions.

LEARNING MORE
Projects for the Reader

1. Look up several recent issues of psychiatry journals in the library. In some of them you will find advertisements for tranquilizing drugs. Read an ad carefully. How does it depict psychological problems that the drug is intended to help? What aspects of the ad seem to perpetuate the illness perspective? What aspects do not?

2. Try to recall the last time you were coming down with the flu. Can you recall your psychological state then? On a scale of "good," "fair," "poor," rate your own psychological functioning at the time, in the following areas: affect or emotional expression, memory, orientation to time (e.g., date, and so on), judgment, interpersonal relations, mood. Does this exercise help you to see how biological events can affect your psychological state? How different or similar do you think this is to the phenomena of abnormal behavior such as disorientation, mood swings, confusion, and so on?

3. Look at a dozen or so recent columns of "Dear Abby" or "Ann Landers" in your local newspaper. Locate some letters in which the person is advised to seek psychological help or is described as "mentally ill." Do the behaviors described fit the illness perspective? Which aspects fit and which do not?

4. Can you recall some recent public education films or advertisements indicating that "mental illness is an illness like any other illness?" Do you think these campaigns are effective in educating the public? What do you think the public learns from them? Try writing a one-minute public education "spot" that promotes the illness perspective. Now try one that promotes Szasz's idea that "mental illness is just a problem in living." Which do you think would elicit contributions from the public? Why?

5. If there is an important genetic component in serious forms of abnormal behavior, then one form of prevention would involve genetic counseling of parents who have the potential to transmit the disorder genetically. What do you think of this idea and its ethical implications?

5

тHE LEARNiNq pERspEctivE

Skinner on Contingencies

Listen as B. F. Skinner transforms a young man's identity crisis into a description of what is wrong with the reinforcement contingencies in the world.

Consider a young man whose world has suddenly changed—he has graduated from college and is going to work, let us say, or has been inducted into the armed services. Most of the behavior he has acquired up to this point is useless in his new environment. We can describe the behavior he actually exhibits and translate the description as follows: he lacks assurance or feels insecure (*his behavior is weak and inappropriate*); he is discouraged (*he is seldom reinforced, and as a result his behavior undergoes extinction*); he is frustrated (*extinction is accompanied by emotional responses*); he feels anxious (*his behavior frequently has unavoidable aversive consequences that have emotional effects*); there is nothing he wants to do or enjoys doing well—he has no feeling of craftsmanship, no sense of accomplishment (*he is rarely reinforced for doing anything*); he feels guilty or ashamed (*he has previously been punished for idleness or failure, which now evokes emotional responses*); he is disgusted with himself (*he is no longer reinforced by the admiration of others, and the extinction that follows has emotional effects*); he becomes hypochondriacal (*he concludes that he is ill*) or neurotic (*he engages in a variety of ineffective modes of escape*); and he experiences an identity crisis (*he does not recognize the person he once called "I"*).

The italicized paraphrases suggest the possibility of an alternative account, which alone suggests effective action. What the young man tells us about his feelings may permit us to make some informed guesses about what is wrong with the contingencies, but we must go directly to the contingencies if we want to be sure, and it is the contingencies we must change if we are to change his behavior (Skinner, *Beyond Freedom and Dignity*, 1971).

In his alternative account, Skinner has done more than just substitute one descriptive language for another. The learning perspective he has applied to the person's behavior has suggested both a new way to view the young man's dilemma and a new approach to coping with it. This is the hallmark of the learning perspective.

THE PERSPECTIVE

Introduction

The learning perspective is currently one of the most rapidly growing and influential approaches to the study of abnormal behavior. Part of its appeal is undoubtedly because the perspective carries with it a quality of scientific respectability. Adherents of the approach usually take pains to point out that its basis is modern learning theory. As such, the learning perspective draws upon basic concepts from learning theory as well as a sizeable body of empirical information.

Another reason for its appeal is the fact that the learning perspective offers not only a formulation of abnormal behavior, but also a relatively well-defined program of treatment based upon the same principles. Thus, typically, the formulation of a particular case within the learning framework suggests at the same time a means of changing the behavior in question.

Although scientific respectability and the promise of effective treatment techniques were the early reasons for interest in the learning perspective, new research developments promise still more. For example, experimental research and theoretical developments on learned helplessness (Seligman, 1975) stimulated by learning concepts suggest new insights into the nature of depression.

Some History

The history of the current learning movement can certainly be traced as far back as John Locke's (1632–1704) doctrine of man as a *tabula rasa* (blank slate). However, the recent history of the perspective as it is applied to abnormal behavior is perhaps more informative in understanding the current state of the field.

In 1950 Dollard and Miller published *Personality and Psychotherapy*, in which they attempted to reexamine some traditional psychoanalytic principles of psychotherapy in light of learning concepts. Although theirs was an impressive attempt, the reaction of fellow professionals, after an initial burst of enthusiasm, was to view the book as little more than a translation of one set of principles into another with the addition of little that was new or innovative.

Shortly thereafter, in 1953, Skinner published *Science and Human Behavior,* an attempt to apply the principles of operant conditioning to a wide variety of human behaviors. Its strength

B. F. Skinner on Understanding Human Behavior

"We must go directly to the contingencies if we want to be sure, and it is the contingencies we must change if we are to change [the] behavior." (Skinner, 1971)

was and remains Skinner's ability to convince us of the power of his approach with his striking examples. Skinner's work was considered impressive by many, but it did not deal in detail with the problem of abnormal behavior and thus did not have great impact on those specifically concerned with this problem.

It remained for Wolpe's *Psychotherapy by Reciprocal Inhibition* (1958) to produce this impact. In this volume Wolpe described his laboratory work on the conditioning of anxiety in animals and the therapeutic technique of systematic desensitization of fear responses which developed out of this work. From this point on, acceptance of the learning perspective increased rapidly. The journal *Behavior Research and Therapy* was established in 1963, to be devoted to theoretical and empirical contributions to the learning approach to abnormal behavior.

Early in the 1960s two distinguishably different orientations within the learning perspective began to emerge. One approach was based largely upon principles of classical conditioning as described by Wolpe (1958) and Eysenck (1960b). The other approach was Skinnerian in orientation and relied much more heavily upon the principles of operant conditioning. The work of Ullmann and Krasner (1965) was greatly influenced by the Skinnerian orientation, and, although it was based largely upon operant principles, it also extended the learning perspective to encompass a much broader range of social phenomena associated with abnormal behavior.

The seventies has been a decade that has seen a number of different lines of development. First, treatment technologies based on learning principles have developed in a wide range of settings (Kanfer & Phillips, 1970). In addition to the psychotherapist's consulting room, behavior modification, particularly that of the Skinnerian variety, has appeared in classrooms, juvenile correctional settings, mental hospital wards, factories, sexual dysfunction clinics, and self-help books. Self-control techniques based on behavioral principles have been developed to reduce weight, stop smoking and drinking, and increase work productivity, motivation, and satisfaction (Thoresen & Mahoney, 1974). Thus the last ten years have seen the establishment of behavior modification techniques as a large and important aspect of American psychology.

Formulations of the nature and development of abnormal behavior from a learning perspective have also developed in this period, though not as rapidly. In some areas, however, as we shall see, major gains have been made.

Basic Processes and Clinical Phenomena

Before we can begin to appreciate the learning perspective on abnormal behavior in detail, it is necessary to examine briefly some of the most fundamental concepts of learning theory. These concepts are given in Box 5-1.

Classical Conditioning

You will recall that we defined classical conditioning as the process whereby an originally neutral conditioned stimulus, through continuous pairing with an unconditioned stimulus, acquires the ability to elicit a response originally given to the unconditioned stimulus. Figure 5-1 describes the standard classical conditioning paradigm. You can see from Figure 5-1 that it is the *pairing* of the neutral conditioned stimulus with the unconditioned stimulus that is crucial for conditioning to occur.

But how is the mechanism of classical conditioning presumed to operate in the development of abnormal behavior? The answer is that a neutral stimulus (CS) is paired in the natural environment with a traumatic or noxious stimulus event that serves as an unconditioned stimulus (UCS). An example of classical con-

BOX 5–1
Language and Concepts of the Learning Perspective

Stimulus   Any objectively defined situation or event that is the occasion for an organism's response.

Response   Any behavioral event whose strength can be manipulated by changing antecedent stimuli or consequent events.

Reinforcer   Any event following a response which changes the strength of that response.

Reinforcement   The process by which response strength (i.e., the probability of a response) is changed as a result of either classical conditioning or operant conditioning.

Classical conditioning   The process whereby an originally neutral conditioned stimulus, through continuous pairing with an unconditioned stimulus, acquires the ability to elicit a response originally given to the unconditioned stimulus.

Instrumental conditioning   Process of development of behavior in which the organism must emit the response before reinforcement can occur. Therefore, the response is **instrumental** in receiving reinforcement.

Modeling   A learning mechanism involving the observation and imitation of others. Advocates of the learning perspective believe it is one mechanism by which abnormal behavior develops.

Discrimination   The reinforcement of a response in the presence of a particular stimulus but not in the presence of other stimuli. The outcome of this procedure is that the response will occur in the presence of the stimulus associated with reinforcement and not in other situations.

Generalization   A failure of discrimination. A response reinforced in the presence of a particular stimulus may also occur to stimuli that are similar to the original stimulus, even though the response was never reinforced in their presence.

Extinction   The removal of the reinforcer used in conditioning a response; the resulting decline in response strength.

Maladaptive behavior   Behavior that (1) is inappropriate in the eyes of those who control the reinforcements for the person, and (2) leads to a decrease in the amount of positive reinforcement given the person behaving abnormally.

ditioning in the production of a phobia is illustrated in the now famous case of Albert (Watson & Rayner, 1920).

The classical demonstration of the development of a phobia was provided by Watson and Rayner in 1920. Having first ascer-

Conditioned
  Stimulus   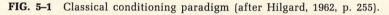 --------------------→ No Response
(before conditioning)

Conditioned -------   (learned)
  Stimulus   ----------
                                  ------------→ Conditioned Response

Unconditioned   (unlearned)   Unconditioned
  Stimulus   --------------------------→   Response

FIG. 5–1   Classical conditioning paradigm (after Hilgard, 1962, p. 255).

tained that it was a neutral object, the authors presented an eleven-month-old boy, Albert, with a white rat to play with. Whenever he reached for the animal the experimenters made a loud noise behind him. After only five trials Albert began showing signs of fear in the presence of the white rat. This fear then generalized to similar stimuli such as furry objects, cotton, wool, white rabbits. The phobic reactions were still present when Albert was tested four months later.

To see how Albert's fear is conceptualized with the classical conditioning paradigm, look at Figure 5–2. Although the process is assumed to operate in the development of numerous maladaptive behaviors, it is extremely difficult to document actual life experiences in children and adults that follow a strict classical conditioning paradigm.

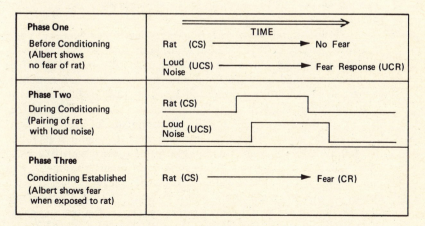

FIG. 5–2   Classical conditioning of Albert's phobia.

Little Hans's Phobia Reinterpreted

In Chapter 3 we discussed the psychoanalytic interpretation of the development of phobias and illustrated it with the famous case of "Little Hans." He was, as you recall, terrified of horses. Freud's interpretation was that the phobia was the product of an Oedipus complex and that, as Cameron (1963) put it,

> The little patient harbored hostile aggression against his only male rival for his mother's love, but at the same time he also loved his father dearly.
>
> Reduced to its simplest terms the phobic solution was about as follows. The love this boy bore his mother was repressed; it disappeared. The love for his father was retained, while the hatred for him was displaced on the horses. This had the added advantage that the horse could easily be avoided, whereas his father could not. In the usual role reversal of fantasies and dreams, the boy expected primitive retaliation from his father for the primitive hostility he himself felt. This expectation likewise was displaced. It became the regressive oral fear that horses would bite him. (p. 294)

This case has been repeatedly cited by advocates of the psychoanalytic perspective as evidence for the dynamic view of the development of phobias. Wolpe and Rachman (1960) have provided an alternative interpretation based on classical conditioning principles. After a scathing attack on the factual basis of the original account, they say:

> We shall show how Hans's phobia can be understood in terms of learning theory, in the theoretical framework provided by Wolpe (1958). . . .
>
> In brief, phobias are regarded as conditioned anxiety (fear) reactions. Any "neutral" stimulus, simple or complex, that happens to make an impact on an individual at about the time that a fear reaction is evoked acquires the ability to evoke fear subsequently. If the fear at the original conditioning situation is of high intensity or if the conditioning is many times repeated the conditioned fear will show the persistence that is characteristic of *neurotic* fear; there will be generalization of fear reactions to stimuli resembling the conditioned stimulus. Hans, we are told, was a sensitive child who "was never unmoved if someone wept in his presence," and long before the phobia developed became "uneasy on seeing the horses in the merry-go-round being beaten." It is our contention that the incident to which Freud refers as merely the exciting cause of Hans' phobia was in fact the cause of the entire disorder. . . . The evidence obtained in studies on experimental neuroses in ani-

mals on phobias in children indicate that it is quite possible for one experience to induce a phobia. . . .

Just as the little boy Albert [in Watson & Rayner's classic demonstration of 1920] reacted with anxiety not only to the original conditioned stimulus, the white rat, but to other similar stimuli such as furry objects, cotton, wool, and so on, Hans reacted anxiously to horses, horse-drawn buses, vans and features of horses, such as their blinkers and muzzles. In fact he showed fear of a wide range of generalized stimuli. . . .

Hans's recovery from the phobia may be explained on conditioning principles in a number of possible ways, but the actual mechanism which operated cannot be identified, since the child's father was not concerned with the kind of information that would be of interest to us. It is well known that especially in children many phobias decline and disappear over a few weeks or months. . . . But since Hans does not seem to have been greatly upset by the interpretations, it is perhaps more likely that the therapy was actively helpful, for phobic stimuli were again and again presented to the child in a variety of emotional contexts that may have inhibited the anxiety and in consequence diminished its habit strength. . . . (pp. 143–146)

Thus, the mechanism for the development of the phobia is seen as classical conditioning by Wolpe and Rachman. Fear of other similar objects is viewed as the result of generalization, and the child's recovery is attributed to extinction rather than to any insights derived from interpretation.

Instrumental Conditioning

A second major process by which the development of abnormal behavior is assumed to occur is instrumental or operant conditioning. In the case of instrumental conditioning, the organism must emit the response before reinforcement can occur. Thus the response is *instrumental* in producing a reinforcer. The operant paradigm is shown in Figure 5–3.

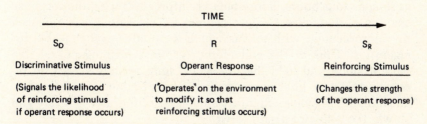

TIME		
S_D	R	S_R
Discriminative Stimulus	Operant Response	Reinforcing Stimulus
(Signals the likelihood of reinforcing stimulus if operant response occurs)	("Operates" on the environment to modify it so that reinforcing stimulus occurs)	(Changes the strength of the operant response)

FIG. 5–3 Operant conditioning paradigm.

A well-known example of the application of operant principles in the acquisition of deviant behavior has been provided
by Haughton and Ayllon (1965). They reported a case in which
they attempted to develop a "symptom" in an individual and
then removed it, thus demonstrating, presumably, the effects of
reinforcement on the behavior. The investigators selected a patient
from an experimental research ward in a psychiatric hospital, a
fifty-four-year-old female patient who had been hospitalized for
23 years. They began by observing the patient every thirty minutes
and recording her behavior in terms of both activity and location.
After a number of days of observation they found, not surprisingly, that the patient typically stayed in bed, smoked heavily,
and refused to work on the ward. Having recorded the necessary
base-line data, the patient was deprived of cigarettes with the
exception of one cigarette after each meal. Following this, a period
of response shaping took place. The investigators selected a response arbitrarily. The response they selected was to stand upright
holding a broom. The procedure for instituting this response in
the behavior of the patient was described by Haughton and Ayllon
(1965) as follows: "a period of response shaping was initiated
during which a staff member gave the patient a broom and while
she held it, another staff member approached the patient and gave
her a cigarette" (p. 96).

Once the response was established, various "reinforcement
schedules" were initiated and response shaping occurred. As different reinforcement schedules were applied to the patient's behavior, fewer and fewer reinforcements, that is, cigarettes, were
given for longer and longer periods of holding the broom in the prescribed manner. Finally, toward the end of the response shaping
period, the patient was receiving the reinforcement of a cigarette
as infrequently as every 240 minutes and yet, interestingly enough,
the broom-holding "symptom" remained strong. This means that
at the end of the response shaping period, Haughton and Ayllon's
patient would in some cases maintain the prescribed behavior for
as long as four hours before being reinforced. During the response
shaping period, direct reinforcement by cigarettes was replaced
by reinforcement with tokens which were later exchangeable for
cigarettes. Thus at the end of the response shaping period, the
patient stood and held the broom for long periods simply to receive a token. A final phase of the demonstration involved extin-
guishing the response. Reinforcement was withdrawn entirely and
slowly the behavior disappeared.

Thus we see that the learning perspective argues that symptoms are developed according to the contingencies obtaining among responses, stimuli, and reinforcers. Of course, this case is a demonstration of how operant conditioning *might* be involved in the acquisition of maladaptive behavior rather than evidence that abnormal behavior does in fact develop by operant processes.

Once maladaptive behaviors are developed, we may ask how the learning perspective argues that they are maintained. The answer is, in essentially the same way they were developed, that is, by reinforcement. Ullmann and Krasner do point out, however, that although reinforcement is assumed to maintain the maladaptive behavior, it is not necessarily true that the reinforcer which led to the development of the behavior will also maintain it. Thus, for example, a behavior may be developed because it allows avoidance of certain aversive consequences in an individual's life. However, once the behavior is developed, it may be maintained by some other positively reinforcing event.

Modeling

A third possible learning mechanism thought to play a role in the development of abnormal behavior is the observation and imitation of others. Albert Bandura has conducted extensive work in this field exploring modeling both as a basis for the development of abnormal behavior, and as a means of treatment. A moment's reflection suggests that observational learning may play an important role even in cases in which no direct conditioning responses are applied to the person's behavior.

An example is that of *vicarious conditioning* of phobic behavior demonstrated by Bandura and Rosenthal (1966). A model (actually an accomplice) was observed by subjects while attached to electrical apparatus designed to appear as if the model were to receive a shock. After a number of trials during which observers watched a buzzer signal apparent shocks to the model, the observers also observed increased emotionality to the sound of the buzzer *even though no direct pairing of an aversive event with the buzzer had occurred.*

One can imagine this sort of vicarious conditioning occurring in children who observe the reactions of their parents or playmates to feared events or objects. How important a role vicarious conditioning actually plays in the acquisition of phobias is far from clear, however.

Photo 5–1 illustrates how behavior sometimes considered maladaptive such as aggression can be acquired through modeling. In a now famous demonstration Bandura et al. (1963) exposed

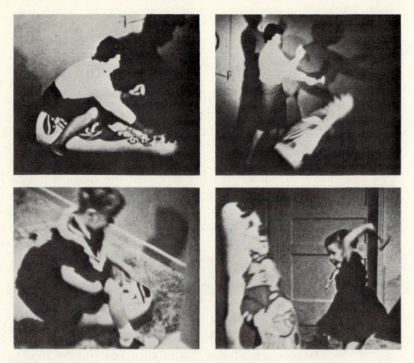

PHOTO 5–1 These photos show aggressive behavior performed by a child as a result of modeling (courtesy of Albert Bandura).

children to adult models who acted aggressively toward a doll. Children who observed such models were often highly aggressive later in the same setting when given the opportunity, while children in a control group who did not observe such models were much less aggressive. Thus, modeling is a plausible learning mechanism for the development of abnormal behavior.

Abnormal Behavior As Learned: "The Symptom Is the Disorder"

Advocates of the learning perspective begin by asserting that abnormal behavior is *maladaptive behavior.* Such behavior has several characteristics or attributes. First, it is not assumed to differ from any other presumably normal behavior either in terms of its development or maintenance. Since there is presumed to be no discontinuity between adaptive and maladaptive behavior, the decision to call any particular behavior pathological must depend to a large extent upon social factors. Specifically, Ullmann and

Krasner (1965) assume in their account that all societies prescribe certain roles which have a particular range of reinforcement associated with them. These roles are then maintained by reinforcement.

Thus, for Ullmann and Krasner, maladaptive behavior has two identifying characteristics. First, it is considered inappropriate by those individuals in a particular person's life who control the reinforcers or reinforcing events for that person. Second, maladaptive behavior tends in general to lead to a reduction or decrease in the amount of positive reinforcement given to the individual who engages in that behavior.

Eysenck further clarifies what is meant by the term "maladaptive," particularly in the case of neurotic behavior:

> As nearly all human behavior may be said to be learned, how do we distinguish neurotic behavior from other types of behavior? The answer must be that neurotic behavior is maladaptive; the individual who adopts a neurotic behavior pattern fails to achieve what he is trying to do and succeeds in doing what is highly disadvantageous to him (p. 3).

From this point of view of the learning perspective then, abnormal behavior is learned and maladaptive in the sense that it is self-defeating for the individual engaging in it.

There is another point on which most advocates of the learning perspective are in fundamental agreement. It is argued that the "symptom" of observable behavior *is* the disorder, rather than some underlying state of affairs. Eysenck and Rachman (1965) make this point quite explicitly when they say,

> The point, however, on which the theory here advocated breaks decisively with psychoanalytic thought of any description is in this. Freudian theory regards neurotic symptoms as adaptive mechanisms which are evidence of repression; they are "the visible upshot of unconscious causes." Learning theory does not postulate any such "unconscious" causes, but regards neurotic symptoms as simply learned habits; there is no neurosis underlying the symptom, but merely the symptom itself. *Get rid of the symptom (skeletal and autonomic) and you have eliminated the neurosis* (p. 10).

Thus, abnormal behavior, at least in the case of neurosis, is not thought to be due to some underlying dynamic or organic set of factors. Similarly, the term "symptom" is regarded only as a convenient label.

While the term "symptom" may be retained to describe neurotic behavior, there is no implication that such behavior is "symptomatic" of anything (Eysenck & Rachman, 1965, p. 277).

Most adherents of a learning perspective believe that the assertion that "the symptom is the disorder" provides a clear-cut distinction between their view and that of the illness or psychoanalytic perspective. Furthermore, the assumption that the symptom is the disorder places the behavior therapist in a position to treat the symptom directly without concerning himself with the problem of "symptom substitution."

The notion of symptom substitution—that removal of a symptom will lead necessarily to the development of some new maladaptive behavior—has been vigorously attacked by adherents of the learning perspective (Ullmann & Krasner, 1965; Yates, 1958). Ullmann and Krasner (1969) have offered two forms of argument against this notion. They indicate that "symptom substitution" is much less frequent than is commonly assumed. Rachman (1963) estimates that symptom substitution occurs after symptom removal in no more than 5 percent of the cases examined.

Ullmann and Krasner (1969) also suggest several alternative interpretations of the re-emergence of maladaptive behavior. First, maladaptive behavior may reoccur because the individual is re-sensitized to threatening stimuli in which he or she had previously been desensitized. Second, a new maladaptive behavior may occur because it is next in response strength in the individual's repertoire. Third, behavioral change in the individual may alter the stimulus situation, thus eliciting new maladaptive behaviors. Finally, symptom removal may lead to inconsistent behavior patterns. That is, newly acquired behavior may not be consistent with other ongoing behavior displayed by the individual and this inconsistency may be perceived as symptom substitution.

Learned Helplessness

So far we have examined the learning perspective on abnormal behavior only in a general fashion. But, can the concepts of the learning perspective illuminate a particular clinical phenomenon in detail? Recent research and theory by Seligman (1975), Eastman (1976), Ferster (1973), and others on the problem of depression suggest that it can.

Seligman argues that important effects occur for people and animals when environmental circumstances occur in which they are *helpless*. Specifically, Seligman argues that helplessness occurs when there is no relationship between the efforts of the organism to receive reinforcement and the outcomes of those efforts. As Yager (1975) puts it, "When nothing works, why bother?"

The Theory

More formally, Seligman (1975) portrays the relationship among behavior, reinforcement, and their contingencies. When there is no relationship between responses (either responding or not responding) and reinforcement, a condition of *response independence* occurs. In this condition, the animal or person cannot predict or control important outcomes and is said to be helpless.

How did Seligman arrive at this formulation? In the original experiments Seligman and his colleagues subjected dogs to a series of inescapable shocks and then placed them in a shuttle box where a warning signal came on before shock occurred. The task of the animals was to learn to leap over a hurdle in order to escape or avoid the shock. Animals that had been previously exposed to inescapable shock did not learn to escape when placed in the shuttle box. On the other hand, animals that had not been previously exposed to shock learned the task easily. Seligman and his colleagues concluded that the inability of the animals that had been exposed to inescapable shock to learn simple escape or avoidance behavior was an example of "learned helplessness." That is, they had previously learned that shock was inescapable and therefore did not try to escape. Furthermore, Seligman and his colleagues showed that the same dogs could be "immunized" against learned helplessness by exposing them to escapable electric shocks and allowing them to develop effective escape behavior. When these same dogs were later exposed to inescapable shock and then placed in an escape situation, they learned to escape quickly. They were not helpless.

To understand why Seligman attaches such significance to these findings, look at Figure 5–4. Here we see the three basic components of the theory of learned helplessness. According to

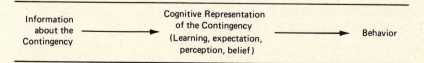

FIG. 5–4 Three basic components of Seligman's (1975) theory of learned helplessness.

this view, the organism receives information about the likelihood of reinforcement, develops an expectation based on it, and behaves on the basis of that expectation. Thus, the dogs in Seligman's experiment had developed the expectation that trying to escape the shocks was futile and therefore "gave up" and became helpless.

Depression

Seligman also believes that the mechanisms involved in the development of learned helplessness can tell us something about the nature and determinants of clinical depression. One of Seligman's most important contributions has been to carefully examine the clinical literature on depression in the light of his own research on helplessness in animals and humans and to carefully draw out parallels between the two sets of phenomena. These parallels are summarized in Table 5–1.

Notice that Seligman has attempted to look at similarities in learned helplessness and depression across four areas that he believes are important. He has looked for similarities in symptoms, in causes, in cures, and in prevention.

It is worth pausing for a moment to think about how Seligman's theoretical work on helplessness provides us with an example of the displacement of concepts. Seligman (1975) notes that using helplessness as a concept to illuminate the concept of depression has several effects. First, applying the idea of learned helplessness selects from and clarifies what we mean by "depression." As he neatly puts it, the concept of learned helplessness "clips the concept of depression at the edges." Furthermore, the fact that a clinical phenomenon is being investigated means that the researcher begins to look among laboratory findings for phenomena that correspond to "symptoms," "cause," "cure," and "prevention," as you can see in Table 5–1.

Thus, the research and theory on helplessness provides us with an example of the learning perspective in action and an example of the mutual adaptation of concepts in the scientist's thought.

Another Learning View:
Rate of Reinforcement and Depression

We have discussed Seligman's learned helplessness view of depression because it presents a clear case of the application of the learning perspective to the phenomenon of depression. But within

TABLE 5–1   Summary of Features Common to Learned
Helplessness and Depression (from Seligman,
1975, p. 106)

	LEARNED HELPLESSNESS	DEPRESSION
Symptoms	Passivity	Passivity
	Difficulty learning that responses produce relief	Negative cognitive set
	Dissipates in time	Time course
	Lack of aggression	Introjected hostility
	Weight loss, appetite loss, social and sexual deficits	Weight loss, appetite loss, social and sexual deficits
	Norepinephrine depletion and cholinergic activity	Norepinephrine depletion and cholinergic activity
	Ulcers and stress	Ulcers (?) and stress
		Feelings of helplessness
Cause	Learning that responding and reinforcement are independent	Belief that responding is useless
Cure	Directive therapy: forced exposure to responses that produce reinforcement	Recovery of belief that responding produces reinforcement
	Electroconvulsive shock	Electroconvulsive shock
	Time	Time
	Anticholinergics; norepinephrine stimulants (?)	Norepinephrine stimulants; anticholinergics (?)
Prevention	Immunization by mastery over reinforcement	(?)

the learning perspective other influential formulations of depression have also developed. Perhaps the major competing formulation has been developed by Lewinsohn (1974a, b). He argues that depression is best thought of as resulting from a *low rate of response-contingent reinforcement*. We will briefly examine Lewinsohn's view because it amply demonstrates how, even within the same perspective, apparently different accounts of the same phenomenon can emerge.

Lewinsohn's account of depression is based on three major assumptions. First, a low rate of response-contingent positive reinforcement acts as a condition that elicits some depressive behavior such as fatigue and unhappiness. Second, Lewinsohn argues that this low rate of contingent positive reinforcement is *sufficient* to explain the low rate of behavior seen in depression. In effect the depressed person is on a schedule of prolonged extinction. Finally, Lewinsohn argues that the total amount of positive reinforcement that the person receives depends on (1) the number or range of events that are potentially reinforcing for that person, (2) the environment's capacity to supply those events, and (3) the person's skill in eliciting those events from the environment.

As you can see in Figure 5–5, each of these factors combines to produce the low rate of positive reinforcement, which in turn produces the verbal and somatic behavior we call depression. Note, too, that this formulation suggests that the sympathy and concern expressed by others constitutes a source of social reinforcement for the depressed behavior, thus maintaining it at a high level.

In a thoughtful comparison of Seligman's and Lewinsohn's views, Blaney (1977) notes that the unique contribution of Lewinsohn's view is its emphasis on the *rate* of reinforcement received by the depressed person. The learned helplessness view, in contrast, emphasizes the degree to which the depressed person can *control* rewarding events in his or her life.

How, then, do we choose between these two versions of depression? Ideally experimental evidence should be the arbiter of the debate. But, as Blaney notes, such evidence does not yet exist and may be difficult to obtain since it may be the *perceived*, rather than the actual, degree of control or rate that is crucial.

Summary

We have seen that the learning perspective defines abnormal behavior as learned maladaptive behavior. Drawing on the fields of learning, the concepts of stimulus, response, and reinforcement provide the basic framework of the perspective. The mechanisms of classical and operant conditioning and modeling both are invoked to explain the development of abnormal behavior. Symptoms are said to be learned rather than produced by some underlying process or disposition.

We examined the theoretic underpinnings of helplessness research and saw how concepts of controllability and helplessness

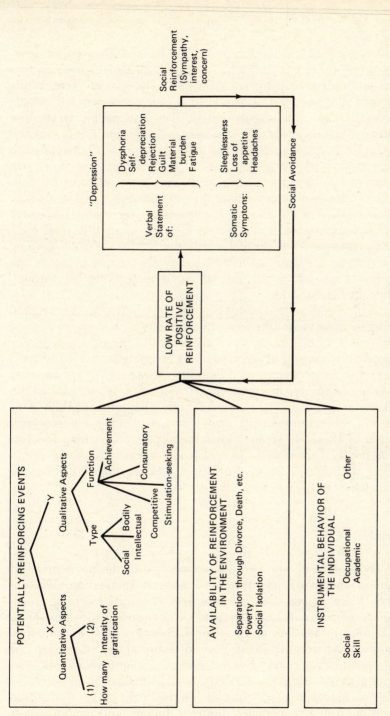

FIG. 5-5 Schematic representation of the causation and maintenance of "depressive" behavior according to Lewinsohn (adapted from Lewinsohn, 1974b, and used by permission).

could be applied to the clinical phenomenon of depression. Lew-insohn (1974a, b) has developed a formulation of depression that is an alternative to Seligman's learned helplessness view. While Seligman emphasizes the degree to which depressed individuals can control rewarding events in their lives, Lewinsohn stresses the depressed person's low rate of response-contingent reinforcement.

As the basic concepts of the learning approach are applied to new and more molar events outside the learning laboratory, we can see the displacement of concepts in operation. Learning concepts are changed to encompass the phenomenon to be explained. Our conception of the phenomenon itself changes as well when we begin to look at abnormal behavior in terms of stimuli, responses, and reinforcers. Thus mutual adaptation of the original learning concepts and the situation to which they are applied is part of the ongoing process in which the metaphor underlying the learning perspective is elaborated.

One result of the mutual adaptation between the original learning concepts and the new situation to which they are applied is that new concepts emerge or are added to the perspective. For example, the concept of adaptation (as in "maladaptive behavior") is found to be necessary as a defining characteristic of abnormal behavior. Similarly, the concept of "helplessness" is used to de-scribe a set of behavioral expectations about the likelihood of affecting the reinforcement contingencies in one's environment. Neither of these concepts is an integral part of learning theories as originally formulated. They become necessary, however, in dealing with complex social behavior and are therefore incorpo-rated as part of the learning perspective.

COMMENTARY

The application of the learning perspective to the phenomena of abnormal behavior has produced several interesting develop-ments. First, as we shall see, the application of learning proce-dures to complex clinical phenomena has produced a number of conceptual difficulties in the use of concepts such as stimulus, response, and reinforcement. Second, many of the phenomena of abnormal behavior are covert, or private cognitive events. The learning perspective has recently been extended to account for these "covert responses," especially in treatment programs directed at self-control. Expectancies, internal dialogs, and cognitive sets all are part of the newly expanded learning perspective. Finally, learning formulations of clinical behavior have not gone unchallenged, and we will look at a biochemical challenge to the learning view.

Throughout our discussion of the learning perspective thus far we have focused on questions of how abnormal behavior is defined, how it evolves, and how it is maintained. This may create the misleading impression that the learning perspective began as a formulation of abnormal behavior and was then later extended to the problem of treatment. In fact, just the opposite is true. Learning procedures typically have been first applied to clinical problems and, in the formulation of treatment strategies, a conceptual scheme for understanding the "learned" nature of the problem has been worked out.

As we shall discover later in our commentary, this approach has led some advocates of behavior modification to the untenable position that because a behavior can be modified by the use of learning principles, it also follows that those behaviors were produced according to the principles of learning.

Another Look at Fundamental Concepts: Stimulus, Response, and Reinforcement

Advocates of a learning theory formulation of maladaptive behavior would probably agree with Ullmann and Krasner (1965), who say: "At present only the broadest, most thoroughly established concepts, those common to all learning theory, are used in the clinical setting" (p. 15). If most advocates of the learning perspective on abnormal behavior agree on basic concepts, then we should examine the three concepts fundamental to all learning approaches: those of *stimulus, response,* and *reinforcement.*

Perhaps one of the best known and most effective attacks on basic learning theory concepts has been launched by Noam Chomsky in his review (1959) of B. F. Skinner's book, *Verbal Behavior* (1957). As a linguist Chomsky was deeply concerned with many of the problems Skinner considered in his attempt to extend a stimulus-response conception to verbal behavior. In many ways the extension of Skinner's thinking from the laboratory to verbal behavior occurring in a natural setting is similar to the extension of learning concepts to clinical phenomena. Chomsky's comments should be especially significant for us.

The concept of stimulus

Chomsky begins by restating what Skinner stated long ago: that stimuli and responses may be called such only if they can be shown to be lawfully related to one another. That is, we can assume that a particular environmental event may be called a "stimulus" only if we can show that this event has "stimulus control" over a particular bit of behavior.

How then, asks Chomsky, can we explain or give an account of any particular response? The answer is that we must do a "functional analysis." Put more simply, this means we must look for the stimulus which was presumably responsible for the response which we have observed. But, Chomsky argues, the "stimulus" cannot possibly be found until the response is known. Thus we can never predict the response from a knowledge of the stimulus alone since the stimulus is inferred *post hoc*, once the response is known. As Chomsky puts it, "We cannot predict verbal behavior in terms of the stimuli in the speaker's environment, since we do not know what the current stimuli are until he responds" (p. 32).

Furthermore, in most cases involving either verbal behavior or clinical phenomena, it is not some physical stimulus of the environment which constitutes the response, but instead some psychological property of the physical event. Therefore it follows that many responses are under the "stimulus control" of the psychological properties of a particular object or event. This, says Chomsky, necessarily drives the concept of stimulus back into the organism and is, therefore, nothing but a retreat into mentalism. Thus Chomsky argues that despite the objective and scientific flavor of the concept of stimulus, it may hide more than it reveals about the nature of human behavior and in particular about potentially lawful relationships which may exist between environmental events and the behavior of an organism.

Our judgment of this difficulty is not as harsh. Although it is true that "radical behaviorism" would require objective specification of the stimulus, in recent years the learning perspective has moved in the opposite direction. Cognitive events are now being incorporated into the perspective and, as we shall see, this greatly increases the scope of the views while simultaneously blurring its original concepts.

The concept of response

As with the concept of stimulus, the concept of response may be identified as that set of behaviors which can be shown to be functionally related to one or more controlling environmental events or stimuli. Chomsky points out that the concept of response presents us with little difficulty when we are dealing with carefully controlled experimental situations. When the concept of response is extended to the less controlled aspects of behavior such as speech, however, the problem of identifying the response becomes very complex indeed. Chomsky argues that no means of identifying the controlling variables of a particular response, that is, the stimulus, is suggested by Skinner. Furthermore, the boundaries of a particular response are virtually impossible to identify in the stream of behavior. Thus identifying the response and its boundaries in more complex situations, such as those involving abnormal behavior, becomes an extremely serious problem. Perhaps even the utility of a concept such as "response" may be questioned when one goes beyond the narrowly confined and experimentally controlled limits of laboratory phenomena.

A concept related to that of the response is the concept of *response strength*. Of course, response strength plays an important role in any learning analysis, since it constitutes the basic dependent variable in any such approach. Skinner suggests that response strength may be inferred in verbal behavior from such variables as pitch, speed, rapidity of emission, and immediate repetition. The use of any one of these indicators of response strength is sufficient to infer an increase in response strength according to Skinner. Skinner would suggest, for example, that if we are being shown a prize work of art and exclaim, "Beautiful!" the speed and energy of the response is not lost on the listener. However, this may not be as straightforward as it seems. Chomsky says,

> It does not appear totally obvious that in this case the way to impress the owner is to shriek "Beautiful" in a loud, high-pitched voice, repeatedly, and with no delay (high response strength). It may be equally effective to look at the picture silently (long delay) and then to murmur "Beautiful" in a soft, low-pitched voice (by definition, very low response strength) (p. 35).

Chomsky's example is right on target. It would appear that the concept of response strength as it is used within the stimulus-response framework is defined by Skinner as variables for which exceptions can very easily be found. We might suggest that similar problems will be encountered in the complexities of abnormal behavior as well.

The concept of reinforcement

Both Chomsky and, more recently, Breger and McGaugh (1965) have undertaken an analysis of the concept of reinforcement. In the *Behavior of Organisms* (1938) Skinner defines the concept of reinforcement:

> The operation of reinforcement is defined as the presentation of a certain kind of stimulus or a response in a temporal relation with either a stimulus or a response. A reinforcing stimulus is defined as such by a power to produce the resulting change (in strength). There is no circularity about this; some stimuli are found to produce the change, others not, and they are classified as reinforcing and nonreinforcing accordingly (p. 52).

Breger and McGaugh point out that this is a reasonable definition and is not necessarily circular, particularly if reinforcement is defined according to class membership, but independently of findings which show the occurrence of learning. This is usually done in a case of laboratory examples; however, when attempts are made to use the concept of reinforcement in a broader context, difficulties arise.

> Care is usually not taken to define reinforcement independently from learning as indicated by response strength. This leads to a state of affairs where any observed change in behavior is said to occur *because* of reinforcement, when in fact, the change in behavior is itself the only indicator of what the reinforcement has been (p. 346).

Of course, this sort of formulation does not avoid the circularity involved in the concept of reinforcement. The stimuli which are assumed to be "reinforcing" cannot be characterized in any other way except in terms of the rather circular assertion that they raise response strength when they follow a particular response.

Chomsky points out in Skinner's book *Verbal Behavior* (1957), the term "reinforcement" is used so loosely in many cases that it appears as if people may be reinforced even if they emit no response at all. In some cases, a "reinforcing stimulus" need not impinge on the individual or even exist as an identifiable event. Chomsky goes on to suggest that the term reinforcement is being used in what can only be characterized as a ritualistic way. It is being used to replace words such as "want," "like," and "wish." To replace terms of this kind with the term reinforcement adds nothing by way of conceptual clarity or explanatory power. We might note here that the use of reinforcement as an explanatory concept to replace these terms—want, like, wish—may obscure important differences between these states as well.

All too often, it appears, the concept of reinforcement is not used as it was originally intended by Skinner. As Chomsky points out, when the term reinforcement is extrapolated to behaviors outside of the laboratory, even Skinner himself fails to use the concept appropriately. When used in less controlled settings, the concept typically takes on a circularity which blunts any of its explanatory sharpness and tends to be used in a rather mechanical, ritualistic way to account for increases in the probability of an observed behavior.

Despite the criticisms we have just considered, we should recognize the power that the concepts of stimulus, response, and reinforcement have had in formulations of both normal and abnormal behavior. This appeal results in part from the simplicity of the concepts. A second aspect of their appeal is their range of application. Both normal and abnormal behaviors are considered within the same framework.

Chomsky's great contribution is in showing us that the basic concepts may require modification if we are to use them to rigorously describe the world of behavior.

Cognitive Influences

A major development within the learning perspective in the recent past has been an increased concern with cognitive events. When we consider the origins of the learning perspective in the radical behaviorism of John B. Watson, the development is a bit surprising. In an early statement of the principles of behaviorism, Watson seemed to rule out the study of internal or private events when he said,

> Introspection forms no essential part of [behaviorism's] methods, nor is the scientific value of its data dependent upon the readiness in which they lend themselves to interpretation in terms of consciousness (Watson, 1913, p. 158).

Latter day behaviorists take a much more relaxed position about including internal events as part of the subject matter of the learning perspective. For example, Thoresen and Mahoney (1974) state,

Recent developments in behavioral research have emphasized the long overdue need for controlled inquiries into cognitive-symbolic processes. Differentiating between radical (metaphysical) and methodological behaviorism, investigators have come to realize that these cognitive processes can be studied, predicted, and controlled with the same precision as external events (p. 110).

Indeed, Seligman's (1975) work on learned helplessness that we reviewed earlier has a strong cognitive flavor. As Yager (1975) notes,

> The formulation is primarily cognitive: While animals and people can actively learn that their own efforts may bring about or stave off pleasurable or unpleasurable events, they can also actively learn that their efforts are without any effect whatsoever on these important events. This learning occurs through insight—the "magic moment" when abstract principles are appreciated. The cognitive set, a learned expectation, that one's own efforts are without any important effect, can develop after actual experiences where no relationship exists between efforts and contingencies, and can also develop when an authority figure leads one to believe a situation is uncontrollable or that one is ineffectual. Moreover, being helpless in one situation may create a persistent belief, hard to unlearn, that one is forever helpless, even when the situation has changed so that one could be effective (p. 291).

One of the major focuses of the new interest in cognitive events by advocates of the learning perspective has been on the problem of *self-control*. This is understandable when we reflect that much of our own self-control–oriented behavior involves wishes, fantasies, hopes, and other cognitive events. In fact, consistent with the learning orientation, Thoresen and Mahoney call such private events *covert responses* and Homme (1965) has called these same events *"coverants"* (covert operants).

Thus, within the learning perspective a number of events previously excluded from study by doctrinaire behaviorists can now be considered. Presumably hallucinations, delusions, fantasies, obsessive thoughts, and irrational beliefs are now legitimate material for study and modification.

The concept that allows private events to become legitimate phenomena in the learning perspective is what Thoresen and Mahoney call the homogeneity principle. This is the assumption that there is no important qualitative or behavioral difference between thoughts and overt behavior.

Table 5–2 summarizes recent work described by Thoresen and

TABLE 5-2   Use of Covert Responses in Treatment of
Undesired Behavior

Covert Responses as Antecedents	Covert Responses as Target Behaviors	Covert Responses as Consequences
Images of feared situations (Wolpe, 1958): Images of feared social situations, heights, etc., used in desensitization	*What clients say to themselves: Self-statements* (Meichenbaum et al., 1974): "Crazy talk," creative ideas, task instructions, fearful self-statements	*Covert sensitization* (Cautela, 1971): Fantasy of aversive event following undesired behavior (e.g., violent nausea following urge to smoke)
"Flooding—implosion": (Stampfl et al., 1967) intense use of feared situations without relief	*Coverants* (operants of the mind) (Homme, 1965)	*Covert responses as positive reinforcement: Self-reward* (Kanfer, 1970)

Mahoney in the role of cognitive events in behavior modification research. The studies cited are divided into those in which covert responses are *antecedents*, or are the target *"behaviors"* themselves, or are used as *consequences* in treatment techniques.

It is clear that researchers working within the learning perspective have shown no lack of imagination in their attempts to include private cognitive events within the realm of behavior.

A Biological Challenge to the Learned Helplessness Concept of Depression

Recall for a moment the basic findings of the learned helplessness research conducted by Martin Seligman and his colleagues. First, Seligman exposed dogs to conditions where they were exposed to escapable or inescapable shock. After this, they were placed in a box requiring them to jump over a hurdle when they were given a warning signal. Dogs that had previously been exposed to inescapable shock could not learn the simple task of escaping over the hurdle. They moved around the box and ultimately became immobilized. Seligman explained the behavior of these dogs by saying that those animals exposed to inescapable shock have learned to be helpless. That is, they have learned that nothing they could do would help them to escape the shock. Therefore they became hopeless and then later helpless.

Beginning with these basic experiments, Seligman went on to show both compelling parallels between clinical depression and learned helplessness in humans. Today many researchers feel that he has made a persuasive case for learned helplessness as an explanation for at least some forms of depression.

In fact, scientists exposed to the learning perspective as a way of thinking about behavior find themselves particularly persuaded by Seligman's work. The passivity, low levels of activity, and other indicators of depression do indeed appear to have been learned in response to an environment that indicates that nothing animals can do will make any difference in whether they are punished or not. But, how would a researcher whose primary interest was in the biochemistry of the brain interpret Seligman's results? Recall in our earlier discussion of perspectives, we noted that perspectives help us to notice certain aspects of phenomena and to pay less attention to others. Weiss (1974a, 1974b) and his colleagues are concerned with biochemical aspects of depression. They have examined Seligman's results and come up with a very different interpretation. They noticed that dogs tested 24 hours after inescapable shock displayed learned helplessness while dogs tested 48 hours later displayed no difficulties. Weiss and his colleagues believe that this recovery is just the sort of thing one would expect if one were observing a *temporary physiological problem* rather than learned helplessness. Specifically, Weiss believes that it is the depletion of a brain chemical called *norepinephrine* that produces the behavior described as learned helplessness. Here we have a classic confrontation of perspectives, two apparently different explanations for the same phenomenon.

What research evidence have Weiss and his coworkers developed to support their contention? In one study these researchers exposed laboratory rats to the experience of swimming for three and one-half minutes in cold water. This experience has been shown to result in decreased norepinephrine activity in the brain. When these rats were then placed in a shuttle box situation, similar to that of Seligman's dogs, they behaved in strikingly similar ways. They were unable to cross the hurdle to avoid shock in most cases and showed a behavior that otherwise resembled learned helplessness. Thus, a condition that depleted norepinephrine in the brain was capable of producing a behavior that resembled learned helplessness.

In another study, the investigators obtained direct measures of the brain level of norepinephrine in laboratory animals that had been exposed to one session of inescapable shock, another group that was exposed to repeated sessions, and a third group that was not exposed to inescapable shock at all. The levels of norepinephrine in the brains of these animals directly paralleled the behavioral results we would expect. That is, one session produced norepinephrine depletion, but repeated sessions and no sessions of inescapable shock showed similarly high levels. This, Weiss and his colleagues argue, favors the idea that helplessness is a biochemical condition to which the body can adapt rather than a learned condition.

What exactly are we to conclude from this? Is it reasonable to conclude that the learned helplessness hypothesis is incorrect? Does it mean that the credibility of biologically oriented illness perspectives on abnormal behavior are greatly enhanced? Perhaps it is most accurate to say that these studies broaden our understanding of depression. A biochemical link involving norepinephrine appears to exist between the experience that produces helpless behavior and the behavior itself. These findings do not rule out the important role of learning or the power of the environment to affect behavior, but make it clearer to us what mechanisms may be involved in linking the environment, the brain, and behavior in the development of depression.

It is also important to notice that evidence can have the effect of altering perspectives. Although much evidence will be assimilated to existing perspectives, new findings can also have the effect of broadening our perspective. Here, for example, the norepinephrine evidence helps us to realize that findings from biological and learning views may be complementary rather than contradictory.

Inferring Origins of Abnormal Behavior from Treatment Results

It is tempting to conclude that abnormal behavior develops according to learning principles when we look at the often impressive effects of behavior modification. This would be a dangerous logical error. As Buchwald and Young (1969) argue, the fact that a particular behavior or set of behaviors can be *changed* by certain procedures does not tell us necessarily anything about how the behaviors were *produced* in the first place. All behavior therapy studies of this sort can do is to demonstrate further the empirical law of effect and the fact that it holds for hospitalized individuals as well as for laboratory animals and normal individuals. To conclude that evidence of the kind tells us anything about how the behavior was originally produced is not warranted. An excellent example offered by Buchwald and Young underscores this point:

It is important to remember that behavior is a final common path-
way, that it is susceptible to a large number of influences. The way
in which responses are changed need not parallel the way in which
they were originally acquired. The asymmetry between the source
of a behavioral disorder and the method of treatment may be illustrated by the case of aphasic patients. They have lost the ability to
speak as a result of a vascular accident or other brain lesion, but
they can sometimes be taught to speak again. The behavioral loss is
due to a physiological insult, but there is no known physiological
or medical technique for overcoming this handicap. That the only
known successful treatment is a behavioral one implies nothing
about the origin of the deficit. Similarly, if a mute schizophrenic
can be taught to speak again by shaping and reinforcement (and
such efforts have had some limited success), there is no implication
that his speech was lost due to the operation of reinforcing factors
in his social environment (1969, p. 618).

This example makes it quite clear that one cannot infer the
origin of "maladaptive behavior" from the techniques used to
change that behavior. There is no necessary relation between the
two, and to suggest that there is can be quite misleading.

Summary

We also noted that the concepts of stimulus, response, and reinforcement are fundamental to all learning accounts of abnormal
behavior. A critical analysis of these concepts suggests that,
despite the apparent rigor they seem to provide, they present as
many logical problems as they appear to solve. Furthermore,
when these concepts are applied to complex human behavior it is
seldom possible to do so with great precision.

But despite these logical problems, the extension of learning
concepts to previously unexplored areas of inquiry has been fruit-
ful. New research on cognitively oriented treatment approaches
may dilute the theoretical purity of the perspective while it ex-
pands its therapeutic usefulness. The present generation of learning advocates seems to recognize the necessity of expanding the
domain of the learning perspective if it is to be equal to the task
of comprehending complex clinical phenomena.

One of the great strengths of the learning perspective is that
it describes environmental events and behavior with enough precision to invite challenge. This is a great asset, as our brief examination of a biological interpretation of the helplessness phenomenon suggests. The result of the challenge was not a decisive

victory for either view but, instead, a broader view of helpless behavior and, perhaps, depression as well.

Finally, we noted that some advocates of the learning perspective have erroneously concluded that because a particular behavior or symptom can be altered by the application of learning principles, it follows that the symptom originated according to those principles. This is, of course, not necessarily the case. We should not be too surprised by such conceptual leaps. The adherents of most of the perspectives we will discuss are convinced of the power of their own formulation and consequently, they may extend their explanations to phenomena beyond the scope of their concepts.

We should remember, however, that it is precisely these extensions to new phenomena and the alteration of concepts to fit new observations that create scientific development.

Suggested Reading

1. Bandura, A. *Principles of Behavior Modification.* New York: Holt, Rinehart and Winston, 1969.
   Bandura's discussion of social learning concepts and behavior therapy is still one of the most comprehensive and carefully done of all such sources.
2. Seligman, M. E. P. *Helplessness: On Depression, Development, and Death.* San Francisco: W. H. Freeman, 1975.
   This is an excellent and highly readable application of learning theory principles to the problems of controllability, depression, anxiety, emotional development, and death. Seligman does not sacrifice readability for solid scholarship. He presents his theory of "learned helplessness" in detail and draws out novel and important implications.
3. Skinner, B. F. *Beyond Freedom and Dignity.* New York: Knopf, 1971.
   This is Skinner's manifesto. In it he asks us to cast aside our illusions of "freedom" and "dignity" and to make a better world using, naturally, Skinnerian behavioral principles.
4. Thoresen, C. E., & M. J. Mahoney. *Behavioral Self-Control.* New York: Holt, Rinehart and Winston, 1974.
   This short book emphasizes two emerging themes in the behavioral and learning perspective: self-control and the reemphasis on internal psychological processes. Theoretical and practical

suggestions for behavior change are offered as a means of giving "power to the person."

1. In order to begin to view behavior according to the learning perspective, try some naturalistic observation. For example, go to a grocery store where parents and young children are likely to be together. Carefully observe the behavior of the parent. Can you see the stimuli, responses, and reinforcements that exist in the parents' ongoing behavior as they interact with the child? Can you see what contingencies exist between the child's behavior and the parents' reinforcements? Of course, children also "shape" their parents' behavior as well. Turn the situation around and ask yourself how the child acts as a "stimulus" for the parent. What behaviors or responses does he or she emit? How is the parent reinforced or extinguished by the child's behavior?

2. Consider violent programs on television. Do you think they serve the function of models for children? Is there the possibility of vicarious conditioning? Consider how you would test this question with an experiment. Violence, of course, is not the only form of learning that television transmits. Watch an episode of *Sesame Street* and see if you can pick out examples of vicarious reinforcement, modeling, discrimination learning, and stimulus generalization.

3. One of the most promising aspects of the learned helplessness idea is that it suggests ways in which we might "immunize" children against learned helplessness and therefore against depression. Discuss how a day care center environment might be arranged to immunize children against learned helplessness.

4. One way to learn more about the reinforcement contingencies in your own life is to chart a particular behavior of your own over the period of a week or so. It might be interesting to choose a habit you would like to change, such as nail biting or smoking. Carry a 3 × 5 card with you and make a note each time you recognize yourself engaging in the habit. Try to notice the events that occur right before you engaged in the behavior and those that occur right afterward. Can you begin to see reinforcement contingencies operating? Do they suggest ways in which you might develop a program of change?

6

The social perspective

A Thought Experiment

Sometimes when social scientists want to think through an issue or question they will conduct a "thought experiment." That is, they will speculate on what would happen if certain events that ordinarily do not occur actually did. Consider this thought experiment.

> Suppose that in your next conversation with a stranger, instead of looking at his eyes or mouth, you scrutinize his ear. Although the deviation from ordinary behavior is slight (involving only a shifting of the direction of gaze a few degrees, from the eyes to an ear), its effects are explosive. The conversation is disrupted almost instantaneously. In some cases, the subject of this experiment will seek to save the situation by rotating to bring his eyes into your line of gaze; if you continue to gaze at his ear, he may rotate through a full 360 degrees. Most often, however, the conversation is irretrievably damaged. Shock, anger, and vertigo are experienced not only by the "victim" but, oddly enough, by the experimenter himself. It is virtually impossible for either party to sustain the conversation, or even to think coherently, as long as the experimenter continues.
>
> The point of this experiment is to suggest the presence of a public order that is all pervasive, yet taken almost completely for granted. During the simplest kinds of public encounter, there are myriad understandings about comportment that govern the participants' behavior-understandings governing posture, facial expression, and gestures, as well as the content and form of the language used. In speech itself, the types of conformity are extremely diverse and include pronunciation; grammar and syntax; loudness, pitch, and phrasing; and aspiration. Almost all of these elements are so taken for granted that they "go without saying" and are more or less invisible, not only to the speakers but to society at large. These understandings constitute part of our society's assumptive world, the world that is thought of as normal, decent, and possible (Scheff, 1975, pp. 5–6).

You may find yourself reluctant to actually conduct this experiment, and it is instructive to ask why. Perhaps it is because you realize that breaking the rather minor rule of face-to-face etiquette might lead the stranger to draw some hasty and incorrect conclusions about your own psychological stability. If you agree, then you already appreciate one of the basic premises of the social perspective we are about to examine—that merely violating social norms can, under the right circumstances, lead to being labeled as "mentally ill."

THE PERSPECTIVE

Madness in the Eye of the Beholder

A unique perspective on abnormal behavior is developing exemplified by writers such as Goffman (1963b), Lemert (1951), Scheff (1967, 1975), and Rosenhan (1973, 1975). The central thesis of the approach can be put quite simply, although its implications are far from simple. Rosenhan (1968) captures the spirit of the perspective when he says,

> Beauty, we know, exists in the eye of the beholder. But what of madness? Is it possible that a profitable conceptualization of madness can emerge from the examination, not of the mad, as both psychoanalysts and learning theorists have done, but of those who call them mad? (p. 360).

This approach offers a direct challenge to the essentially individual orientations to abnormal behavior that have their roots in psychiatry and clinical psychology and have dominated the field for so long. Sociologists and social psychologists, perhaps because of the unique viewpoint of their discipline, have offered us a fresh look at abnormal behavior.

The social perspective differs from others in at least two important ways. First, for the most part, psychiatrists and clinical psychologists think of mental illness or abnormal behavior as something arising within the individual. The social view, on the other hand, argues that "mental illness is something ascribed to persons as a function of the definition given certain types of acts by certain audiences" (Spitzer & Denzin, 1968, pp. v–vi). Second, the social perspective focuses upon the ascription process. That is, the perspective asks, "Who is labeled as mentally ill and under what circumstances?"

These viewpoints have a number of consequences. One consequence of adopting the social perspective is that considerably more attention will be given to the *social context* in which the abnormal behavior occurs. One of the strongest criticisms made by proponents of the social view is that other approaches have isolated the symptoms displayed by individuals from the context in which they occur. The social view attempts to remedy this deficiency, sometimes emphasizing context at the expense of descriptive precision of the symptoms themselves.

Another consequence of adopting the social perspective is that new elements are introduced into the problem. Whereas individual approaches to abnormal behavior operate in what is essentially a contextual vacuum, the social approach focuses on *social reactions to symptoms,* the social institution of mental illness, and the diagnostician as well as those who are diagnosed. Thus, the social rule which is broken and the consequences of breaking it become at least as important as the rule-breaker.

BOX 6-1
Language and Concepts of the Social Perspective

Social role A pattern of behavior associated with a distinctive social position (e.g., father, teacher, employer, or patient).

Norm violator One who disturbs or disrupts the agreed-upon rules of the group within a particular social environment.

Rule-breaking Behavior that clearly violates agreed-upon rules of the group. Examples are crime, perversion, drunkenness, or bad manners.

Residual rule-breaking Norm violations that do not fall into an explicit rule category but which may result in others labeling the rule violator as "mentally ill."

Deviance The response of other people to the rule-breaker. Deviance is a quality of people's response to an act and not a characteristic of the act itself. **Primary deviance** and **secondary deviance** are distinguished from each other to refer to the fact that abnormal behavior can arise in response to being labeled, or hospitalized (secondary), or as a result of some internal (primary) cause, such as brain damage.

Labeling Acknowledgment in some public way of a person's role. Once labeled (e.g., as "ex-mental patient"), a person is subject to many contingencies of that role, according to the social perspective adherents.

Stigma A stigmatized person is one with a discrediting identity. Persons who have been labeled "mentally ill" or "ex-mental patients" are usually said to be stigmatized.

Deviant career "The sequence of movements from one stigmatized position to another in the sector of the larger social system that functions to maintain social control" (Scheff, 1966, p. 39).

Looking at abnormal behavior through the eyes of sociologists or social psychologists gives us a sense of immediacy about the problem. One reason for this is the wide range of data on which they draw. Material from newspapers, television, and our own social experience appears in a new light and the commonplace takes on new meaning. The sociologist looks where we have been looking all along but sees things there we never saw.

In our discussion of the social perspective we will begin by discussing work of Thomas Scheff (1966). His writing is particularly suited to our purpose because it represents a clear example of the social perspective, is moderately well formalized, and reflects the thinking of some of the most influential theorists in this area. Scheff's account traces the career of the person as he or she becomes a mental patient. The story begins innocently enough with the breaking of rules for face-to-face interaction. By the time our story is finished, however, we should be able to fully appreciate Goffman's (1959) comment that "one could say that mental patients *distinctively* suffer not from mental illness, but from contingencies" (p. 127).

Violating Unstated Norms: Residual Rule-Breaking

Think again for a moment about the experiment we proposed at the beginning of the chapter. The social perspective begins with the idea of social rule-breaking or "norm violation." But what sort of rule would you be breaking if you persisted in staring at the ear of a stranger during your first meeting? Scheff (1966, 1975) calls it a *residual rule* because it is a "rule" or norm for which we have no specific category. He says,

> we can categorize . . . psychiatric symptoms as instances of residual rule-breaking or residual deviance. The culture of the group provides a vocabulary of terms for categorizing many norm violations: crime, perversion, drunkenness, and bad manners are familiar examples. Each of these terms is derived from the type of norm broken, and ultimately, from the type of behavior involved. After exhausting these categories, however, there is always a residue of the most diverse kinds of violations, for which the culture provides no explicit label. For example, although there is great cultural variation in what is defined as decent or real, each culture tends to reify its definition of decency and reality, and so provides no way of handling violations of its expectations in these areas. The typical norm governing decency or reality, therefore, literally "goes without saying" and its violation is unthinkable for most of its

Theodore Sarbin on Mental Illness

"The language and thought defects noted in hospitalized schizophrenics are products, resultants or outcomes of *certain describable social events associated with labeling a person as mentally ill and with the . . . instru-*mental acts and rituals carried out by medical, legal, or other profes-sional personnel." (Sarbin, 1969, p. 192)

members. For the convenience of society in construing those instances of unnameable rule-breaking which are called to its attention, these violations may be lumped together into a residual category: witchcraft, spirit possession, or, in our own society, mental illness. In this discussion, the diverse kinds of rule-breaking for which our society provides no explicit label, and which, there-fore, sometimes lead to the labeling of the violator as mentally ill, will be considered to be technically *residual rule-breaking* (pp. 33–34).

Thus we can see that residual rule violations are those left over when we have difficulty in accounting for the rule-breaking with more conventional categories. For our discussion, psychi-atric symptoms are the most important examples of residual rule-breaking.

Goffman (1963a) has described a number of acts which fall into the category of residual deviance and are also taken to be psychiatric symptoms. Perhaps the best example of this sort of norm violation is what Goffman calls the "away." The "away" violates norms of involvement. When an individual allows his or her attention to wander or sinks into reverie in the presence of others while engaged in social interaction, he or she is violating involvement norms. However, the act of "away" is not in itself a norm violation and will not in itself bring censure. Only when these acts are performed in inappropriate social contexts or by unqualified persons will they be seen as a breach of the implicit rules of face-to-face interaction. Under these circumstances violations of involvement norms may be seen as "withdrawal" or "hallucination" and be taken as evidence of "mental illness."

Having gained a somewhat clearer idea of the nature of residual rule-breaking, we may ask some additional questions. What are the origins of residual rule-breaking? How frequently does it occur? What is the public response to residual rule-breaking? Scheff (1966) offers answers to each of these questions.

Causes of Rule-Breaking

For Scheff, residual rule-breaking arises from diverse causes. Four general sources are mentioned. These include organic defects typically involving genetic or physiological disturbances. A second source is the psychological background of the individual. Scheff refers to this source only generally, assuming that any variables having to do with child-rearing are included. A third general cause cited is external stress. Included in this category are a variety of phenomena such as food deprivation, sleep deprivation, and combat stress. A final source of residual rule-breaking is volitional acts. Scheff cites two movements in history as examples of deliberate breaking of residual rules: French Impressionism and Dadaism. Both of these movements engaged in deliberate rule-breaking that evoked strong societal reaction but in time actually changed social and esthetic evaluations. Perhaps a more contemporary example of volitional breaking of residual rules can be found in the Youth International Party or "Yippie" movement (Hoffman, 1968).

The actual sources of residual rule-breaking are of only marginal interest to Scheff and this is typical of the social perspective. As we suggested in the introduction, the social viewpoint focuses upon the social reaction to rule-breaking and has little interest in the origins or "etiology" of the behavior in question. We shall discuss this point in more detail in the commentary.

Frequency of Rule-Breaking

How frequent is residual rule-breaking? Scheff argues that "relative to the rate of treated mental illness, the rate of unrecorded residual rule-breaking is extremely high" (1966, p. 47). As evidence for this, Scheff cites a number of epidemiological studies which have attempted to estimate the actual or "true" rate of mental illness in various populations and which compare that rate to the rate of actual treatment. After reviewing a number of different studies, Scheff concludes that approximately 14 untreated cases exist in a community for every case that is actually treated. Hence his statement that the unrecorded (untreated) rate is high.

Thus relatively few cases of residual rule-breaking actually receive social recognition and censure or treatment. The residual rule-breaker is not necessarily given the status of one who is "mentally ill."

Rule-Breaking Is Usually Ignored or Denied

We may ask then what processes are operating to allow the rate of actual residual rule-breaking to be so much higher than that of recognized or treated cases? This leads us to Scheff's next proposition. He argues that the vast majority of instances of residual rule-breaking tend to be "denied" and are of little or only transitory significance. By denial, Scheff means that people respond to much residual rule-breaking by inattention, ignoring the behavior, or rationalizing its existence.

Although evidence on this point is scanty, at least two pieces of research offer support for Scheff's proposition that much residual rule-breaking is denied, or at least minimized, by significant others in the rule-breaker's environment. A study by Yarrow, Schwartz, Murphy, and Deasy (1955) examined the reactions of wives to their husbands' behavior prior to the husband's first psychiatric hospitalization. The most striking finding in their study was that wives tolerated prolonged and extreme amounts of deviant behavior from their husbands before reluctantly acknowledging the possibility of a "mental" problem. Hallucinations, delusions, physical abuse, and even threats on the wife's life were rationalized, excused, or "normalized" by elements in the husband's past behavior that were consistent with his current bizarre actions. In many cases, only when it was abundantly clear that the husband or wife's life was in danger would the wife recognize the problem as one requiring psychiatric attention.

Another example of minimization of residual rule-breaking is offered by Bittner (1967) in his study of police discretion in dealing with mentally ill persons.

> In one observed instance a young man approached an officer in a deteriorating business district of the city. He voiced an almost textbook-type paranoid complaint. From the statements and the officer's response it could be gathered that this was a part of a sequence of conversations. The two proceeded to walk away from an area of high traffic density to quieter parts of the neighborhood. In the ensuing stroll the officer inspected various premises, greeted

passers-by, and generally showed a low level of attentiveness. After about twenty-five minutes the man bade the officer goodbye and indicated that he would be going home now. The officer stated that he runs into this man quite often and usually on the same spot. He always tries to lead the man away from the place that apparently excites his paranoid suspicions. The expressions of inattentiveness are calculated to impress the person that there is nothing to worry about, while, at the same time, the efforts the man must make to hold the officer's interest absorb his energies. This method presumably makes the thing talked about a casual matter and mere small-talk. Thus, the practices employed in sustained contacts involve, like the practices of "psychiatric first aid," the tendencies to confine, to disregard pathological material, and to reduce matters to their mundane aspects (p. 290).

Although the reasons for denial and minimization of residual rule-breaking may be diverse, evidence that even extreme cases may be denied exists, as Scheff suggests. Another factor that may modify the reaction to norm violation is the role or status of the rule-breaker. Although Scheff does not discuss this point in detail, it is important to recognize. For example, a professor who talks to him- or herself may be excused as preoccupied or "absent minded," but someone without such a role justification might be thought to be hallucinating. Similarly, the observation that "the difference between eccentricity and schizophrenia is about forty thousand dollars a year in income" reflects the recognition that socioeconomic status can also play a part in the denial of norm violation.

So far we have seen that there are diverse causes of rule-breaking and that not all rule-breaking will be of the "residual" sort which may or may not be classified as symptomatology. Furthermore, even if the rule-breaking is of the residual sort it will not necessarily be recognized or labeled as a manifestation of mental illness. The vast majority of residual rule-breaking will be episodic and transitory, and will be denied or go unrecognized.

If most norm violation is ignored, then how can it play a role in the development of abnormal behavior? Scheff suggests an answer to this question:

the most important single factor (but not the only factor) in the stabilization of residual rule-breaking is the *societal reaction.* Residual rule-breaking may be stabilized if it is defined to be evidence of mental illness, and/or the rule-breaker is placed in a deviant status, and begins to play the role of the mentally ill (pp. 53–54, author's italics).

In the following section we will examine the processes that transform the social identity of the residual rule-breaker into that of chronic mental patient.

Learning the Deviant Role

Stereotypes of Madness

If, as Scheff suggests, the chronic residual deviant is a person who has accepted certain role prescriptions and is playing the role of mental patient, then at least two conditions must be fulfilled: first, the chronic residual deviant must have available to him or her the basic elements of the rule; and second, he or she must have knowledge of how mental patients behave, and must be motivated to act that way.

The first question raised by this analysis is, how does the chronic residual deviant know how to behave like one who is mentally ill? Among the sources of the final stabilization of the deviant role adopted by the residual rule-breaker is the stereotyping of mental symptoms. Scheff offers two propositions concerning the stereotyped imagery of mental illness that are intended to establish the fact that these stereotypes are (1) learned early in childhood and (2) continually reinforced and reaffirmed in our everyday life.

Let us consider Scheff's (1966) first proposition concerning the stereotype of mental disorder. Scheff states that "stereotyped imagery of mental disorder is learned early in childhood" (p. 64). He suggests that it is commonly observed that children learn the literal meaning of the word "crazy" early in life. Furthermore, adults are often evasive and unclear in their responses to questions concerning the meaning of the term "crazy." Hence the stereotypes that arise around the term "crazy" continue to have associated with them many of the childhood uncertainties and fears typified by concepts such as "the bogeyman."

In one study Lamy (1966) was able to demonstrate convincingly that we have fairly specific stereotypes about what ex-mental patients are like, and those ideas are quite different from those that we hold about other deviants such as ex-convicts.

Media Stereotypes

Scheff's second general proposition concerning the stereotype of mental disorder is that "the stereotypes of insanity are continually reaffirmed, inadvertently, in ordinary social interaction" (p. 67). Scheff draws on a wide variety of evidence to support this assumption. In particular he implicates the mass media. Both traditional stereotypes of mental disorder learned early in childhood and more sophisticated views may exist side by side in individuals whom one would presume to have a more informed notion of abnormal behavior. Scheff argues that the mass media tend to reinforce our stereotype of mental disorder, and he draws upon data from the work of Nunnally (1961) to support his claim. For example, Nunnally shows that of all the televised films depicting mental illness in some form the vast majority of such accounts are fictional rather than documentary programs. Typically, these features and films use the stereotype of mental disorder, while there are few documentaries that attempt to produce a more realistic picture of the disorder.

The following quote from Scheff (1966) concerning the manner in which newspapers strengthen our traditional stereotypes of mental disorder speaks for itself.

In newspapers it is a common practice to mention that a rapist or a murderer was once a mental patient. Here are several examples: Under the headline, "Question Girl in Child Slaying," the story begins, "A 15-year-old girl *with a history of mental illness* is being questioned in connection with a kidnap-slaying of a 3-year-old boy." A similar story under the headline, "Man Killed, Two Policemen Hurt in Hospital Fray" begins, "*A former mental patient* grabbed a policeman's revolver and began shooting at 15 persons in the receiving room of City Hospital No. 2 Thursday."

Often acts of violence will be connected with mental illness on the basis of little or no evidence. For instance, under the headline, "Milwaukee Man Goes Berserk, Shoots Officer," the story describes the events and then quotes a police captain who said, "He may be a mental case." In another story under the headline, "Texas Dad Kills Self, Four Children, Daughter Says," the last sentence of the story is "One report said Kinsey (the killer) was once a mental patient." In most large newspapers there is apparently at least one such story in every issue.

Even if the coverage of these acts of violence was highly accurate, it would still give the reader a misleading impression because negative information is seldom offset by positive reports. An item like the following is almost inconceivable: "Mrs. Ralph Jones, an ex-mental patient, was elected president of the Fairview Home and Garden Society at their meeting last Thursday" (pp. 71–72).

It seems clear from these examples that Scheff is justified in asserting that the stereotypes of mental disorder are reaffirmed and strengthened by our mass media. Thus the individual who may embark on a career of chronic deviance has available the elements necessary to learn the mental illness role. Now it remains for us to examine the mechanisms by which he is actually compelled to adopt the role.

Becoming a Mental Patient

It is one thing to argue that people will think you are peculiar if you violate norms of face-to-face conduct and to assert that our culture shares stereotypes of mental illness. It is quite another thing to argue that *social* forces can lead a person ultimately to occupy the role of chronic mental patient. Yet advocates of the social perspective have developed an account of how this process can occur.

In the following discussion we will trace the path of a hypothetical individual from the initial instance of residual rule-breaking to the point of chronic hospitalization. In doing so we will review a number of studies that lend support to the social perspective. We will also broaden our account well beyond that offered by Scheff in his original formulation of the social perspective.

Briefly, Scheff argues that four factors contribute to the stabilized role of mental patient: (1) the increased suggestibility of the person at the time of personal crisis and rule-breaking, (2) the subtle rewards offered by professionals for accepting the role of mental patient, (3) the labeling of the person through diagnosis and other social means, and (4) punishment for attempts to return to the role of a "normal" individual. In what follows we will find some support for these assumptions and also discover that the process is more complex than Scheff suggests.

Crisis

The path of our hypothetical person begins when people, perhaps the spouse or employer, first notice behavior that seems strange or peculiar to them. At first they may deny or minimize this peculiarity, but if the behavior becomes public or especially frightening, they may tentatively conclude that the person has a "mental problem" (Mechanic, 1962; Smith & Hall, 1963).

Smith and Hall (1963) were concerned with the question of the types of incidents that lead to hospitalization. These incidents are often described by the family of the patient as the "last straw" that led to hospitalization. The authors studied 100 decisive incidents that resulted in the subsequent hospitalization of diagnosed schizophrenic patients. They found that the incidents were quite varied and had no systematic relationship to the age, sex, marital status, religion, or social class of the person. Instead, what appeared to make an incident "decisive" depended on the specific sensitivities of the family or community member observing the behavior. If the behavior elicited fear, shame, or disgust in the observer, it was likely to become a "last straw."

Consider the following example:

> A male patient hit his mother periodically, talked in a loud and hostile manner to the voices, used profane language, and masturbated openly at home for one year. The decision to seek hospitalization occurred promptly when he carved obscenities on the new grand piano. The mother acted because she was afraid that her spouse, the patient's step-father, would leave her, since the piano was a status symbol and the carvings would present tangible evidence to the neighbors that the family was indecent (Price & Denner, 1973, p. 76).

Not only is the public instance of norm violation a crisis for those around the violator, but it is also a crisis for the person. Therefore, another mechanism by which the deviant role becomes stabilized has to do with the crisis that occurs when an individual is publicly exposed for rule-breaking and is labeled as a result. Scheff summarizes this assumption in the following way:

> In the crisis occurring when a residual rule-breaker is publicly labeled, the deviant is highly suggestible, and may accept the proffered role of the insane as the only alternative (p. 88).

Thus, an individual may break residual rules and be recognized for doing so. An issue is then made of the residual rule-breaking. At this point the rule-breaker is expected to become confused and ashamed, but most important of all, he or she should also become *suggestible*. Naturally, to those around the rule-breaker in the crisis situation, his or her behavior is incomprehensible. This leads to a strong need among the rule-breaker's associates for collective action. Furthermore, the need for collective action and the action itself are typically based on the stereotype of mental disorder. Because the rule-breaker is sensitive to the cues of others and accepts their evaluation of his or her behavior, he or she begins to behave according to the stereotype.

Those especially concerned with the person may then contact one or more of a variety of people: the family physician, the clergyman, the police, or a psychiatrist (Clauson & Yarrow, 1955). Depending on who is consulted, the person's path to the mental hospital may turn in one direction or another. If the police are called in, they may simply administer "psychiatric first aid" (Bittner, 1967) and leave the person to his or her own devices. If it is the clergy, perhaps assurances and moral support will be offered. If the family doctor or a psychiatrist is consulted, the person may be referred for psychiatric treatment.

Commitment Proceedings

For some people, a step on their path to the mental hospital will involve a court hearing in which their competence to care for themselves will be judged. Research on the nature of these hearings (Scheff, 1966) suggests that these hearings are often arbitrary and that it is *presumed* that the people are suffering from mental illness before the hearings even begin.

However, a more subtle and interpersonally oriented picture emerges in research reported by Miller and Schwartz (1966). They observed courtroom proceedings involving petitions to commit people to psychiatric hospitals and were able to provide an answer to the question of who is committed and why. Although these authors make it clear that the commitment proceeding does not yield a simple pattern of results, they do confirm Scheff's finding that commitment proceedings often proceed on the presumption of the insanity of the defendant.

The authors also find that the likelihood of commitment depends heavily upon the interpersonal skills of that defendant. If he is able to present himself as being in control and interpersonally effective, he is likely to be released. At least two patterns emerge that result in commitment. If the person offers no objection to the proceeding and is generally passive, he is likely to be committed. On the other hand, if he objects violently, this may be taken as evidence of his unstable mental state and he will be committed.

Table 6-1 shows how the authors classified people in terms of their *alignment* (general orientation) to the hearing. As we can see, the hearings are brief to the point of being cursory, but the likelihood of being released depends on whether the person appeared bewildered or defiant, or had volunteered for hospitalization.

But, as Miller and Schwartz point out, we should not con-

TABLE 6–1   Type of Alignment by Number Released and
Average Time of Hearing (adapted from
Miller & Schwartz, 1966)

		RELEASED		
TYPE	Total Number of Patients	No.	Percent	Avg. Time Minutes
Defiance (resistance to the commitment procedure)	21	7	33	5.7
Bewilderment (general air of bewilderment at the hearing)	16	3	19	3.8
Nonparticipation (remained mute during hearing)	8	1	13	2.9
Volunteer (claimed were "sick and needed help")	13	2	18	3.8
TOTAL	58	13	22	4.4

clude that relatives, who are often the complainants in such hearings, are necessarily eager to "railroad" the patient into the hospital. Relatives who testify against the defendant are often under considerable strain and are very much concerned about the breach of family loyalty that such a legal action may represent. To the relatives of the patient, the decision for hospitalization often appears to be the only solution to an intractable problem.

Diagnosis and Labeling

At the point of hospitalization and once hospitalized, the patient is subject to medical decisions. These decisions are often strongly affected by the use of a "conservative" decision-making strategy by the examining physician or psychiatrist. That is, when in doubt about the patient's mental state, the psychiatrist may decide to hospitalize or retain the person in the hospital (Scheff, 1963).

Scheff examined the decision rules used in medicine to determine whether a person would receive treatment or not. Scheff concluded that the operative decision rule in medical practice takes the form: "Better to treat an individual who is not sick than to fail to treat a person who might be ill." The psychiatrist's implicit rule is "when in doubt, continue to suspect and treat illness." In the case of physical diseases, this sort of bias may benefit the patient, but in the case of abnormal behavior, the application of this decision rule may have very different effects. Scheff suggests that it is possible that physicians may actually be "creating" cases of mental illness by applying this medical decision rule to psychiatric practice.

Once the patient has been admitted to the hospital, it is very likely that he or she will be examined by a psychiatrist or psychologist and a decision will be made about a diagnosis. Often the final decision about an individual's diagnosis will be made in a large staff meeting attended by psychiatrists, psychologists, and social workers.

The usual assumption is that the patient's psychological history, current behavior, and possibly psychological test results will form the basis for diagnosis. This may often be the case, but research by Temerlin (1968) shows that the mere suggestion by a prestigious psychiatric colleague can markedly bias the diagnosis. Temerlin presented a recorded interview by a trained actor carefully designed to portray a psychologically healthy man to psychiatrists, clinical psychologists, and graduate students in clinical psychology. When a prestigious psychiatrist suggested that the individual might actually be psychotic, Temerlin found that this suggestion had a marked effect on the diagnosis produced by all three groups.

Temerlin appears to have uncovered yet another variable that may contribute to the "pathological bias" manifested in mental health professionals' diagnoses. It is quite possible that this pathological bias, whatever its source, may actually contribute to the longer hospital stay or custodial treatment of many patients who might benefit from early release from the hospital. Again we see that the patient's career can be affected by a variety of factors which have little to do with his or her psychological condition.

In still another study, Langer and Abelson (1974) videotaped an interview of a young man recounting his job history and personal difficulties. The tape was shown to behaviorally oriented and dynamically oriented clinicians. One-half of each group were told the patient was a job applicant and the other half were told the young man was a patient, thus "labeling" him. The authors found that labeling produced judgments of poor adjustment (for the same tape) and that the effect of labeling on judgments of adjustment was much stronger for dynamically oriented clinicians. Thus, it appears that both labeling and one's *perspective* on abnormal behavior can affect judgments of severity of psychological disturbance, even those made by experienced clinicians.

Mental Hospitals as Insane Places

The social environment of the mental hospital can also help to stabilize a person in the role of chronic mental patient according to the social perspective. A number of social forces in the hospital environment have been identified that are capable of having this effect.

For example, Goldman, Bohr, and Steinberg (1970) described the experiences of two psychologists who, disguised as mental patients, had themselves admitted to a large state psychiatric hospital. One of the two psychologists was assigned to a treatment and the other to a custodial ward. Both experienced intense feelings of fear of being forgotten in the mental hospital or of being betrayed by their friends, and both suffered from intense boredom. They also found that minor events took on disproportionate significance. In addition, the lack of information about events in the outside world created considerable disorientation and confusion. Clearly, these effects were the result of the situation into which they placed themselves. Thus, it is possible that mental status examinations administered by psychiatrists may reveal disorientation attributed to the patient's disorder rather than to the patient's situation in the hospital.

The authors note that, from the perspective of the patient, the staff is divided into two groups. Professional personnel work a conventional eight-hour day and are seen as remote from the patient. On the other hand, the attendants who work around the clock in shifts are forced into closer relationships with the patients. These investigators found that in the acute treatment ward, an exchange system developed between the attendants and the patients. The attendants rewarded patients for help with minor duties which the attendants themselves did not have time to perform. This system of mutual reward placed the patients in a dependent position with respect to the attendants, and the authors feel that this dependency may have a great deal to do with the development of chronicity and institutionalization among the patients. The mutual exchange system was much less obvious on the custodial ward where negative sanctions for noncooperation seemed to be the typical method of control. Goldman and his colleagues make it clear that the attendants are forced into a controlling role and forced to make the patients dependent on them. The demands of the attendants' jobs, understaffing, and other difficulties force them to utilize the patients in this way.

Recall again the study reported by Rosenhan (1973) and described in Chapter 4, in which a number of professionals requested and received psychiatric hospitalization based on a vague complaint of hearing voices sounding "empty, hollow, thudding." Rosenhan notes the way staff responded to simple requests by pseudopatients. Typically the staff member simply moved on with head averted ignoring the pseudopatient. Rosenhan compared encounters in the hospital with responses by faculty on a nonmedical campus and responses on a university medical campus. Clearly, as Table 6-2 shows, responses to people in the mental hospital are very different from those elicited in other contexts.

Finally in many cases other patients in a psychiatric setting exert social pressure on a new arrival to accept being "sick."

> NEW PATIENT: "I don't belong here. I don't like all these crazy people. When can I talk to the doctor? I've been here four days and I haven't seen the doctor. I'm not crazy."
> ANOTHER PATIENT: "She says she's not crazy." (Laughter from patients.)
> ANOTHER PATIENT: "Honey, what I'd like to know is, if you're not crazy, how did you get your ass in this hospital?"
> FIRST PATIENT: "That's what they all say." (General laughter.)
> (Scheff, 1966, p. 86)

Patient Counterpower: Impression Management

One might be tempted to conclude that the mental patient is a helpless person controlled by the social forces and pressures of the mental hospital. But some research suggests that some mental patients may have their own form of "counterpower." The person often finds his or her own way of "making it" in the mental hospital. In fact, some patients may actually use their symptoms as a means of managing the impressions that they make on the staff in order to pursue their own goals in the hospital setting. Braginsky and his colleagues (1969) suggest that mental patients may actually express or withhold the expression of their symptoms as a way of managing the impression they make on the treatment staff. By managing these staff impressions, the authors argue, patients may be able to convince the staff that they are ready for discharge if that is what they wish, or perhaps that they should remain in the hospital if that is what they desire.

In one study, Braginsky et al. suggest that not all patients wish to leave the mental hospital. Some patients ("old-timers") appear to prefer the hospital setting to the outside world and will behave in any way that assures them their place in the hospital.

TABLE 6–2 Self-initiated Contact by Pseudopatients with Psychiatrists and Nurses and Attendants, Compared with Contact with Other Groups (from Rosenhan, 1973)

CONTACT	PSYCHIATRIC HOSPITALS		UNIVERSITY CAMPUS (NON-MEDICAL)	UNIVERSITY MEDICAL CENTER — PHYSICIANS		
	(1) Psychiatrists	(2) Nurses and attendants	(3) Faculty	(4) "Looking for a psychiatrist!"	(5) "Looking for an internist!"	(6) No additional comment
Responses						
Moves on, head averted (%)	71	88	0	0	0	0
Makes eye contact (%)	23	10	0	11	0	0
Pauses and chats (%)	2	2	0	11	0	10
Stops and talks (%)	4	0.5	100	78	100	90
Mean number of questions answered (out of 6)	*	*	6	3.8	4.8	4.5
Respondents (number)	13	47	14	18	15	10
Attempts (number)	185	1283	14	18	15	10

* Not applicable.

Other patients ("short-timers") seem anxious to leave the hospital and will also report their symptoms in whatever way seems appropriate to gain their freedom.

In another study, Braginsky et al. tested their impression-management hypothesis in the context of the psychiatric interview. Their findings suggest that mental patients will respond according to their beliefs about the purpose of the interview. If they believe that the purpose of the interview is to decide whether they should be placed on a less desirable closed ward, they will suppress complaints to demonstrate that they are capable of remaining in the open ward setting. If, on the other hand, they believe that they may be discharged, and do not wish to be, they will present themselves as "sick" and ineligible for discharge. This research suggests that mental patients are not necessarily the ineffective, passive people that they are usually thought to be. Their behavior can be purposeful and goal-directed. Of course, the mental patient's skill in impression management will vary, just as it does for people in everyday life, and will depend on how severely disturbed he or she is (Price, 1972, 1973).

Labeling and Stigma

So far we have seen that the *presumption* of mental illness can affect medical decisions about the person presumed mentally ill. And we also saw that mental patients can use their deviant behavior as a form of "counterpower" (Price & Denner, 1973) to fulfill their own needs. But the social perspective goes further. It argues that persons who have been labeled as mentally ill are *stigmatized*. Their social identity as mental patients or even as ex-mental patients is deeply discrediting.

One of Scheff's propositions—that the labeled deviant is punished for attempts to return to conventional roles—takes account of the phenomenon of stigma but does not treat the problem in detail. The stigma phenomenon is worthy of more extended discussion, both because it illustrates the potential power of the labeling phenomenon so well and because it emphasizes the importance of audience reaction to the labeled deviant. These are both central themes in the sociological perspective. In addition, the phenomenon of stigma extends our view well beyond the narrower limits to which other perspectives of abnormal behavior adhere.

Goffman describes the origin of the idea of stigma in the following way:

The Greeks, who were apparently strong on visual aids, originated the term *stigma* to refer to bodily signs designed to expose something unusual and bad about the moral status of the signifier. The signs were cut or burnt into the body and advertised the bearer as a slave, a criminal, or a traitor—a blemished person ritually polluted, to be avoided, especially in public places. Later, in Christian times, two layers of metaphor were added to the term: the first referred to bodily signs of holy grace that took the form of eruptive blossoms on the skin; the second, a medical allusion to this religious allusion referred to bodily signs of physical disorder. Today the term is widely used in something like the original sense, but is applied more to the disgrace itself than to the bodily evidence of it (1963b, pp. 1–2).

One of the most notable qualities about the stigma of mental illness is that it occupies what Hughes (1945) has described as a "master status" in the minds of others. That is, a person who has been socially defined as mentally ill is considered mentally ill or deviant above all else. All other attributes or social roles that the individual may carry are relegated to the background. Consequently, when the patients are released from the hospital— even if they have been described as "cured" by the hospital staff— they cannot be cured of the stigma of mental illness from which they will suffer. Although society provides a wide variety of rituals to allow the normal individual to gain entrance to deviant status, there are no formal rituals for removing the stigma of mental illness from an individual so designated.

The stigma associated with having been a mental patient may affect both the way in which others view a person and behave toward him and the way he views himself. Miller and Dawson (1965) have interviewed over a thousand ex-mental patients one year after discharge from mental institutions. They have found that one-third of their patients reported difficulty in obtaining or maintaining a job once prospective employers discovered that they had previously been mental patients. In addition, many ex-mental patients reported that once they had been identified as ex-mental patients, this strongly affected the way in which their families and friends related to them.

Tables 6-3 and 6-4 summarize some of Miller and Dawson's (1965) findings. Of course, there is no way of separating the degree to which increased unemployment and lowered job status are due to stigma or to psychological disability, although Miller and Dawson make a strong case for the stigma interpretation.

Of course, the stigma of mental illness has the quality of

TABLE 6–3 Employment Status of Patients Prior to and
after Hospitalization (from Miller &
Dawson, 1965)

	PRIOR TO ADMISSION		AFTER RELEASE	
STATUS	Number	Percent	Number	Percent
Employed, full-time	209	19	133	12
Employed, part-time	180	17	77	7
Psych. or phys. disabled	82	8	219	20
Seeking employment	29	2	94	9
Not in the labor market	582	54	559	52
Total	1,082	100	1,082	100

TABLE 6–4 Occupational Identity of Patients Prior to
and after Release from a Mental Hospital
(from Miller & Dawson, 1965)

	PRIOR TO ADMISSION		AFTER RELEASE	
OCCUPATION	Number	Percent	Number	Percent
White collar	174	22	83	10
Blue collar	292	36	235	30
No occupation	326	42	474	60
Total	792	100	792	100
	N=792			

a self-fulfilling prophecy. An employer may reject an applicant because he has been a mental patient. It may also be that ex-mental patients are viewed as unemployable because employers reject them. Thus the discrimination associated with the stigma of mental illness may in a sense "create" the social fact of the mental patient's inferiority.

The stigma of institutionalization can affect the relatives of the mental patient as well. The behavior of the wife of a mental patient provides a good example.

Concealment often becomes cumbersome. Thus, to keep the neighbors from knowing the husband's hospital (having reported that he was in a hospital because of suspicion of cancer), Mrs. G. must rush to her apartment to get the mail before her neighbors pick it up for her as they used to do. She has had to abandon second breakfasts at the drugstore with the women in the neighboring apartments to avoid their questions. Before she can allow visitors in her apartment, she must pick up any material identifying the hospital, and so on (Goffman, 1963b, p. 89).

The wife of another mental patient reports,

> But I've cut off all our other friends [after citing five who "knew"]. I didn't tell them that I was giving up the apartment and I had the phone disconnected without telling anyone so they don't know how to get in touch with me.
>
> I haven't gotten too friendly with anyone at the office because I don't want people to know where my husband is. I figure that if I got too friendly with them, then they would start asking questions, and I might start talking, and I just think it's better if as few people as possible know about Joe (Goffman, 1963b, p. 99).

The effect of such stigma is not restricted to persons who have been hospitalized at some time in psychiatric institutions. A study by Phillips (1963) indicates that the act of seeking help for psychological problems is *in itself* ground for rejection by other members of an individual's community. Phillips found that members of the community display increasing amounts of rejection toward an individual depending upon where he or she has gone for help. For identical descriptions of disturbed behavior, the amount of rejection increased according to what help the person sought: no help, a clergyman, a physician, a psychiatrist, hospitalization in a mental hospital. Thus the act of seeking help may identify the person as someone with mental problems and may in turn discredit his or her identity.

A person who has been identified as a mental patient or someone with mental problems may attempt to hide this fact and to "pass" for normal (Goffman, 1963b). Passing provides the possibility of re-entry into normal role status, but it may provide pitfalls of its own. People who attempt to conceal the fact that they have been in a mental hospital or have had psychiatric difficulties may go to great lengths in order to accomplish this act of passing. Difficulty may arise when their attempts to conceal their stigmatized status become in themselves instances of residual rule-breaking. If this occurs, or if the individual is discovered concealing his or her status, this may lead to a new cycle of disturbed behavior and a new public crisis. The unsuccessful passer will then be relabeled as a mental patient and again embark on a career of deviance.

We can see, then, that the stigma of mental illness and the

failure to pass as normal successfully may lead the deviant even deeper into a career of chronic deviance.

Summary

The sociological perspective begins with an analysis of rules for social interaction. Most rules for social interaction are un-named social conventions. Breaking social norms or rules is thought of as "residual" deviance because we have no formal rule category to account for it, such as legal codes or etiquette. Norm violation may be the result of a variety of biological, psycho-logical, and social factors. Most residual rule-breaking is denied, minimized, or ignored by others despite the fact that the prev-alence of residual rule-breaking is quite high.

However, some residual rule-breaking becomes labeled as mental illness. It is at this point in the crisis—when the rule-breaker is publicly labeled as deviant or mentally ill—that he or she may become highly suggestible and accept the label as the only alternative. Now the rule-breaker is embarked on a career of chronic deviance and may begin to play the role of one who is mentally ill.

Labeled deviants are products of our culture and as such know a good deal about the social institution of insanity and how "crazy" people are supposed to behave. From early childhood they have been exposed to stereotypes of madness. As they pro-ceed in a career of chronic deviance, they are rewarded for playing the stereotyped role and are punished for any attempts to leave the role. "Insight" into the fact that they are "sick" will be rewarded by their therapists and the stigma of their identity as mental patients will block their entrance into normal roles, such as seeking a job after release from the hospital.

But we have also seen that the person need not be a passive recipient of social definitions. On the contrary the research we described on impression management and on commitment hear-ings shows that the patient can indeed play a decisive role in his or her own fate.

Nevertheless the social perspective argues that in the process of becoming a mental patient, a person follows a fairly predictable "career path" of the sort shown in Figure 6-1.

One of the notable features of this summary figure is that it includes a large number of "feedback loops." These feedback loops are intended to characterize situations in which the deviant may be caught in a "vicious circle" in the social system. To take

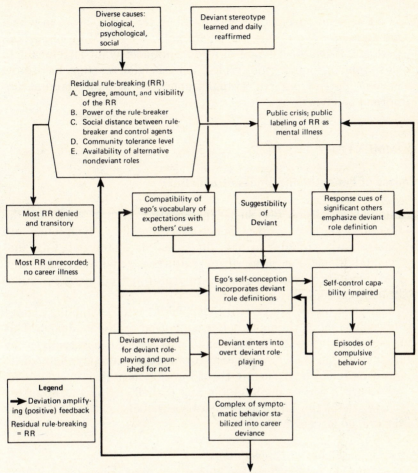

FIG. 6-1 Flow chart: stabilization of deviance in a social system. (Redrawn from T. J. Scheff, *Being mentally ill: A sociological theory*. Chicago: Aldine, 1966. Reproduced by permission.)

an example from the flow diagram, a public crisis may lead to increased suggestibility of the deviant, incorporation of the deviant role definition, and impairment of self-control capability, followed by episodes of "compulsive" behavior, which in turn lead back to the crisis module; the same process may be repeated almost indefinitely. A number of different feedback loops of this kind exist within the system. As Scheff points out, these feedback loops may serve to create a *stabilized* or even amplified system.

The social perspective has given us yet another way in which we may view the problem of abnormal behavior. More important, perhaps, it has broadened our conception of what is relevant to the problem. Social rules, roles, and societal reaction have now become part of our conceptual framework in understanding abnormal behavior.

COMMENTARY

Causes of Patienthood: Illness or Labeling?

Implicit in all of the social perspective is a critique of the illness view. The social perspective implies that "symptoms" are merely norm violations, that "diagnosis" is merely labeling, that "mental illness" is primarily a culturally sanctioned idea, and that "chronic mental patients" are really just occupying a stabilized social role.

Here truly, we have two perspectives with competing claims. But which set of claims is better supported by the evidence? This is a difficult question to answer in part because perspectives, by their very nature, are seldom formulated precisely enough to allow a crucial test. The merits of the evidence have been argued, however, in recent books defending (Scheff, 1975) and attacking (Gove, 1975) the labeling point of view. Let us look at some of the crucial issues.

Craziness as Cause or Consequence

Another reason for the slippery nature of the debate between the illness and labeling perspectives is that they frequently point to different events in supporting their own view. An example of this is provided by Lemert's (1951) early distinction between *primary* and *secondary* deviance. Briefly the distinction refers to the fact that abnormal behavior can arise in response to being labeled, or hospitalized (secondary), or as a result of some internal (primary) cause such as brain damage or perhaps lead poisoning. Scheff (1975) simply states that there are no uniform causes of deviant (primary) behavior, but that they are "diverse."

We have reviewed ample evidence earlier in this chapter to support the notion that court proceedings, hospitals, diagnosis, and treatment are capable of producing secondary deviance. But ample evidence also exists for organic (primary) determinants of abnormal behavior. Which position is correct? Perhaps both positions are correct in part. After all, proponents of the labeling perspective typically refer to events that occur *after* some initial episode of deviant behavior. Supporters of the illness view (Gove, 1975) usually offer evidence focusing on etiology of initial episodes of abnormal behavior. Labeling can, after all, be both cause and consequence of abnormal behavior.

Does Society Create Deviants?

Frequently behavorial scientists attempt to decide a theoretical "either-or" question on empirical grounds. The usual strategy for doing this is to ask whether one set of factors "accounts for more variance" than another. That is, the scientist asks whether heredity or environment, early experiences or adult trauma, or others are the more powerful sets of determinants of abnormal behavior. In deciding about the importance of various causes in a controlled experimental situation this strategy may be quite acceptable. But in the competition between perspectives in which agreement about what constitutes relevant evidence is seldom reached, this method for deciding between competing accounts often cannot be used effectively.

Thus, deciding whether society "creates" deviants or not on empirical grounds is quite difficult. Howard Becker (1963) has advanced a very different kind of argument. He argues that *society by its very nature creates deviants.* He says,

> [This is] the central fact about deviance: it is created by society. I do not mean this in the way it is ordinarily understood, in which the causes of deviance are located in the social situation of the deviant or in "social factors" which prompt his action. I mean, rather, that *social groups create deviance by making the rules whose infraction constitutes deviance,* and by applying those rules to particular people and labeling them as outsiders. From this point of view, deviance is not a quality of the act the person commits, but rather a consequence of the application by others of rules and sanctions to an "offender." The deviant is one to whom that label has successfully been applied; deviant behavior is behavior that people so label (pp. 8–9).

The implications of Becker's remarks are obvious. Society creates the rules for conduct. Without rules there can, quite obviously, be no deviation from rules. Thus, society's propensity for rule-making can be thought of as a "causal" factor in the production of deviance. In this sense, at least, society creates deviance.

Is the Labeled Deviant a Passive Victim?

Reading the accounts of Goffman, Scheff, and others leaves one with the impression that the victim of labeling is passively processed in the machinery of psychiatric diagnosis entirely against his or her will. After all, the social perspective places considerable emphasis on the process of labeling and its consequences for the mental patient. Scheff (1966) has argued that the social fact of labeling is perhaps the single most important factor in establishing an individual in a career of chronic deviance. Certainly labeling represents an important part of the social institution of mental illness. Audience reaction to the labeled deviant is a crucial element of the social perspective. Yet this emphasis may lead us to neglect the role of the labeled deviant or predeviant in the social process, as Spitzer and Denzin (1968) point out.

> This view of deviant behavior has quite profitably shifted attention in research to the interactional settings within which the labeling and deviance ascription process occurs; yet, it has deficiencies which may mislead the researcher. Most notable has been a tendency to slight the role played by the deviant or pre-deviant in the actual labeling process. Erikson, Kitsuse, and H. Becker have insightfully noted that the actual province of a sociology of a deviant behavior is "audience reactions," but *it must be recognized that the actor himself may and, in fact, quite frequently does play an important determining part in the labeling process.* If the burden of theoretical attention is placed upon the audience's reaction to social acts, the implication is that the pre-deviant is under the complete control of the audience members whenever interpretation of social acts becomes an issue. . . . It is our position that investigators in the sociology of mental illness, regardless of theoretical orientation, have overlooked the fact that quite frequently persons labeled as mentally ill react to this label and often attempt to dissuade audience members of their allegations (p. 462, italics added).

As we noted earlier, evidence now available suggests that hospitalized psychiatric patients are at least capable of engaging in a variety of interpersonal strategies in order to fulfill their own goals. Braginsky, Braginsky, and Ring (1969) have reported a series of studies showing that mental patients are able to manage the impressions they make upon hospital staff in order to remain at or leave the hospital, remain on a custodial ward, or to achieve various other goals. Evidence of this sort will cer-

tainly counteract any overemphasis on audience reactions implied in the social perspective.

In addition, new more interactional approaches to understanding abnormal behavior (Berne, 1964) now also emphasize the
reciprocal nature of all social transactions including those involving deviant behavior.

Ideology and Value Issues

Despite all attempts at "objectivity," students of abnormal behavior have ideological commitments. Often researchers may
not be aware that they have such commitments and may vigorously deny any bias when asked. The social perspective certainly
may contain a bias. Spitzer and Denzin (1968) suggest what it
may be:

> By ignoring the process of self-indication in social interaction,
> theorists have presented what at times appears to be an ideological
> defense for the underdog—e.g., "the poor mental patient." While
> this defense is seldom if ever explicitly stated, the implication is
> that the mental patient has virtually no control over his environ-
> ment and that once he has been so labeled, he will carry for life a
> deeply discrediting and stigmatizing label (p. 462).

Scheff (1975) actually appears to agree with this view when
he describes labeling theory as a "protest against the practices
it describes" (p. 2). In fact, Scheff believes that the primary value
of the social perspective is a "sensitizing" one. That is, it alerts
the reader to issues otherwise too easily obscured.

There may well be a place for such ideological commitments
in the study of abnormal behavior. However, if such commitments
are going to be made they should be explicit, and their implications must be fully explored. Unfortunately this is seldom
done. Instead, sociological data are often examined and interpreted as if no value orientation or ideological commitment
existed. Only recently has the value issue emerged as central
(Denner & Price, 1973; Price & Denner, 1973; Ryan, 1971).

Becker (1964) distinguishes between two types of ideological
commitment that can occur in social research. The first type he
calls "conventional sentimentality." The social scientist who
refuses to examine the possibility of professional incompetence
in the disposition of persons who become labeled as mental

patients is guilty of conventional sentimentality. In many cases the error of conventional sentimentality takes the form of unquestioning acceptance of myths that mental health workers hold about themselves or their profession. For example, they may commit the "sentimental" fault of believing that the treatment that mental patients receive is "for their own good" and that therefore these people's rights are not being violated. Perhaps worse, the acceptance of a conventional sentimentality may lead social scientists to design their research in ways which do not allow evidence of possible incompetence to be gathered.

A different sort of error is what Becker (1964) calls "unconventional sentimentality." Unconventionally sentimental people assume that things are always worse than they appear. Furthermore, they do not acknowledge any evidence that refutes this assumption. They may believe that the underdog is always right or perhaps that the mental patient is always the "poor mental patient" who is being systematically discriminated against and mistreated.

Much of the research and theory on the problem of abnormal behavior written from the social perspective has erred in the direction of unconventional sentimentality. Becker (1964) suggests that

> this, after all, is the lesser evil. If one outrages certain conventional assumptions by being unconventionally sentimental, a large body of opinion will be sure to tell him about it. But conventional sentimentality is less often attacked, and specious premises stand unchallenged (pp. 5–6).

Perhaps the ideal stance for the student of society to take in investigating the problem of abnormal behavior might be described as the study of "folk medicine" (Scheff, 1967). This idea, which borrows a term from anthropology, implies that the researcher seeks to describe the way in which members of a particular society (including the society's "medicine men") behave toward illness and those who are designated as ill without necessarily subscribing to the assumptions made by that society about the illness.

Developmental Emphasis of the Social Perspective

The social perspective examines the development of abnormal behavior over time. Psychologists usually refer to this as a "developmental" or a "longitudinal" approach. Concepts like "path," "career," "sequence," or "contingencies" in the social perspective give evidence of the preoccupation with the sequence of events unfolding in the life of the individual. Following Becker (1963), we will use the term "sequential" to describe it. As we shall see, the sequential method of description has a variety of useful features.

Becker (1963) distinguishes between simultaneous and sequential approaches to the description of abnormal behavior. The principle methodological tool of simultaneous methods is multivariate analysis. An assumption often made when multivariate analysis is the methodology employed is that all of the factors which produce the event or phenomenon we are studying operate "simultaneously." The question implicit in the multivariate approach is: what variables or combination of variables will best predict the occurrence of the behavior being studied? For example, in the study of abnormal behavior, we might wish to ask what variables predict whether psychiatric hospitalization will occur, and we might begin by trying to discover whether socioeconomic class, marital conflict, traumatic childhood events, or a combination of these factors are involved.

However, we know that these factors do not operate at the same time and we need instead an approach that accounts for the fact that *behavior patterns develop in sequence.* The idea of events being sequential is of great importance, because a particular factor may have to occur at a certain point in the sequence in order to operate causally. If it occurs at other points in the sequence its effects may be negligible.

Becker (1963) offers the example of habitual drug use:

Let us suppose, for example, that one of the steps in the formation of an habitual pattern of drug use—willingness to experiment with the use of the drug—is really the result of a variable of personality or personal orientation such as alienation from conventional norms. The variable of personal alienation, however, will only produce drug use in people who are in a position to experiment because they participate in groups in which drugs are available; alienated people who do not have drugs available to them cannot begin experimentation and thus cannot become users no matter how alienated they are. Thus, alienation might be a necessary cause of drug use, but distinguishable between users and nonusers only at a particular stage in the process (pp. 23–24).

Perhaps now we can better appreciate the reason for the use

of the term "career" in the social perspective. The concept of career implies a sequence of movements from one social position to another. In addition, the idea of career contingencies—those factors which are responsible for mobility from one position to another—may seem more real and useful to us.

Social accounts of the development of deviant behavior often have the idea of career contingencies implicit in them. For example, Goffman (1959) writes of the "moral career of the mental patient" and Becker (1963) describes "becoming a marijuana user."

The flow diagram used to describe Scheff's (1966) account of the career of the chronic residual deviant is a specific application of the sequential approach. Buckley (1966) notes that this method of description is a product of modern systems research; to place a general verbal theory within this more rigorous context, he finds, carries with it a number of advantages.

First, such a system allows the explicit labeling of propositions and variables within the theory and allows relations and potential relations between propositions to be specified. Second, as a result of this increase in explicitness, research hypotheses are easily formulated from an examination of the propositions and the relationships that exist between them. Third, the systematic nature of theories cast in this form implies not merely the consideration of the relations of single variables to each other but also the relations between whole complexes of variables. The variety of problems as elaborate as those posed by the systematic study of abnormal behavior seems to require an approach that allows enough complexity to consider the problem at hand.

Finally, an approach of this kind incorporates as a natural part of the system certain mechanisms that seem important in capturing the process involved in the development of abnormal behavior. For example, within Scheff's own system, a number of "feedback loops" are incorporated to depict the manner in which sets of events lead from one to another and may produce stabilized or even amplified sequences of events.

Thus a sequential approach to the description of abnormal behavior, particularly if it is cast in a flow chart, would seem to recommend itself strongly to the study of abnormal behavior. Perhaps other perspectives on abnormal behavior considered in this way could profit from the explicitness of this approach.

The Social Perspective and the Community
Mental Health Movement

In recent years mental health professionals have begun to change their thinking about the best way of providing mental health services to people in need of them or to those in "high risk" groups known to be more likely to develop some form of psychological disorder. Much of this new thinking is part of the community mental health movement (Denner & Price, 1973).

Although the idea of community based help for people in distress is an old one, the most recent impetus for the community mental health movement came from the efforts of President Kennedy in the early sixties. His concern with providing mental health care to the entire population and with preventing disorders before they occur stimulated legislation resulting in a nationwide network of community mental health centers in the United States.

An examination of some of the basic assumptions and strategies of the community mental health movement reveals many themes in common with the social perspective. For example, advocates of community mental health argue in favor of *early intervention* for people experiencing the psychological distress of crisis. The rationale for early intervention is that helping people to cope with problems early in their development will prevent more serious later developments, including the negative consequences of labeling and institutionalization.

Another major common theme in both the social perspective and the community mental health movement concern *deinstitutionalization*. In recent years the federal government has strongly encouraged the placement of hospitalized mental patients back into the community. The impetus for this movement has been in part a recognition of the debilitating effects of long-term mental hospitalization (Price & Denner, 1973). As Kurt Back (1975) has noted, it is likely that the impact of labeling theory or social policy has had much less to do with the evidence in favor of labeling theory than with the psychological impact of the idea of labeling on policy makers.

In any case, in their focus on social components of abnormal behavior and in the common concern with the negative effects of the patient role, community mental health and the social perspective share common assumptions about the nature and treatment of abnormal behavior.

Summary

We have seen that trying to untangle the question of what "causes" people to become mental patients is extremely difficult, although the distinction between primary and secondary deviance is helpful. The social perspective focuses for the most part on secondary deviance that occurs in reaction to being labeled or hospitalized. But it is also true that in a larger sense, society does "create" deviants by defining the rules for conduct in the first place.

But people labeled as deviant and even those who are hospitalized are not necessarily passive victims of social forces. Impression management can be and is used as a form of patient counterpower to cope with the hospital environment.

The social perspective takes a longitudinal or developmental view of behavior that can provide us with insights that are not immediately obvious. Looking at the development of deviant behavior over time allows us to trace the "career" of the individual and to discover the choice points for both the person labeled and the labeler.

The social perspective has a clearly visible value stance or ideological position in favor of the underdog, the victim of social forces. Perhaps we should recall that all perspectives on abnormal behavior contain ideological positions, some better concealed than others. As one of Theodore Sarbin's students recently noted (Sarbin, 1974), psychology is only beginning to discover the ideological positions implicit within its concepts and perspectives.

Finally we noted some similar themes in the social perspective and the community mental health movement. Although the conceptual wellspring of both approaches is similar, it is still too early to tell if the community mental health movement will act on its social insights or move the illness perspective into the community context.

Suggested Reading

1. Braginsky, B. M., D. D. Braginsky, & K. Ring. *Methods of Madness: The Mental Hospital as a Last Resort.* New York: Holt, Rinehart and Winson, 1969.
   This social psychological analysis of the plight of mental patients suggests that they may often use symptoms as a means of man-

aging the impressions of psychiatrists and others. It clearly conveys the idea that mental patients are not always the passive victims of social focus.

2. Denner, B., & R. H. Price (Eds.) *Community Mental Health: Social Action and Reaction.* New York: Holt, Rinehart and Winston, 1973. This collection of articles raises issues of deviance and its control in the community context. Ethical, moral, and political implications of current community mental health practices are examined.

3. Goffman, E. *Asylums: Essays on the Social Situation of Mental Patients and Other Inmates.* Garden City, N.Y.: Anchor Books, 1961.
No one sees the world quite like Erving Goffman. This classic analysis of the careers of mental patients has stimulated much research and controversy.

4. Gove, W. R. (Ed.) *The Labeling of Deviance: Evaluation of a Perspective.* Beverly Hills, Calif.: Sage, 1975.
A strongly critical attack on the labeling perspective in the fields of mental health, criminal justice, alcoholism, and elsewhere, this book is a useful antidote to the frequently uncritical acceptance of the labeling point of view.

5. Price, R. H., & B. Denner (Eds.) *The Making of a Mental Patient.* New York: Holt, Rinehart and Winston, 1973.
This collection of articles traces the path of a mental patient from the time deviant behavior is first observed through encounters with police, courts, diagnosis, hospitalization, and finally, release into the community.

6. Scheff, T. J. (Ed.) *Labeling Madness.* Englewood Cliffs, N.J.: Prentice-Hall, 1975.
These essays summarize recent theoretical developments and research by labeling theorists. They also venture into the fields of demonic possession and thought reform in China.

LEARNING MORE
Projects for the Reader

1. To get an idea of how people react when unstated social rules are broken, try the "ear watching" experiment described at the beginning of this chapter. How did the other person react? What were your own feelings? Was the residual rule-breaking denied? If not, how did the other person cope with it?

2. Popular conceptions of the nature of mental illness are portrayed all around us in our environment. The social perspective argues

that these public stereotypes often condition our own ideas of deviant behavior and, more importantly, how we react to them. For the next week carefully scan your newspaper. Look for news stories involving apparent "mental cases." Look in "Ann Landers" or other advice columns and note the writers who are advised to "seek psychiatric help." Look at the comics. How are "crazy" people portrayed there? Also survey television and movie offerings. At the end of a week you should have a substantial collection of evidence. What stereotypes did you find? Do you think they condition the ways in which we behave toward labeled deviants?

3. Consider David Rosenhan's experiment in which he and some confederates had themselves admitted to a mental hospital. Would you have participated in his experiment? Consider the reasons for your answer. Do they support or refute any of the assumptions of the social perspective?

4. Interview the police in your community to discover the techniques they use to deal with psychologically disturbed persons. How do they encounter such people? How can they tell if they are disturbed? What do they do with them under various circumstances? How do the police feel about dealing with such cases? Can you trace the "flow chart" used by the police similar to the one in this chapter used to describe the "career" of mental patients?

7

tHe hUMANiSTic peRSpEcTive

A Brief Test in Concept Formation

What do all these names and ideas have in common?

> Altered States of Consciousness
> Biofeedback
> Sufism
> I-Ching
> LSD
> Zen Meditation
> Gestalt Therapy
> Hypnosis
> PSI Processes
> Self-Actualization
> Schizophrenia

To most readers, this seems to be an extremely diverse list of ideas, concepts, and terms. As you have probably guessed by now, the common theme that runs through them is that they are part of the humanistic movement in psychology. This movement is developing a coherent view of the nature of abnormal behavior and human consciousness. Along with the view, a set of concepts about the treatment and transcendence of personal difficulties is developing. The very diversity of the movement produces the expected effects of seeming incoherence. And yet, as we will see, common themes do run through the humanistic movement and its paradigm of the nature of abnormal behavior.

THE PERSPECTIVE

In the study of abnormal behavior, particularly in the United States, two perspectives have until recently been dominant forces. These viewpoints are behaviorism and psychoanalysis. Recently, however, a third approach has captured the imagination of mental health professionals and laymen alike. The name usually given to this "third force" is humanistic psychology.

Although "third force" suggests a monolithic or univocal point of view, this is not accurate. Instead, the humanistic perspective has at least three distinct viewpoints: self-theories, some elements of existentialism, and some of phenomenology. Among the authors usually identified with the humanistic perspective are Rogers (1961), Maslow (1955), May (1969), Laing (1967), and Bugental (1965).

What unifies these various authors under the rubric of humanistic psychology is a general *view of human nature.* Sutich and Vich (1969) define this view by contrasting it to behaviorism and psychoanalysis.

> Two main branches of psychology—behaviorism and psychoanalysis—appear to have made great contributions to human knowledge, but neither singly nor together have they covered the almost limitless scope of human behavior, relationships, and possibilities. Perhaps their greatest limitation has been the inadequacy of their approach to the positive human potentialities and the maximal realization of those potentialities (p. 1).

In recent years, the third force has reflected still another influence. The exclusively Western view of human potential has been supplemented by ideas from the East including Sufism, Zen, and other religious disciplines. Blended with these ideas, an emphasis on altered states of consciousnes as avenues for personal growth has emerged. As disparate as these intellectual traditions seem, we shall see that the humanistic psychology of today revolves around several common themes and ideas about the nature of abnormal behavior.

Beginnings of Humanistic Psychology: Rogers and Maslow

The "third force" in addition to psychoanalysis and behaviorism in American psychology is not a single viewpoint. But two psychologists stand out as major representatives of the earlier period in humanistic psychology. Carl Rogers and Abraham Maslow both emphasized a concern for the subjective life of the individual and both theorists were particularly concerned with the idea of *self-actualization*—activities concerned with pursuing the human potential within each of us. Their belief in the human potential of each person and the value of the subjective experience of each person is the core of humanistic psychology. We will briefly review the positions of Carl Rogers and Abraham Maslow because they represent "classic" examples of humanistic psychology as it existed in the 1940s and 1950s in American psychology.

Rogers the Humanist

Carl Rogers stands as a widely known and admired advocate of the humanistic perspective. Although Rogers is basically a self-theorist, his approach exhibits the optimistic view of human

BOX 7-1
Language and Concepts of the Humanistic Perspective

Experience (as a verb) To experience is to receive the impact of exterior and interior events at a given moment in time. Events that are perceived at the level of consciousness are said to be experienced.

Self-concept The person's self-experience that then develops into the perceptual object the person experiences as "me" or "I."

Self-actualization Important theme of the humanistic movement. A process described by Maslow and others in which one develops the ability to perceive reality efficiently, be detached and objective, be interested in one's fellow human beings, and discriminate between means and ends. Self-actualized people are creative, have a sense of humor, and are able to resist the forces of the culture in which they live.

Actualizing tendency The actualizing tendency is the tendency of the organism as a whole to develop all its potentialities in a manner that serves to maintain or enhance itself. The actualizing tendency involves both meeting biological needs and striving for autonomy from external forces. It is the only motive postulated in Rogers' system.

Need hierarchy A listing of human needs set out by Maslow, a proponent of the humanistic perspective, in which basic human needs are listed at the bottom and needs less basic to human existence occupy higher levels. The higher needs function only when lower needs have been satisfied.

Human potential movement A portion of the movement emphasizing personal growth.

Gestalt therapy A therapeutic approach to expanding awareness and maximizing human potential. The basic injunctions include being centered in the present, observing rather than analyzing, and attempting to relive and identify with past events or experiences (e.g., through psychodrama).

Altered state of consciousness (ASC) State of consciousness other than the normal state. Methods for achieving ASC include psychedelic drugs, meditation, yoga, hypnosis, and fasting. ASCs are seen as a means to personal growth.

---

nature so characteristic of the humanistic perspective. Furthermore, Rogers is, at least in part, a phenomenologist, deeply concerned with the phenomena of individual human experience. Furthermore, many of the concepts Rogers uses—"actualization," for instance—are a part of the intellectual tradition of the humanistic perspective.

Early Development

In order to understand Rogers' ideas about the development of abnormal behavior, we must first examine his theory of the development of the normal individual from infancy.

For Rogers (1959), infants' experiences constitute the whole of their reality. Any particular infant alone has access to his or her unique internal frame of reference. Furthermore, infants have an inherent tendency toward *actualizing* themselves. The goal-directed behavior of infants—reaching, sucking, touching—is an attempt to actualize themselves in terms of their reality as each perceives it. Thus infants come to value experiences which they perceive as serving that actualizing process. Similarly, infants learn to avoid unpleasant experiences which they find are hindering the actualization of their biological and psychological being.

As children engage in the actualizing process, their experiences become more and more differentiated from each other. They begin to symbolize, that is, to view their own behavior as a separate entity. This emerging awareness of their own behavior and functions is the beginning of the experience of themselves as independent entities. As children continue to grow and interact with other people, the self-experience develops into a *self-concept*. The self-concept then becomes a perceptual object which each child may experience as "me" or "I." They may come to think of themselves as good or bad, clever or ineffective, as a result of their experiences with others and others' reactions to them.

As children's self-concepts develop, they also develop a need for others' *positive regard*. Rogers avoids any explicit statement of whether the need for positive regard is learned or inherent, but he does hold that it is a pervasive and persistent characteristic of the individual. For Rogers the need for positive regard is a "universal" need.

The need for positive regard is usually satisfied by children in a reciprocal way. That is. in satisfying another person's need for positive regard they will also satisfy their own need. However, we must realize that this need may become more compelling than the need for actualization. Children may seek positive regard from others rather than seeking experiences that would serve to actualize themselves.

Positive regard applied to oneself or to those experiences that refer to the self is termed positive self-regard. The need for positive self-regard is a learned need, and children come to value or devalue themselves independently of how others may see them.

Conditions of worth develop in people when they selectively respond to their self-experiences as more or less worthy of positive regard. If a child always experienced unconditional regard, then no conditions of worth would develop and the child would experience the self in terms of positive self-regard regardless of the external experience. The child would in this case remain psychologically adjusted. In reality, however, conditions of worth exist for everyone since no child receives only unconditional positive regard from others. Thus the child is valued for competent performance in school or play and less valued for poor performance, valued for "good" behavior and less valued for the "bad." As we shall see, the child who has incorporated many or intense conditions of worth is vulnerable to threat or anxiety when encountering experiences which are contrary to his or her conditions of worth.

As individuals grow they continue to need self-regard, but, as we suggested above, they have also acquired conditions of worth. That is, they come to value certain behaviors and experiences which they find others value. Similarly, they devalue those behaviors and experiences which others do not value, or disapprove of, or punish.

Since people retain their need for self-regard, they begin to perceive their experiences in a selective fashion. They either deny awareness of or selectively view those experiences that are contrary to their conditions of worth, even to the point of making them appear to be conditions of worth. They may deny or rationalize a failure, for example.

As a result of this distortion or selective perception an incongruence develops between the person's actual experience and concept of self. The individual is now vulnerable to anxiety and, to some degree, is psychologically maladjusted. That Rogers' concept of incongruence is very closely tied to his notion of conditions of worth is central to his idea of psychopathology. It tells us, as well, a good deal about his view of human nature and the humanistic tradition in which his theory clearly fits.

The Development of Defensive and Disorganized Behavior

When incongruity exists in the person, he or she is vulnerable to threat. The basic threat is that experiences which are incongruent with the self-structure endanger the integrity of the self as a consistent structure. The person will not meet his or her conditions of worth and will then experience anxiety.

Defensive behaviors develop as the person attempts to pre-

Rogers on Values and Science

"We can choose to use the behavioral sciences in ways which will free, not control; which will develop creativity, not contentment; which will facilitate each person in his self-directed process of becoming. . . ."
(Rogers, 1956, p. 1064)

vent the anxiety from occurring. In general, defensive behavior is a distortion or selective perception of experience that makes the experience consistent with the self-structure as it currently exists. Rogers (1959) offers the following example of defensive behavior:

> Let us consider for a moment the general range of defensive behaviors from the simplest variety, common to all of us, to the more extreme and crippling varieties. Take first of all, rationalization ("I didn't really make that mistake, it was this way . . ."). Such excuses involve a perception of behavior distorted in such a way as to make it congruent with our concept of self (person who doesn't make mistakes). Fantasy is another example ("I am a beautiful princess, and all men adore me"). Because the actual experience is threatening to the concept of self (as an adequate person, in this example), this experience is denied, and a new symbolic world is created which enhances the self, but completely avoids any recognition of the actual experience (p. 228).

In Figure 7-1, the development of defensive behavior is shown in schematic form. Our diagram recapitulates the development of the person as Rogers describes it. The lack of unconditional positive regard and unconditional positive self-regard in the life of the person leads to conditions of worth. Once conditions of worth are firmly established as part of the self-concept, the person may encounter threatening experiences which are incompatible with his or her self-concept. Thus, incongruence may develop between the self-concept and experience.

Incongruence makes the individual vulnerable to anxiety, an unpleasant state. At this point the person's defenses come into

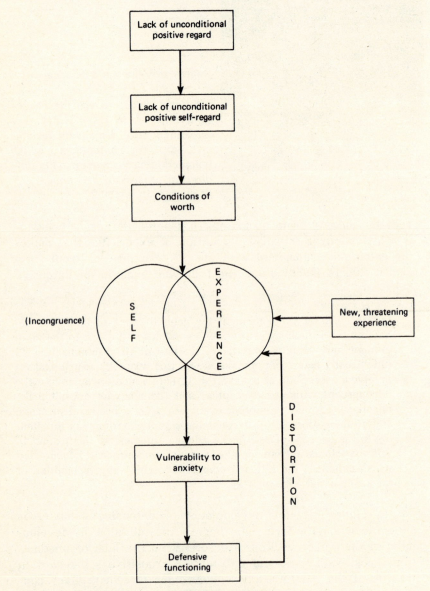

FIG. 7–1   The development of defensive behavior.

play. Defenses serve the purpose of distorting experience to make it more compatible with the self-concept. But it is an artificial compatibility, one that occurs only at the expense of distorted experience.

Rogers makes a general distinction between defensive behaviors as we have just described them and disorganized behaviors. This distinction provides a crude typology of abnormal behavior. Among the defensive behaviors are included behaviors conventionally thought of as "neurotic"—for example, rationalization, projection, phobias—as well as some behaviors often regarded as psychotic—for example, paranoid behaviors such as suspicion or projection. Disorganized behaviors, on the other hand, include much of what is usually associated with "acute psychotic" reactions. We will now turn to the development of this second type of abnormal behavior. The degree of incongruence between the self and experience may be great for a particular individual. Furthermore, a person may undergo an experience that confronts him or her with the incongruence suddenly and without warning. If this occurs, the process of defense may not operate successfully. When defenses are unable to operate with any degree of effectiveness the experience will not be distorted but instead will by symbolized accurately in experience. In this case disorganization, rather than defensiveness, will result.

Rogers suggests that in cases of disorganization, the behavior pattern that will result is one in which at times the person will act in terms of his or her self-concept and at other times in terms of the discrepant experiences; thus the behavior will alternate between these two modes. Examples of disorganized behavior are the "psychotic break" or the "acute psychotic episode."

Once individuals have shown the psychotic behavior, they may resort to two possible processes of defense. First, they may defend against their awareness of themselves. They may in effect deny their identity and perhaps even take on a different identity. A person may, for example, be perplexed about who he or she is or may even claim to be a famous figure from the past. The latter claim is usually regarded as a "paranoid delusion." A second possibility is for the concept of self to change, and, as Rogers puts it, now exist as "a self-concept which includes the important theme, 'I am a crazy, inadequate, unreliable person who contains impulses and forces beyond my control.' Thus it is a self in which little or no confidence is felt" (Rogers, 1959, p. 230).

In Figure 7–2, the development of disorganized behavior is sketched. We can see that the early stages of the development of

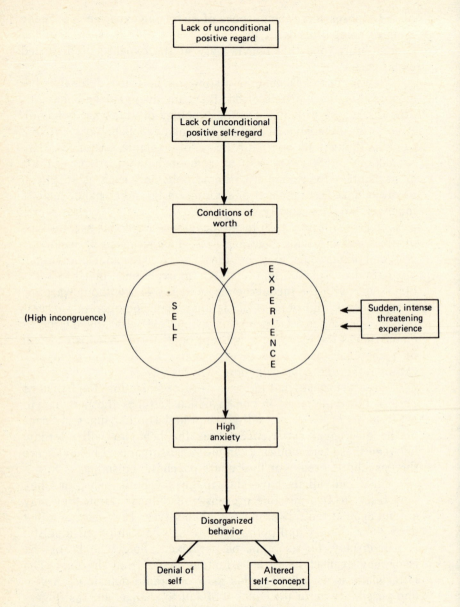

FIG. 7–2 The development of disorganized behavior.

disorganized behavior are the same as those of defensive behavior. In this case, however, the incongruence-evoking experience is sudden and intense, producing extreme incongruence and
high anxiety. The defenses are unable to operate under such cir-

cumstances, and the result is disorganized behavior which is resolved either by the denial of the current self-concept or an altered self-concept.

Maslow's Concepts: Self-Actualization, Need Hierarchy, and Psychological Health

Unlike most perspectives on psychopathology, the humanistic movement places at least an equal emphasis on the positive aspects of behavior. The single most important theme that runs through the work of many theorists within this movement is the concept of *self-actualization*. Goldstein (1939) was one of the first to use the term "self-actualization"; Erich Fromm (1941) described the concept as the "productive orientation." Karen Horney (1950) used the term "the real self and its realization," while for Allport (1955) the concept was best expressed as "creative becoming."

What sort of person is a self-actualized individual? Maslow (1954) has attempted to provide a general description by a list of characteristics. He indicates that these are not merely speculative ideas but the result of his study of a number of self-actualizing people.

Maslow believes that self-actualizing people are more efficient in perceiving reality, more accepting of themselves and others, more spontaneous, more problem centered, and capable of being detached and objective. In addition, they are autonomous, capable of a fresh appreciation of things, and open to mystical experiences. Self-actualizers show a good deal of interest in others, possess democratic character structures, experience deep and profound interpersonal relationships, and are able to discriminate between means and ends. Finally, self-actualizers have a sense of humor, are creative, and yet at the same time are able to resist many of the forces of the culture in which they live.

These characteristics are by no means mutually exclusive but overlap with each other to a great extent. In addition, it is fairly clear that Maslow owes much to Erich Fromm (1941), since his list is quite similar to Fromm's description of the characteristics of persons with a "productive orientation." Yet it serves to provide an explicit example both of what is meant by the concept of self-actualization, and at the same time, of the positive, optimistic orientation so typical of the humanistic perspective.

Maslow (1954, 1955) postulates *a hierarchy of needs,* with the most basic needs at the bottom. As one progresses up the hierarchy, these needs become less basic to human existence. He argues that the higher needs only function when lower needs have been satisfied. Further, Maslow believes that these needs are universal and independent of specific cultural influences. Thus he describes them as "instinctoid," by which he means that although they exist in all people, many of these needs are not strong enough to be observed unless conditions are favorable.

Maslow places the *physiological needs* at the bottom of the hierarchy. These are needs such as hunger and thirst. Since in our society few people are in danger of starvation, this need is almost always satisfied.

Second in the hierarchy are the safety needs. Like the physiological needs, the safety needs may dominate behavior if they are not satisfied. Among the safety needs are, for children, the need to protect themselves from sudden noises or being dropped, or, in slightly older children, the need to protect themselves from strangers. In times of war, disease, or natural catastrophe, the safety needs dominate behavior.

Next in the hierarchy are the *belongingness* or *love needs*. In general, these needs are manifested by the hunger for affectionate relationships with other people. Again, these needs will not manifest themselves until prior needs in the hierarchy are fulfilled. Maslow believes that belongingness and love needs are often frustrated and this frustration is an important basis for the development of maladjustment or abnormal behavior.

Next are the *esteem needs*. These needs represent a desire for a firmly based high evaluation of oneself. The need for self-esteem or self-respect and a need for respect from others are examples of esteem needs. In adults these esteem needs often show themselves as a desire for dominance, recognition, prestige, or status. When these needs are gratified, the person will feel self-confident, strong, capable, and adequate.

Finally, the highest need in the hierarchy is that of *self-actualization*. The characteristics of self-actualizing people that have already been outlined implicitly describe the needs of the self-actualized person. They include the need for spontaneity, the need to be creative, and the need to show an interest in other people.

Maslow believes that the gratification of all of the needs in the hierarchy is crucial to the psychological well-being of the individual. When these needs are not met, there exist, Maslow says, "deficiency conditions." Maslow argues that the hierarchical needs are basic to mental health for a number of reasons. First, if these needs are not satisfied, psychological health is not possible. Second, when these needs are satisfied, illness is prevented. Third, if a person is already maladjusted, the satisfaction of the needs will overcome the maladjustment. Finally, Maslow believes that in healthy, fully functioning persons, these needs are fulfilled (Maslow, 1955).

It is interesting to note that Maslow strongly believes that this hierarchy of needs is not specific to any particular culture but is universal. Unlike Freud, who holds a relatively pessimistic human view, the growth theorists such as Maslow and Rogers hold as a basic premise the idea that destructiveness is not instinctual in human nature. Instead, the growth theorists view aggression and destructiveness as learned reactions.

Thus, it is not people who are indicted as the "cause" of abnormal behavior but society. Both Maslow's concept of "deficiency conditions" and Rogers' idea of "conditions of worth" are central to their view of how abnormal behavior develops. Both concepts attribute the source of human unhappiness not to people themselves but to society and the socialization process. We will see this theme again later in our commentary.

The New Wave: Human Potential and Altered States of Consciousness

Perhaps more than any other perspective, the humanistic perspective has been affected by the cultural changes of the late 1960s and the early 70s in the United States. The questioning of assumptions about conventional modes of dress and conventional modes of behavior, increasing doubts about the validity of many of our cultural assumptions, and even doubts about the nature of reality influenced the humanistic movement in psychology. The earlier thinking of Rogers, Maslow, and other representatives of the humanistic movement was supplemented by the cultural changes of the sixties. The earlier emphasis on actualization and human potential remained, but a much stronger emphasis on the value of altered states of consciousness through drugs or meditation was emphasized. Indeed, the counterculture gave the humanistic movement new vigor in a time when all conventional wisdom was being questioned.

In retrospect, authors such as Robert Ornstein (1973), Charles Tart (1975), and others make two points. The first was that we must open up the scientific enterprise, and particularly, scientific psychology, to make altered states of consciousness a legitimate field of study. These scientists argued that studying the effects

of mind-expanding drugs, meditation, and other methods to expand consciousness might help us to understand various forms of
abnormal behavior. The second message of the new wave of
humanistic psychologists was that various attempts to alter our
own consciousness had the power to unlock untapped human
potential within each of us. Although there was no disagreement
about the potential of altered states of consciousness, many ways
to alter our consciousness were suggested. Mind-expanding and
psychedelic drugs, meditation, hypnosis, yoga, and fasting were
all put forth as methods of coming closer to our own human
potential.

In the sections that follow we will note both of these themes.
The new humanistic psychology is a psychology that has its
roots in phenomenology and in the value of human experience,
but the new emphasis is on altered states of consciousness and
the insights they may provide about various forms of abnormal
behavior. And we will see that even behaviors conventionally
regarded as abnormal are seen as a source of growth.

Schizophrenia as an Altered State of Consciousness

We have noted that recent developments in the humanistic
perspective focus heavily on new sources of human potential
and on altered states of consciousness. But what about serious
disorders such as schizophrenia? How does the humanistic perspective view these forms of abnormal behavior? Pelletier and
Garfield (1976) have noted that one can think about schizophrenia
as simply another example of an altered state of consciousness.
Furthermore, they suggest that there is nothing inherently pathological about the phenomenology of schizophrenia. That is,
everyone has experienced many of the feelings and subjective
states of schizophrenia at one time or another. This seems a
relatively neutral stance and implies that we can think of schizophrenia as just another state of consciousness. But there are
advocates of the humanistic perspective who will go much
further. For example, R. D. Laing (1967) suggests that schizophrenic experience may be a glimpse of states of consciousness
now denied by us through our socialization and social conventions. He suggests that if the human race survives it may be that
we will look back on our time as a dark age and that schizophrenics may be seen as "the light that began to break through
the cracks of our all too closed minds."

The notion that schizophrenic experience is pathological

in the sense that a disease is pathological is strongly criticized by Pelletier and Garfield. They note that,

> three antitherapeutic consequences of regarding schizophrenia as exclusively a pathological condition are: (1) the rejection of the validity of multiple realities; (2) the definition of the schizophrenic as a non-responsible object; and (3) the lack of attention directed at the positive aspects of altered states of awareness. It is the third consequence, that is, the conceptualization of schizophrenia as an altered state of awareness or an ASC with both positive and negative potential for the individual that is our major concern (1976, p. 52).

Thus, we see that Pelletier and Garfield have been able to simultaneously criticize the illness perspective and more clearly define the humanistic position. They emphasize the value of multiple realities, an existential orientation toward responsibility, and the idea that altered states of consciousness can have positive insight-promoting effects.

A hallmark of the recent developments within the humanistic perspective is, as we have said, the valuing of alternate realities. Altered states of consciousness are seen as alternative ways of seeing the world and are believed to contain valuable insights about ourselves and the world around us.

One well-known method for chemically altering one's psychological experience has been to take certain "psychedelic" substances such as LSD-25. Typically, a person who has taken LSD experiences profound perceptual distortion and feelings of awe or deep insight. In fact, LSD has been used as a therapeutic agent in psychiatry, particularly for people suffering from severe alcoholic problems.

Silverman (1970) has noted a number of common characteristics in the psychedelic experience associated with LSD and in the experience of schizophrenia. These common characteristics are: (1) heightened sensory experience; (2) distractibility and figure ground disorders; (3) thought disorder; (4) blocking; (5) withdrawal; (6) loss of spontaneity in movement and speech; (7) changes in space perspective; and (8) stimulus intensity reduction. Thus, Silverman implies that both schizophrenia and the LSD experience are altered states of consciousness with a number of characteristics in common.

In fact, Cohen (1970) has offered a detailed comparison of the LSD reaction and one particular type of schizophrenic reaction, that of catatonic schizophrenia. The comparison is shown in Table 7-1 below.

TABLE 7–1 Characteristics of Psychotic and Psychotomimetic Reactions [From K. R. Pelletier and C. Garfield, *Consciousness East and West*. New York: Harper and Row, 1976, p. 71. Reproduced by permission.]

TYPE OF CHANGE	MODEL PSYCHOSIS PRODUCED BY LSD	ACUTE CATATONIC EXCITEMENT (SCHIZOPHRENIC REACTION)
PERCEPTION	Illusions, frequent intensified visual perception; pseudohallucinations; hallucinations, mainly visual; other sensory hallucinations are rare	Illusions, rarely intensified perceptions; hallucinations, mainly auditory but also visual; other sensory hallucinations are rare
COGNITION	Impairment of judgment and abstract reasoning for practical problem-solving purposes; blocking; ideas of reference; delusions; disorganized ideation	Marked impairment of judgment and abstract reasoning; blocking; use of metaphor; ideas of reference; bizarre delusions; disorganized ideation
AFFECT	Anxiety; depression or elation, ecstasy; uncontrollable laughter or tears	Anxiety, terror; rarely euphoria or ecstasy; mutism, inappropriate moods, stupor
BEHAVIOR	Passive, rarely restless, and overactive	Gesturing, grimacing, destructive, withdrawn, automatism, negativism, hostility
POSTURE	Slight tremor; slight unsteadiness	Complete immobility; pacing, "caged animal"; posturing
CONSCIOUSNESS	Relatively clear	Relatively clear but preoccupied
REALITY TESTING	Slightly or moderately impaired	Greatly impaired
SPEECH	Blocking, halting, sometimes unimpaired	Condensations, alliterations, blocking, echolalia, slang associations
EGO BOUNDARIES	Depersonalization; derealization	Depersonalization; derealization

The comparison by humanistic psychologists of the LSD experience and schizophrenia has two aspects worth noting. First, from this perspective both experiences are simply altered states of consciousness rather than pathological conditions. They are different ways of being in the world, which are not to be devalued but to be experienced and appreciated in their own right. Second, it is implied that these altered states of consciousness can have either negative or positive potential for the individual. They can be sources of anguish and misery or sources of insight and growth. Indeed, it is the emphasis on the potential growth enhancing qualities of abnormal experiences that we will turn to next.

Schizophrenia as a Growth Experience: R. D. Laing

Nearly all perspectives on abnormal behavior view the development of symptoms in an individual as a negative, unfortunate turn of events. Typically the terms used to denote the development of psychological disturbance are negative. Behavior is described as "maladaptive," "disorganized," "disintegrated," or "regressed." However, there is a small but growing group of theorists, especially within the humanistic tradition, who regard some forms of abnormal behavior not as negative events, but as a hopeful and positive indication of the possibilities of personal growth.

Such a conception may sound unfamiliar or alien to us. Yet this idea may force a genuine shift in our perspective. Assumptions that are shared by other perspectives—for example, the idea that all abnormal behavior is negative—may not be obvious to us until we are confronted with an exception to the implicit assumption. Thus, the idea that abnormal behavior may actually be an opportunity for personal growth not only represents a genuine shift in our view of abnormal behavior but also exposes an assumption which we may previously have accepted unquestioningly.

Among the major proponents of this view are R. D. Laing (1959, 1967), Kazimierz Dabrowski (1964), and John Perry (1962). As yet no single account of this basic idea has emerged, but there are similarities.

In *The Divided Self,* Laing argues that "madness" is actually a breakdown of an earlier split between the person's real or true inner-self and a false outer-self. As children develop, they may develop a false outer-self which is conforming and compliant and which attempts to fulfill others' expectations. This false outer-self leads other people to believe that the children are adjusted and happy. But meantime a true inner-self is developing which protects itself by withdrawing and disengaging from the relentless demands of others. Thus individuals may smile but not necessarily feel amusement or friendliness. Phenomenologically, they are isolated and alone. The difference between the schizoid experience and the normal experience is shown in Figure 7-3 below.

For Laing, psychosis or madness, in some people at least, is the sudden stripping away of the false outer-self, revealing beneath it the preoccupation, distortions, and fears of the true inner-self. The precariously maintained split or dissociation between the true inner-self and the false outer-self is dissolved, revealing all the terror and anger that had remained hidden.

However, the psychotic break or onset of madness may actually represent a possibility for personal growth. Laing believes once the person has become mad, the split between the inner-self and the false outer-self may now be healed.

But "healing" is not accomplished by the reestablishment of the false outer-self. Instead, for Laing, therapy consists of allowing the person to explore the inner-self freely, since he assumes that only through such exploration and support from others can the person achieve a whole and vital embodied self.

There are several striking parallels in the thinking of Rogers

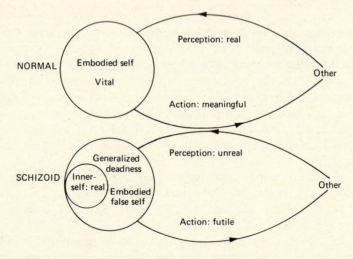

FIG. 7–3 Laing's conception of the "divided self" and the normal self. (Redrawn from R. D. Laing, *The divided self*. Baltimore, Md.: Penguin, 1965. By permission.)

and Laing concerning the development of abnormal behavior. For both Laing and Rogers abnormal behavior arises from a background involving a great deal of pressure to please others. For Laing this results in a "false outer-self"; for Rogers the result is "conditions of worth." Rogers suggests that incongruity is reflected in a discrepancy between the self and experience while Laing describes much the same thing when he suggests that a split develops between a true inner-self and a false outer-self. Finally, the source of these difficulties is attributed by both Laing and Rogers to an oppressive socialization process which values people for what they do rather than what they are.

Mary's Trip through Schizophrenia

To better appreciate what Laing is describing, let us examine briefly a clinical example. James Gordon (1971) describes the case of Mary, a woman who had been seeing R. D. Laing in psychotherapy for some years before her crisis developed. Mary had been hospitalized previously and had been diagnosed as a schizophrenic. She had since left the hospital but continued to lead a dreary, anxiety-laden life in which she continually put up a rigid, constricted front.

Mary went to Kingsley Hall shortly after R. D. Laing opened this special institution. Soon after her admission she began to regress. At night she would tear off her clothes and lie on the floor smearing her feces. For a time, she stopped eating solid food and was fed milk from a bottle by Laing and his colleagues. At one point, Mary regressed even further and even stopped drinking milk from a bottle or performing any other bodily function. Then, slowly, Mary began to recover from her madness. She began to wear clothes again and to play like a child, dancing and playing ball. Throughout this time, Laing and his fellow therapists continued to support her but made no attempt to intervene or to alter in any way the evolution of her psychosis. Soon she began to draw profusely. She drew all over the wall and then began to draw on strips of paper. Since then, Mary has been painting steadily. Dozens of paintings and drawings have appeared on boards, sheets of paper, and the walls. She describes her fascination with painting as her salvation and has become a full-time artist, still living in Kingsley Hall but, nevertheless, by her own account, a new person.

Such a dramatic account of madness and the resulting dramatic personality change may lead us to ask whether Mary's case is an extraordinary exception or whether it is typical of a much

larger group of people who have once been "mad." There is some
evidence to indicate that some patients diagnosed as schizophrenic
may actually benefit from their psychotic experiences as Mary
did.

Silverman (1970) suggests that patients who improve after
the onset of their symptoms are typically people for whom symptom onset is sudden. They have experienced a definite life crisis
or precipitating event immediately before their psychotic break.
He also points out that, in other cultures, behavior which we
call schizophrenic may be treated very differently and thought
of as a kind of initiation rite. He suggests that many religious
figures, among them Saint Theresa, Saint Paul, and George Fox
(the founder of the Quakers), went through experiences which
we might today regard as psychotic episodes. But these were
individuals who, in their own cultural setting, were valued for
the special insights that their psychosis seemed to provide.

It is also interesting to note the implications of the views of
Laing and Silverman for Rogers' account of the development
of disorganized behavior. We will recall that Rogers (1959) suggests two possible results of severe behavioral disorganization.
First, the person may finally deny his or her own identity and
even take on a new "delusional" identity. Second, he may finally
accept an identity as an incompetent, confused, "crazy" person.
If the view that abnormal behavior may in some cases be the
precursor of a growth experience has any validity, then we may
add yet a third possible outcome to the two that Rogers has outlined. In some cases the development of behavioral disorganization may actually signal the beginning of positive personality
growth.

Summary

Humanistic psychology has gone through two distinct historical periods. The first is represented by pioneers like Carl
Rogers and Abraham Maslow. Both theorists emphasized self-
actualization as a fundamental principle of humanistic psychology. Rogers' view is that conditions of worth established by
the socialization of the child can produce incongruity between
inner feelings and external experience. This incongruity can in
turn lay the groundwork for the development of abnormal behavior. When incongruity cannot be resolved it leads either to
defensive behavior of the kind that we often call "neurotic" or
to more severely disorganized behavior.

Maslow, on the other hand, emphasizes the human tendency to fulfill needs that he believes are arranged in a hierarchical fashion. The most basic need for biological fulfillment exists at the bottom of the hierarchy, while higher needs such as the need for growth exist at the top. Maslow consistently emphasizes the need for human growth and offers us examples of "actualizing personalities" who appear to have reached higher levels of human potential.

An abrupt shift in the humanistic movement occurred in the late sixties and early seventies. A new emphasis on altered states of consciousness and the potential for growth in the schizophrenic experience itself came to be emphasized. This is perhaps one of the most important points of recent departure in the humanistic perspective. The idea that abnormal behavior can be a positive growth-oriented experience is unique in the humanistic perspective and sets it apart. This is a truly paradigmatic shift away from most other perspectives on abnormal behavior. Although it is a radically different assumption about the nature of abnormal behavior, it is certainly consistent with the earlier view that all human experience is to be valued for its own sake.

COMMENTARY

Expanding Awareness and Human Potential

The humanistic movement in psychology has explored an extremely wide range of techniques for expanding awareness and maximizing human potential. Earlier in the history of humanistic psychology, client-centered therapy, which involved the reflection of the client's expressed feelings by the therapist, was a major route to self-awareness. The new wave of humanistic psychology has explored an extremely wide range of techniques from both Eastern religion and Western science. So we find body awareness techniques, hypnosis, autosuggestion, biofeedback, Gestalt therapy, and meditation all used or prescribed as awareness expanding methods. We will focus on two approaches to expanding awareness and maximizing human potential. They are the practice of Gestalt therapy (Perls, 1969; Naranjo, 1973) and newer techniques of self-control including biofeedback and hypnotic suggestion.

Gestalt Therapy

Claudio Naranjo (1973) has suggested that the basic injunctions of Gestalt therapy can be fairly easily described. Table

7–2 lists nine general moral injunctions of Gestalt therapy. These injunctions help us to capture the underlying idea that Gestalt therapy values what Naranjo calls *living-in-the-moment*.

This need to be centered in the present can be observed in many of the technical tactics of Gestalt therapy. Usually the patient is asked to express whatever enters his or her field of awareness. The patient is discouraged from reasoning about the awareness, but merely to observe the self. In addition, typically, the technique of Gestalt therapy asks that the individual attempt to relive and identify with past events or experiences. Frequently a re-enactment of the past in scenes similar to psychodrama is used for this purpose. In many cases the therapist will help the patient to become aware of his or her feelings that have been previously suppressed.

> *P.:* I don't know what to say now. . . .
> *T.:* I notice that you are looking away from me.
> *P.:* (Giggle)
> *T.:* And now you cover up your face.
> *P.:* You make me feel so awful!
> *T.:* And now you cover up your face with both hands.
> *P.:* Stop! This is unbearable!
> *T.:* What do you feel now?
> *P.:* I feel so embarrassed! Don't look at me!
> *T.:* Please stay with that embarrassment.
> *P.:* I have been living with it all my life! I am ashamed of everything I do! It is as if I don't even feel that I have the right to exist! (Naranjo, 1973).

We have chosen Gestalt therapy as one example of a technique used by humanistic psychologists to intensify awareness and enhance human potential. It resembles in some ways tradi-

TABLE 7–2   Nine Injunctions of Gestalt Therapy
                (From Naranjo, 1970)

---

1. Live now. Be concerned with the present rather than with past or future.
2. Live here. Deal with what is present rather than with what is absent.
3. Stop imagining. Experience the real.
4. Stop unnecessary thinking. Rather, taste and see.
5. Express rather than manipulate, explain, justify, or judge.
6. Give in to unpleasantness and pain just as to pleasure. Do not restrict your awareness.
7. Accept no *should* or *ought* other than your own. Adore no graven image.
8. Take full responsibility for your actions, feelings, and thoughts.
9. Surrender to being as you are.

---

tional psychotherapeutic techniques but it is strikingly different from treatment strategies prescribed by psychoanalysis or behavior therapy. For us, the primary lesson is that Gestalt therapy requires an intense awareness of one's own inner experiences in order to transcend blocked impulses and maximize human potential.

Other Ways to Human Potential

The humanistic perspective has been bolstered by scientific findings from a variety of unexpected quarters. One advocate of exploring new ways to expand human potential is Theodore X. Barber (Barber et al., 1974). Barber, a research psychologist with a long history of empirical research in the area of hypnosis, has recently turned his attention to the observation that many hypnotic suggestions do not require a hypnotic trance at all in order to exert their effects. On the contrary, it appears that the control of awareness through various cognitive strategies can provide striking therapeutic effects.

Barber argues that the traditional approach to hypnosis substantially underestimates normal human cognitive and behavioral capabilities. Human potential can be maximized, he argues, by simply using techniques that help us to control the focus of our awareness. Barber offers a number of examples of research that illustrate this idea. For example, he has shown that substantial control of pain can be accomplished by the simple cognitive strategy of focusing on other events. Barber has also reviewed research which suggests that so-called hypnotic amnesia is merely a cognitive strategy for avoiding thinking about certain past events. And he reports other suggestive research that indicates changes in skin temperature can be controlled through cognitive strategies, that allergic reactions can be controlled, and even that visual acuity can be improved!

True to his pragmatic origins, Barber has attempted to develop a program of "training in human potentialities" (1974) in which subjects are taught to control pain, to experience a variety of different phenomena including age regression, and to learn deep relaxation and self-control.

Barber, however, is not merely a narrow empirical scientist. He has been willing to examine a range of evidence of feats of human performance by practitioners of Hatha Yoga who appear able to control their heart rate, their metabolism, and even produce striking differences in skin temperature on two sides of the palm of one hand. In fact, these performances have in recent years become commonplace. Such findings, Barber argues, are clear evidence that we have not come close to understanding the human potential available to each of us through various self-control and awareness-altering strategies.

Thus, we see the stress of humanistic psychology being infused not just by an emphasis on mind expansion through psychedelic drugs or meditation, but also by attempts to more nearly approximate human potential from more traditional scientific quarters of psychology.

The Humanistic Movement in Psychology and the Scientific Establishment

As long as there has been a humanistic movement within psychology there has also been a tension between its definition of its subject matter and the more conventional view of psychological science as empirical, laboratory-oriented, experimental research. Earlier in the history of the humanistic movement this conflict manifested itself primarily in a debate about the importance of human values and subjective experience versus the importance of cold, hard facts and scientific objectivity. The epitome of this earlier conflict was a debate between Carl Rogers, champion of the humanistic view, and B. F. Skinner, advocate of the learning perspective and of experimental science as the chief method of understanding in psychology.

As we might expect, the humanistic perspective holds strong views concerning the nature of science, particularly the human science. Perhaps the best known expression of these views exists in the now famous Rogers-Skinner debate (Rogers & Skinner, 1956). This debate paired proponents of two of the major perspectives discussed in this book—the learning perspective, espoused by Skinner, and the humanistic perspective, of which Carl Rogers is a major advocate.

In this symposium, Rogers and Skinner are concerned with the place of science in human endeavor. More specifically, both are concerned with the issue of the control of human behavior. It is not surprising that control would be a pivotal question in the conflict existing between the learning perspective and the humanistic view.

Science and Human Control

Skinner opens the debate by pointing to the fact that our power to influence, to change, to control human behavior has been steadily increasing. He suggests that three broad areas of human behavior supply good examples of our increasing ability to control. First, in the area of personal control, people influence each other in face-to-face relationships.

Second, in the area of education, as Skinner points out, our concept of education implies the control and shaping of human beings. Finally, at the most general level, Skinner points to government as an explicit example of control.

Skinner does not believe that the capacity for human control is necessarily evil; he asserts that it exists. Perhaps the best example of a Skinnerian conception of what positive control can be like at its best is portrayed in his utopian novel *Walden II* (1948). Skinner suggests that his intention in writing *Walden II* was to propose a behavioral technology that would lead to the construction of an effective, productive, workable community based on positive reinforcement. He notes that his idea met violent reaction and that attitudes concerning inherent human freedom directly conflicted with his notion of what a utopian society would be if it systematically applied learning principles to human behavior. Skinner expresses some surprise at the reaction and says:

> One would scarely guess that the authors are talking about a world in which there is food, clothing, and shelter for all, where everyone chooses his own work and works an average of only 4 hours a day, where music and the arts flourish, where personal relationships develop under the most favorable circumstances, where education prepares every child for the social and intellectual life which lies before him, where—in short—people are truly happy, secure, productive, creative, and forward looking (Rogers & Skinner, 1956, p. 1059).

Skinner summarizes his argument by calling for a new conception of human behavior which is compatible with what he feels are the implications of scientific analysis. In short, Skinner asks us to accept the fact that all people control and are controlled. This is a basic fact of our lives. He sees the wise use of this control as a basic challenge to our scientific ingenuity.

Science and Value Choice

Rogers' reply to Skinner well illustrates the humanistic attitude toward the question of human control. Rogers, although he believes that Skinner presents an optimistic view, feels he underestimates the problem of power in societies which value control.

But Rogers' main objection to Skinner's analysis is that he believes that Skinner and his fellow scientists grossly underestimate the place of means and ends, goals and values in their relationship to science. Rogers' principal point is that

> in any scientific endeavor—whether "pure" or applied science—there is a prior subjective choice of the purpose or value which brings the scientific endeavor into being which must always lie outside of that endeavor and can never become a part of the science involved in that endeavor (p. 1061).

Rogers points out that, although the techniques for engaging in the experimentation may be the province of science, to choose to experiment is in itself a value choice. Thus, any endeavor in science is carried on in pursuit of a purpose or value which is at bottom subjectively chosen. He argues further that this basic choice can never be studied by scientific means, and that therefore any discussion of the control of human beings must first concern itself with the subjectively chosen purposes which science is intended to implement.

Since, for Rogers, science must begin with the value choice, Rogers offers a very different set of initial values and purposes from those he attributes to Skinner. He suggests that, instead of valuing control, we might value people as being in a process of becoming and value the goal of developing the potentiality of each individual. In short, Rogers suggests that we turn the methods of science toward discovering how each person can ultimately engage in the self-actualizing process. Rogers argues that the choice between the goal of control and the goal of people as self-actualizing beings cannot be reconciled. But, we can

> choose to use the behavioral sciences in ways which will free, not control; which will develop creativity, not contentment; which will facilitate each person in his self-directed process of becoming; which will aid individuals, groups, and even the concept of science to become self-transcending in freshly adaptive ways of meeting life and its problems (p. 1064).

It appears, however, that Rogers has not had the last word in this debate. Recently Skinner (1971) has reopened the controversy with his book, *Beyond Freedom and Dignity*. In it he argues that the solution to society's problems lies in the systematic application of the principles of his behavioral technology.

The book is a frontal attack on many of the most fundamental concepts of the humanistic perspective. Predictably, the reaction has been violent and the debate continues without a resolution or an end in sight.

Thus we see yet another point of conflict between two of the perspectives we have discussed. For the learning perspective, the goal of the human science is clear. We must face the fact of human control, develop our ability to control human behavior, and use it wisely. For the humanistic perspective, the goals of the human science are value choices which are outside the province of that science and are subjectively chosen.

Paradigm Clash: "Hip and Straight"

The 1960s and 1970s have seen yet another conflict arise between the scientific establishment in psychology and the humanistic movement. The nature of this conflict is aptly illustrated by Charles Tart (1972) who notes that a recent Gallup poll has shown that more than half of American college students have tried marijuana and are well acquainted with its effects. Yet, he notes that the accepted scientific description of the effects of marijuana is "a slight increase in heart rate, reddening of the eyes, some difficulty with memory, and small decrements in performance on complex motor tasks." Tart observes with some amusement, "would you risk going to jail to experience these?" Tart notes that the young marijuana smoker who hears a physician or scientist describe the basic nature of marijuana intoxication as it is described here will simply sneer and have his or her anti-scientific attitude further reinforced. It is clear to the student, says Tart, the scientist has no real understanding of what marijuana intoxication is all about.

Tart sharpens his point even further when he says,

the conflict between experiences in these ASC's (altered states of consciousness) and the attitudes and intellectual emotional systems that have evolved in our ordinary state of consciousness (SOC) is a major factor behind the increased alienation of many people from conventional science. Experiences of ecstasy, mystical union, and other "dimensions," rapture, beauty, space and time transcendence, and transpersonal knowledge all common in ASC's are simply not treated adequately in conventional scientific approaches. These experiences will not "go away" if we crack down more on psychedelic drugs, for immense numbers of people now practice various nondrug techniques for producing ASC's such as meditation and yoga (Tart, 1972, p. 42).

Tart's point is this: there is a widening gap between what conventional science perceives as acceptable knowledge and what the humanistic movement in psychology and other people experimenting with altered states of consciousness believe is the range of human psychological experience.

Tart goes on to argue that this state of affairs is, indeed, a "paradigm clash" of precisely the kind that Kuhn (1962) has described and with which we are now quite familiar. He describes it as a "paradigm clash between 'straight' and 'hip.' " For example, a subject may ingest LSD and tell the investigator that "you and I, we are all one, there are no separate selves," but the investigator may report that his subject showed "a confused sense of identity and distorted thinking processes." Tart remarks that the investigator's implicit paradigm is based on his or her cultural background and scientific training and produces a literal interpretation of the subject's statement. He also notes that it could be argued that the *investigator* is showing the mental dysfunction because he or she is incapable of perceiving the obvious.

The point is an important one. The emphasis of humanistic psychology and, more broadly, the cultural changes occurring in the late sixties and early seventies have expanded the field of relevant phenomena for psychologists. Psychological science is, indeed, experiencing a kind of paradigm clash here in which new phenomena are being assimilated very slowly in the mainstream of psychological thought. Today, however, it appears that we are on the way to accepting some of these phenomena as legitimate subjects of study. Laboratories around the country are now studying biofeedback, meditation, hypnosis, and drug-induced altered states of consciousness—phenomena that would have been consigned to the "lunatic fringe" only a few years ago.

The Humanistic Movement as a Reaction to Social Dilemmas

The humanistic movement is a relatively recent phenomenon, though, as we have seen, many of its themes have been anticipated by earlier theorists. We might wonder why the humanistic perspective, with its optimistic flavor, its emphasis on the individual, and its concern for values, should enjoy such a rapidly growing popularity today.

A number of writers see the humanistic movement as a reaction to a number of features of contemporary life. Conditions such as those described here are thought to have set the stage.

Problems of identity and alienation in a technocratic and overly crowded society provided fertile ground for the growth of new systems of thought that attempted to address explicitly discrepancies in the social system, in man's relationship to himself, and in the relationship between the two. The threat of nuclear annihilation, the rapid technological changes that interfered with long accepted rules and modes of existence, the tendency to value man for what he did rather than what he was—all of these confronted man with a gap between himself as an individualistic, unique person and the demands of a scientifically based industrial society (Anonymous, 1970, p. 13).

In an essay entitled "Modern Man's Loss of Significance," Rollo May (1967) expresses a similar idea. He suggests that there is ample evidence that people have lost their sense of self and their sense of individual significance or importance. Among the examples he cites are the student protests against the "facelessness of students in the modern factory university" (p. 26). He suggests that modern people are victims of feelings of helplessness and insignificance when they confront the ever-present spectre of thermonuclear war. Finally May discusses the problem of the "organization man," who paradoxically can gain personal significance only by giving up his individual significance and becoming a "team man." For May (1967) the results of these dilemmas are

the loss of the experience of one's own significance which leads to that kind of anxiety that Paul Tillich called the anxiety of meaninglessness, or what Kierkegaard terms anxiety as the fear of nothingness. We used to talk about these things as psychological theories, and a couple of decades ago when I was undergoing my psychoanalytic training, we discussed them as psychological phenomena shown by "neurotic" people. Now such anxiety is endemic throughout our whole society. These are some of the considerations which impel me to suggest that there is "no hiding place" with respect to the psychological dilemmas of our time (p. 37).

Although our conclusion can only be speculative, it certainly seems plausible that the dilemmas which May cites have provided fertile ground for the growth of a perspective on human behavior and pathology which attempts to reassert the human sense of self and individuality.

The Humanistic Movement as Social Criticism

In earlier versions of the humanistic psychology movement and in more recent positions there exists an underlying theme of social criticism that deserves special attention. The idea of society as a constraining force is clearly evident in Carl Rogers' idea of "conditional positive regard" in which the children are valued for their achievements rather than for themselves and in R. D. Laing's notion that society encourages children during their socialization to develop a "false outer self." As we have noted earlier, both Rogers' emphasis on the subjective nature of human experience and more recent focus on the expansion of awareness and altered states of consciousness suggest a turning away from the external demands of society and a turning inward toward new insights and new forms of experience.

Thus, the third force in psychology sees human salvation through turning inward, away from external control. Human potential is best reached, the humanistic position argues, not through the creation of better social institutions, but in turning away from social institutions toward inner experence in whatever form it may take.

Some interesting parallels and differences between the social perspective and the humanistic perspective are evident here. The social perspective, as we have noted, also presents a critique of society. The labeling view of abnormal behavior suggests that social institutions such as psychiatry and the mental health movement at the very least require reform. By contrast, the humanistic perspective sees many of the same difficulties in society that are indicted by the social perspective, but the solution is quite different. It advocates turning inward for salvation rather than outward.

Summary

In our commentary, we have seen that the humanistic perspective has done more than just offer a conception of abnormal behavior growth. It has also mobilized diverse techniques of both Eastern and Western origins for consciousness expansion in the name of growth. According to the humanistic perspective, Gestalt therapy, hypnosis, drugs, and other means of altering consciousness have as their common goal increased self-awareness and its presumed benefits.

The scientific establishment has been slow to accept this new thrust. The initial introduction of altered states of consciousness as a legitimate subject of study was met at first with resistance. Now, however, like many other products of cultural changes of the sixties, it is rapidly being assimilated into the mainstream, and "straight" scientists increasingly view such research as acceptable.

The humanistic perspective has also served as the springboard for social criticism. Problems of poverty, the threat of war, and other societal dilemmas have been seen as both the cause and the consequence of feelings of alienation and loss of personal significance. For the humanistic view, the solution is not to turn outward in search of social reform, but to turn inward toward a more authentic self.

Suggested Reading

1. Pelletier, K. R., & C. Garfield. *Consciousness East and West.* New York: Harper & Row, 1976.
   This book is an excellent example of the new humanistic perspective. It covers schizophrenic and psychedelic states of consciousness, psychophysiological evidence, meditation, psychotherapy, and transpersonal therapy. It comes closer than most books to providing an integrating treatment of the new wave in humanistic psychology.
2. Ornstein, R. E. *The Nature of Human Consciousness: A Book of Readings.* San Francisco, Calif.: W. H. Freeman, 1973.
   This book of readings presents over 40 separate articles or chapters ranging from classic discussions by William James on the scope of psychology to the I-Ching. Read them in any order you like. The effect is mind expanding in the best sense.
3. Barber, T. X., N. P. Spanos, & J. F. Chaves. *Hypnosis, Imagining, and Human Potentialities.* New York: Pergamon, 1974.
   Barber has managed to bring together several disparate topics and find a common core of meaning. Both experimental and anecdotal accounts of various approaches to expanding human consciousness are offered.

LEARNING MORE
Projects for the Reader

1. We noted that an important new emphasis in the humanistic perspective is on the expansion of human consciousness. In order

to get an idea of what is meant by this, ask a friend who has tried meditation to describe what the experience is like. Are there experiences of your own that seem similar to you?

2. One of the most important concepts in Carl Rogers' ideas about the development of abnormal behavior is that of "conditions of worth." By this he means, you will recall, that people are sometimes valued for what they can achieve or do rather than for themselves as individuals. Can you remember aspects of your own childhood that were particularly strong conditions of worth? Do you think they had a positive or adverse effect on your later development?

3. Try to recall a personal crisis or extremely difficult time in your own life. Do you feel that the long-term effect of this personal crisis was beneficial? How does your own experience fit the ideas of Laing and others who argue that personal crises and difficulties can be a source of new growth?

4. In order to increase your own body awareness and to experience some of the phenomena discussed by humanistic therapists, try deep body relaxation. Lie down on a comfortable couch. Beginning with your feet and moving slowly up toward your head, deeply relax each part of your body including feet, legs, thighs, hips, stomach, back, shoulders, neck, and head. Imagine that each part of your body is very heavy and very relaxed. Once you have achieved a reasonable state of relaxation, stay with it for a while and let your mind wander. What kind of experiences did you have? Do you think you would have had similar psychological experiences if your body were not relaxed?

PART THREE

integration and application

8

OVERViEW
ANd A look to the future

A BRIEF SUMMARY OF PERSPECTIVES

It should be clear at this point that the perspectives we have discussed differ in a variety of ways and that therefore direct comparison is difficult. Nevertheless, a brief summary of the perspectives may be useful. In Table 8–1 the perspectives we have discussed are summarized in terms of six general dimensions. For each perspective we have listed the basic metaphor underlying the perspective, related subordinate concepts, presumed causal factors, the terms used to describe abnormal behavior, the type of therapeutic intervention implied by the perspective, and the major proponents of the perspective.

In the sections that follow we will summarize some recent trends in the field and make some guesses about the nature of the field of abnormal psychology in the future.

RECENT TRENDS AND A LOOK TO THE FUTURE

In the last ten years each of the perspectives has shifted in emphasis, some more than others. These trends are worth noting because they tell us something about possible future directions of each perspective. Consider some of the recent changes in each view.

The *illness perspective* has recently generated much more and better quality evidence regarding the *biological* nature of some of the more severe forms of abnormal behavior. In particular, the research we reviewed regarding the *genetic determinants* of schizophrenia, the highly specific effects of certain *drugs* on schizophrenic behavior, and the involvement of norepinephrine in depression all suggest that the organic orientation of the illness perspective is gaining support at least for some disorders.

Somewhat paradoxically, while the evidence for biological components of some forms of abnormal behavior gains strength, support for the *medical model* in psychiatry continues to decrease. There is no inconsistency in arguing that some forms of abnormal behavior have biological components while at the same time criticizing the current medical service delivery system available to people suffering from depression or schizophrenia, for example.

The *dynamic perspective* on abnormal behavior has undergone little fundamental change in recent years. The perspective has spread far beyond the boundaries of abnormal psychology and serves as a tool of biographers, writers of psychohistory, and historians themselves. Although the dynamic perspective is not

	PSYCHO-ANALYTIC	ILLNESS	LEARNING	SOCIAL	HUMANISTIC
BASIC METAPHOR	Intrapsychic conflict	Disease	Learning	Deviance; norm violation	Actualization; growth
SUBORDINATE CONCEPTS	Id, ego, superego, anxiety, defense	Nosology, etiology, symptom, syndrome, prognosis	Stimulus, response, reinforcement, classical and operant conditioning	Norms, rule-breaking, career, stigma	Experience, self-concept, incongruity, conditions of worth; consciousness expansion
CAUSAL FACTORS	Intrapsychic conflict	Organic, biochemical, genetic	Reinforcement; classical and operant conditioning	Diverse factors: Organic, psychological, social; labeling	Conditions of worth, deficiency needs; social demands
HOW ABNORMAL BEHAVIOR IS DESCRIBED	Defense and anxiety	Symptoms, syndromes, disorders	Maladaptive behavior; helplessness	Behavior is deviant; audience reaction emphasized	Defensive and disorganized behavior; false outer self
MEANS OF THERAPEUTIC INTERVENTION	Psychoanalysis	Medical treatment; drugs, shock treatment, surgical procedures	Behavior therapy, desensitization, shaping	Institutional reform; community mental health	Client-centered therapy; sensitivity training; Gestalt therapy; yoga; meditation
MAJOR PROPONENTS	Freud	Kraepelin, Meehl, Snyder	Bandura, Eysenck, Krasner, Seligman, Skinner, Ullmann, Wolpe	Becker, Goffman, Sarbin, Scheff	Laing, Maslow, May, Ornstein, Rogers, Tart

currently producing breakthroughs in our understanding of abnormal behavior, it has become a permanent part of our intellectual heritage.

The *learning perspective* has been the scene of rapid change in the last decade. From its doctrinaire beginnings as an attack on the dynamic and illness views, it has matured into a view with its own field of basic research and treatment technology. The most significant recent trends in the learning perspective have to do with the acknowledgment of *internal cognitive events* as important components of abnormal behavior. Both research on *self-control* and on *learned helplessness* rely heavily on a cognitive emphasis. This is an important opening of the perspective beyond the radical behaviorism of J. B. Watson who argued that thought was merely "internal speech."

The *social perspective* has also undergone change, but of a different kind. The illness and learning perspectives have gained their new vigor largely as a result of imaginative research. The social perspective, on the other hand, can credit its development largely to the perceptiveness and energy of a few social critics and policy makers.

Two important trends are discernible in the social perspective. First, the emphasis of the perspective is moving away from an exclusive focus on the effects of social forces on the individual to a more *transactional view*. That is, the interpersonal aspects of labeling processes are being recognized as important, and the role of the labeled person in perpetuating his or her "sick role" is being emphasized increasingly. Second, the social perspective is gaining an action focus of its own in the *community mental health* movement. This is important for the intellectual vitality of the perspective because ideas must be put to the test in some arena if a perspective is to remain viable and develop further.

Finally, the *humanistic perspective* has undergone important changes in recent years. Interestingly, the countercultural movement of the sixties and early seventies has probably had its greatest impact on the humanistic viewpoint. Two major themes come through. First, an emphasis on *altered states of consciousness* as valuable, personally enhancing states has emerged. The sources of the altered states could be meditation, biofeedback, drugs, autosuggesion, body awareness exercises, or psychotherapy. The source seems less important than the emphasis on new forms of awareness. This focus on altered states of consciousness also has helped to transform the humanistic view of abnormal behavior. A new emphasis is emerging on abnormal behavior as an important form of altered consciousness.

A second theme in the humanistic perspective is the desire to maximize *human potential*. This idea is not in itself new and was strongly emphasized by pioneers such as Rogers and Maslow. What is new are the methods advocated. Eastern religion including Sufism and hatha yoga is seen as a legitimate route to enhance human potential. The new emphasis on Eastern ways of thought is joined by the typically Western pragmatic focus on biofeedback and other therapy techniques.

The most rapid shifts in the last decade seem to have occurred in the illness, learning, and humanistic perspectives. In each case the changes have been quite different. In the case of the illness perspective, new methods in biochemistry and neurobiology have greatly sharpened the focus of research on the brain chemistry of major psychological disorders such as depressions (Akiskal & McKinney, 1973) and schizophrenia (Snyder, 1975).

The learning perspective has developed through the application of learning concepts to particular clinical phenomena such as depression. Here the argument has been almost entirely by analogy. Reactive depression, Seligman contends, is analogous to certain laboratory phenomena produced in dogs when there is no contingent relationship between responses and reinforcements. The detailed spelling out of this analogy has produced new research leads and its reification as "learned helplessness" has made its plausibility seem much greater.

The humanistic perspective has changed rapidly, not because of new methodological or conceptual developments so much as because it has embraced related, but essentially new, streams of thought. Both Eastern mysticism, with its highly relativistic view of various states of consciousness, and the Western fascination with self-improvement and diverse treatment technologies, for example, provide a very broad, if diffuse, appeal.

There is little doubt that the major perspectives will continue on their separate paths for some time to come, although new perspectives may emerge and attempts at a grand synthesis will be made. Let us turn now to the nature of the conflict between perspectives.

Perspectives in Conflict

In Chapter 1 we argued that the current state of conflict among perspectives of abnormal behavior represents a distinct stage in the development of the field of abnormal psychology. Kuhn (1962) and other historians and philosophers of science (Hanson, 1965) have pointed out that this stage in growth is characteristic of the early stages of most sciences. It is therefore appropriate to review Kuhn's account and to examine its implications for the future of the field of abnormal psychology.

Kuhn argues that science is not the mere accumulation of facts, as the popular view suggests. Instead the history of science consists of periods of "normal science" where one or perhaps two views are dominant and direct the way in which we see the world. During periods of normal science nearly all practitioners of the science engage in research, which is a "strenuous and devoted attempt to force nature into the conceptual boxes supplied by professional education" (1962, p. 5).

Normal science will, because a single view is dominant, often suppress novel observations because such observations may subvert a basic conceptual commitment. During these periods, the scientific community shares the belief that it knows what the world is like. At times this view may be defended at considerable cost.

This description of normal science is not meant to imply that a period of normal science is unproductive. On the contrary, the very rigidity and strength of commitment to a single conceptual scheme is one of its most redeeming features. It means that a number of problems will be solved because a set of basic assumptions and a particular methodology will be fully exploited.

But even the conceptual commitments of normal science are in some ways arbitrary, and novel observations cannot be permanently suppressed. Sooner or later a normal problem may resist solution if the accepted conceptual and methodological approach is used. Or perhaps a particular method of observation may yield unexpected results. The few practitioners of normal science who choose to follow such leads may then perform experiments which are considered "extraordinary" from the point of view of the prevailing normal science. Kuhn argues that this is the beginning of a "scientific revolution."

New paradigms or conceptual schemes will then emerge to account for the novel observations and the result is what Kuhn has called a "paradigm clash." Almost invariably the paradigm clash is between the prevailing view of normal science and the new emerging conceptual scheme. Often the new paradigm will produce a shift in the problems available for scientific investigation. More important, it will transform the ways in which the scientist sees the world.

Periods of paradigm clash are periods of controversy. But the controversy is not over minor issues of fact or method but over basic metaphysical assumptions. As Kuhn (1962) remarks, in periods of paradigm clash and scientific revolutions "neither side will grant all the non-empirical assumptions that the other needs to make its case" (p. 147).

We would like to argue that the field of abnormal psychology is currently in the midst of such a scientific revolution. The basic conceptual commitments are not over questions of the nature of physical reality, as has been the case in physics. Instead the fundamental controversy is over *the nature of human beings.*

The period of normal science from which we are emerging is not characterized by a single dominant view but is one in which both the illness perspective and the psychoanalytic perspective have been dominant if not always comfortable companions. These perspectives will certainly continue to make substantive contributions to our understanding. New developments in the biological sciences suggest that the illness perspective will continue to be vigorous for some time to come. Nevertheless, the other perspectives we have discussed—humanistic, learning, and social —are all emerging with their own fundamental assumptions about human nature and, by extension, about the way we should view abnormal behavior.

In the following section we will take a closer look at the current state of "the paradigm clash" now underway.

Some Dimensions of the Conflict Among Perspectives

The conflict among perspectives on abnormal behavior is not simple and has a number of dimensions. Three of them are: first, that advocates of different perspectives have difficulty communciating with each other; second, that perspectives operate at different levels of analysis; and third, that perspectives are pretheoretical in nature.

The Communication Problem

Kuhn argues that communication difficulties exist among advocates of different perspectives for at least three reasons. The first is that the proponents of competing perspectives will often disagree about the list of problems that any perspective must resolve. That is, their standards or definitions of science are not the same. For example, the illness perspective may suggest that the fundamental problem to be resolved is the discovery of an organic etiology. On the other hand, the learning perspective asks the question of how abnormal behavior is shaped by reinforcement contingencies; and the social perspective is most concerned not with abnormal behavior itself but how others may react to it.

A second reason for the communication problem has to do with a confusion that arises in the use of scientific vocabulary. Since new perspectives are often derived from old ones, they may incorporate much of the vocabulary and conceptual apparatus that the traditional paradigm had previously employed. But the difficulty is that the new perspective seldom uses these borrowed elements in the traditional way. Consequently, advocates of different perspectives, even when using the same words, may be talking at cross purposes. For example, the term "symptom" may be used very differently by advocates of the illness, behavioral, and psychoanalytic perspectives. For advocates of the illness perspective it is part of a syndrome and a behavioral manifestation of a *disease*. From the learning perspective the symptom may be simply a single behavior that is subject to the principles of *reinforcement*. The psychoanalytic perspective may view a symptom as a defense mechanism indicating *intrapsychic conflict*.

The third reason for the communication difficulty is that the proponents of competing perspectives "practice their trade in different worlds." As Kuhn puts it,

> practicing in different worlds . . . groups of scientists see different things when they look from the same point in the same direction. Again, that is not to say that they can see anything they please. Both are looking at the world, and what they look at has not changed. But in some areas they see different things, and they see them in different relations one to the other. That is why a law that cannot even be demonstrated to one group of scientists may occasionally seem intuitively obvious to another (p. 149).

Perhaps one of the most striking instances of two scientists practicing their trade in two different worlds was the contrast in views of learned helplessness as adopted by Seligman and by Weiss. Seligman's explanation of the helpless behavior of his laboratory animals was based entirely on learning principles. It would have been surprising if he had looked elsewhere for an explanation. Weiss, on the other hand, saw the helpless behavior quite differently. Its temporary effects suggested a reversible neu- rochemical state of norepinephrine depletion—a view consistent with the illness perspective. As we have seen, the result was a series of experiments that promises to further clarify the phe- nomenon of helplessness.

Levels of Analysis

There is perhaps another reason for the conflict among perspectives which is related to the remarks we have just made. It is that the perspectives we have discussed do not all describe the phenomenon of abnormal behavior at the same level of analysis.

The scientific disciplines may be ordered on a rough con- tinuum from molecular to molar levels of analysis, ranging from physics through chemistry, biology, psychology, and social an- alysis. For our purposes we may consider four general levels: biological, intrapersonal, interpersonal, and social. The biological level refers to physiological and genetic events occurring in a single individual. The intrapersonal level refers to intrapsychic events within a single person. The interpersonal level refers to events that occur between individuals, and the social level refers to events that occur between the individual and social institutions. Each of the perspectives we have discussed may be placed at some point or range of points along this continuum.

Of course, in most cases it is more accurate to suggest that a particular perspective occupies some range along this con- tinuum, since it is seldom the case that a particular perspective is described in terms of only a single level of analysis. Figure 8-1 shows the four levels of analysis that we have described and the general placement of the perspectives with respect to the levels of analysis.

In general, the fact that a perspective treats the phenomenon of abnormal behavior at a particular level of analysis has at least two implications. First, the basic metaphor or concept of the perspective will reflect the level of analysis occupied by the per- spective. In addition, inferences about the causal factors in ab- normal behavior are likely to be closely related to the level of analysis of the perspective. Thus, for example, the illness per- spective takes as its basic metaphor the concept of disease, a biological concept. Furthermore, the causal factors in the illness perspective tend to be genetic, biochemical, or physiological.

Placing perspectives at a particular level of analysis suggests

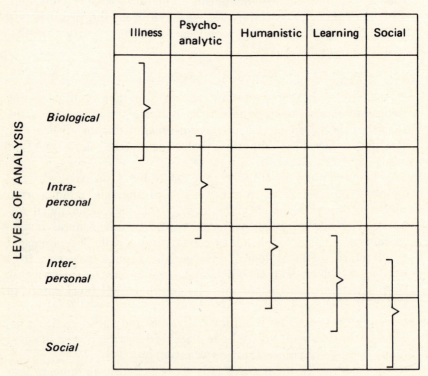

FIG. 8–1   Levels of analysis of the perspectives.

that the advocate of that perspective has made his or her "bet" as
to how the phenomena of abnormal behavior can best be understood. But we will argue here and later that a complete account
of the phenomena of abnormal behavior will *not* be derived from
a single level of analysis. Instead, a more complete account of the
phenomena of abnormal behavior will be one which can encompass observations from a wide range of levels of analysis.

For example, we might imagine some severe forms of schizophrenia being explained in terms of genetic predispositions (illness perspective) interacting with certain life stresses (social and
dynamic perspectives) leading to an altered state of consciousness
(humanistic perspective) that further alters behavior and produces
a stigmatizing societal reaction to norm violations and a drift into
a career of chronic deviance (social perspective).

The problem with such a synthesis is its lack of coherence.

Although such a patchwork increases the number of levels of analysis invoked in the overall account, it is essentially a mixed metaphor. The challenge of any synthesis that attempts to encompass several levels of analysis will be to retain the necessary scope while generating connecting concepts between levels of analysis. This is not an easy task since one level of analysis (e.g., biochemical) may not be translatable into the terms of another (e.g., learning).

Perspectives Are Pretheoretical

It is conventional to refer to what we have called perspectives as "theories," and we have resisted that temptation throughout our discussion for several reasons. First, we argued in Chapter 2 that perspectives were products of a particular process of thought which we described as metaphorical. They are preliminary formulations despite the fact that they often powerfully shape the way in which we see and organize the phenomenon of abnormal behavior.

Furthermore, the perspectives we have discussed do not meet the criteria for a scientific theory as advanced by Nagel (1959). Nagel suggested at least three criteria which might be used in deciding whether a particular conceptual approach can be considered a scientific theory. First, it must be possible to identify explicit consequences that will arise from the assumptions made by the perspective. This is necessary in order to judge the meaning of any empirical data for whatever assumption we are examining. Second, at least some of the assumptions and concepts of the theory must be given definite and unambiguous specifications in terms of some rules of procedure. These rules of procedure are often called operational definitions. Third, the propositions of the theory must be capable of being disconfirmed. Thus, the theory cannot be formulated in such a way that it can be manipulated to fit whatever the evidence at hand may be.

Certainly it is true that the perspectives we have described are not all pretheoretical to the same degree. Perspectives differ in the degree to which the basic metaphor has been spelled out in terms of formal description, operationalization, and the statement of propositions.

Some perspectives have developed in the direction of formal theory only to a small degree. The psychoanalytic and the humanistic perspectives are examples. Other perspectives, or at least aspects of them, are somewhat more advanced. In particular, the illness perspective, the learning perspective, and the social perspective display a higher degree of formalization. But, in general, no perspective has reached the stage of rigor implied by the criteria for a theory that Nagel has described.

If the current state of the field is as we suggest, then advocates of different perspectives have difficulty communicating with one other. Furthermore, the perspectives themselves reflect differing levels of analysis and are pretheoretical. We may then ask, what are the possible solutions to this state of affairs? How will the field develop? It is to those questions that we now turn.

What Is the Goal of Science?

Scientific Progress as Evolution

At the outset of this chapter we suggested that scientific progress is characterized by periods of normal science followed by periods when several alternative perspectives compete for dominance. We also suggested that the field of abnormal psychology may now be entering one of the latter periods. But what then is the nature of scientific progress? Toward what goal, if any, does it move? Kuhn (1962) uses the analogy of biological evolution to describe the course of scientific progress.

> The analogy that relates the evolution of organisms to the evolution of scientific ideas can easily be pushed too far. But [for the present purposes] it is very nearly perfect. The process described . . . as the resolution of revolutions is the selection by conflict within the scientific community of the fittest way to practice future science. The net result of a sequence of such revolutionary selections, separated by periods of normal research, is the wonderfully adapted set of instruments we call modern scientific knowledge. Successive stages in that developmental process are marked by an increase in articulation and specialization and the entire process may have occurred, as we now suppose biological evolution did, without benefit of a set goal, a permanent fixed scientific truth, of which each stage in the development of scientific knowledge is a better exemplar (pp. 171–172).

This is an extraordinary statement. It asserts that *science has no goal toward which it progresses*. Instead, science is a process from primitive beginnings and is characterized by increasingly detailed and refined understanding; but it moves toward no specific goal. If we accept this evolutionary analogy even tentatively we can then ask what will give a particular perspective its "survival value"? What are the characteristics of particular perspectives that will lead them to survive while others will die? Both Kuhn (1962) and Toulmin (1961) have suggested characteristics that may give perspectives survival value. To these we have added some of our own.

A new perspective is more likely to be adopted *if it can solve the problems that led older perspectives into crisis.* For example, the failure of psychoanalysis to form propositions and assumptions which are disconfirmable has had much to do with its current loss of appeal. Similarly, the failure of the illness perspective to deal with the social impact of abnormal behavior has stimulated a great deal of the recent criticism of that perspective. Perspectives that survive will certainly have to be responsive to these and still other problems.

A new perspective is also more likely to have survival value *if it is capable of predicting phenomena that were unexpected while the older perspective prevailed.* To take but one example, the humanistic perspective suggests that abnormal behavior may in some cases present the possibility of positive personality growth.

The degree to which a perspective is *capable of moving from a primitive metaphorical formulation to formalized theory* will certainly be important for its survival. Thus, perspectives must develop operationalized concepts and disconfirmable propositions. The learning perspective has made substantial progress in this regard. In the arena of science, perspectives that are not capable of such development will ultimately become historical curiosities.

A related consideration is that perspectives must be *capable of describing abnormal behavior over a broad range of levels of analysis.* Humans are not merely biological animals or merely psychological or merely social in nature. The function of all these descriptive levels and behavior, both normal and abnormal, can be described at each level.

In a field with an applied clinical aspect, pragmatic results will substantially affect the survival of a perspective. *Perspectives that lead to effective treatment technologies* such as the illness and learning perspectives are good candidates for survival.

Finally, a particular perspective may survive because it appeals to the *scientist's basic prejudices about human nature.* Of course, scientists are not above such concerns. These concerns often play a powerful if tacit role in the choice of a perspective.

We cannot predict with certainty which perspective on abnormal behavior will survive any more than we can predict the precise form that a species will ultimately take in the process

of natural selection. But we can point to some of the characteristics it must possess in order to survive and perhaps to become
the normal science of the future.

LEARNING MORE
Projects for the Reader

1. Conduct a debate on the merits of at least two perspectives. A
   third person should observe the debate and note the ways in
   which communication problems arise. Are they similar to the
   problems cited by Kuhn? Are there difficulties raised by the
   differing levels of analysis of various perspectives?
2. Try to construct a scenario of how abnormal psychology will
   look in the year 2000. Use a group to "brainstorm" the idea and
   then discuss your product. Or try writing a brief "science fiction"
   sketch of the development of abnormal behavior and its treatment in the year 2000. Trace how you extrapolated current trends
   into the future. How plausible do you feel your science fiction
   story really is? Try to decide what aspects are most plausible
   and why.

application of the perspectives

INTRODUCTION

After reviewing the five different perspectives on abnormal behavior, the concepts of each perspective are now probably fairly familiar to you. But how are they applied to clinical material? That is the question we will answer in this chapter.

In studying abnormal psychology, one kind of "raw data" we can use is the case history. Our raw data in the chapter will be a *generalized case history,* and it will be rewritten from the point of view of each perspective.

Remember, in Chapter 2 we said that perspectives have a perceptual effect on the raw material of human behavior. Perspectives shape not only what we *see* but also what we *look for* in formulating a case. As a result, the case histories may at times omit information—for example, earlier life events—that would have seemed crucial to the advocate of a particular perspective in reconstructing the case.

The five versions that result are in some ways caricatures. That is, they systematically distort the generalized case history to conform with the basic assumptions and point of view of the perspective. But a caricature can be instructive. It points up the distinguishing features of the perspective by exaggeration. Thus, while these case histories are in some ways distortions, they also demonstrate how the basic metaphor of each perspective selects from and shapes the raw data of abnormal behavior to produce five different yet coherent views.

Now let's read the generalized case history describing events in the life of Amy J. Watch what happens when it is reexamined from each of the five perspectives.

A Generalized Case History: Amy J.

Mrs. Amy J. is a thirty-four-year-old married woman. She is from a large midwestern town of approximately one-half million people. Amy left school to work when she was 16, even though she had two years of high school to complete before graduation. She is an only child and both of her parents are still living. They live in the same neighborhood as do Amy and her husband. Amy's husband works in a factory at a semiskilled job that involves shift work. Although the family cannot be described as poor, their income seems not to be sufficient to allow substantial savings after all the bills are paid. Amy works as a part-time waitress in a coffee shop to supplement the family income.

The first discernible indications of Amy's difficulties were noticed by her husband. Over a period of several months, he reported, she began to pay less attention to her housework; at times he would come home and no meal would have been prepared. He reported that "It was almost as if she forgot to make dinner, but I didn't say much about it . . . you know how it is when you're tired from work . . . you don't want to talk."

At about this time Amy's parents also reported noting signs of changes in Amy's behavior. Her mother reported that Amy "looked nervous" and that she "didn't seem to be herself." Amy's mother was particularly concerned because, as she put it, "We have always known our Amy well and if something was wrong she would let us know."

Both Amy's husband and her parents mentioned to Amy that they noticed a change in her behavior and inquired about her health on several occasions. As her father put it, "We figured she wasn't getting enough sleep or something. You know, if you don't get enough sleep that can really make you feel bad."

A few weeks after these first signs of difficulty were noted by her husband and parents, Amy began to have crying fits. She would often burst into tears when her husband asked her if she had remembered to do something for him or if he appeared irritated with her. At this time, Amy began to fail to report to work as often as once a week. She had had an excellent record of attendance before this, and although her employer was concerned he decided not to say anything in hopes that things would work themselves out.

As Amy's crying episodes became more frequent, her husband grew genuinely worried and irritated. At this point the husband consulted with her parents. As he described it later, "I figured I should talk to them about Amy since she was an only child. They always seemed to know what she was thinking, even when she didn't herself. They are the kind of parents who really care."

Amy's husband and parents agreed that "she wasn't acting like herself" and that the crying episodes were getting worse. They decided that they would "keep an eye on her" and if things did not improve, they would encourage her to see a physician. Approximately two more weeks passed during which her mother and father visited more frequently in the afternoon and evening. Repeated inquiries concerning her health were met with silence or disclaimers such as "I'm OK, don't worry."

Amy's husband and parents again discussed her behavior. They agreed that Amy was getting not better, but worse, and that recently she had been giving all of them "funny looks" when they

asked how she felt. As a result of their discussion, it was decided
to have Amy see a physician. Amy's parents and husband decided
to tell her together so that she would know that they were all
concerned.

Amy greeted the decision of the husband and parents quietly
but repeated her denial that anything was wrong. They made an
appointment for her to see a physician the following Wednesday.

When Amy's husband returned home after work on Tuesday
evening, Amy was not there. After several hours he became
concerned and went out looking for her. After another several
hours of fruitless search, he called the police department and
reported her missing.

She was found later by a police patrol. The following is an
excerpt from their report:

> Subject was found wandering in a vacant lot at the corner of Green
> and Elm Streets. She was not wearing a coat and had on bedroom
> slippers. Subject was crying and we had difficulty getting her to
> identify herself. Subject kept repeating, "They're working on my
> mind." Since subject would not identify herself she was taken into
> custody.

Amy spent the evening in jail before she was identified and
returned to her husband. Repeated questioning by the husband
failed to reveal Amy's reasons for running away. At this point,
her husband again called her parents and reported the incident.
They came over immediately but their questions yielded no more
information than her husband's had concerning the reason for
her behavior.

It was decided to drive her to the doctor's office to keep the
appointment previously made. Amy strongly resisted going but
was finally convinced to go along. On arriving in the doctor's
waiting room she burst into tears, repeating over and over, "I
don't want to see him . . . I don't want to see any doctors." She
could not be calmed and finally the physician gave her a sedative
and recommended that she be put under observation at the state
psychiatric hospital. As he described it later, "This woman was
quite agitated and seemed somewhat irrational. I thought under
the circumstances the best thing was to put her under observation."

When Amy learned that she was to spend two weeks in the
state psychiatric hospital, she glared at her husband and ceased
talking altogether. Repeated explanations that she "was just

going for a rest and a checkup" seemed only to drive her into deeper withdrawal. She refused to speak to her husband or parents but muttered at several points that "they are trying to get rid of me."

Amy was placed on the admissions ward of the state psychiatric hospital. She was given a grey smock to replace her own clothing and her personal effects were taken away and kept in safekeeping for her. She was placed under intense observation; the following is taken from the nurses' notes in Amy's folder.

> Patient is quiet and withdrawn. She will not socialize with other patients and ignores them when they approach her. Her manner appears very suspicious and she replies to questions by asking, "Why do you want to know?" Patient goes to meals with the rest of the ward but eats very little. Patient is not cooperative about ward routine and seems somewhat disoriented. She tries the doors frequently during the day even though she knows they are locked.

After two weeks of observation, Amy was interviewed by a psychiatric staff conference which included a social worker, the nurses on her ward, the ward physician, and a psychologist. What follows is the physician's report of that staff conference.

> Patient is a 34-year-old, white, married female. At the time of admission she appeared withdrawn and depressed. Prior to admission she had been found wandering in a field by the police.
>
> Her behavior on the ward has been withdrawn and generally uncooperative. Nurses' report indicates some suspiciousness and the report of the referring physician suggests some ideas of influence. Affect is somewhat flattened. Memory for remote and immediate events is not markedly impaired but she is unable to report with accuracy the events surrounding her arrest. Judgment is somewhat faulty and she insists she is just here for a rest, although she admits that she is in a psychiatric hospital. Orientation for place is intact but she is somewhat disoriented for person. She does not know the name of the ward personnel or the ward physician. Orientation for time is fair. She does know the month and the year, but is vague about the exact date and day of the week. Insight appears somewhat impaired. She does not know exactly why she is here but reports that she feels she is being watched by ward personnel. She appeared quite guarded in my interview with her but did admit that she was afraid that her relatives might be trying to get rid of her. She also said she felt as if people were "trying to read my mind and to work on it."
>
> Current diagnostic impression is: *Schizophrenic reaction, acute undifferentiated type with depressive features and paranoid trends.*

It is recommended that hospitalization be continued and that the case be reviewed again in one month.

A conference with Amy's husband and parents, the ward physician, and the social worker followed, and the recommendations of the staff were communicated to the relatives. It was explained that the staff felt a brief stay in the hospital would be beneficial to her and that it was hoped she could be sent home in the husband's custody in about a month. Amy was then brought in and informed of the staff decision in the presence of her mother, father, and husband. She was told that everyone felt it was the best thing for her and that she would be "back to normal in no time." Amy greeted this news with a flash of anger and resentment, shouting, "You want to get rid of me!" and bursting into tears. Following this outburst she was returned to the ward and given an extra dose of medication.

Amy was discharged the following month as "much improved." She no longer had the fits of uncontrollable crying, but she had become quite taciturn. In his discharge report the ward physician stated that "no schizophrenic ideation could be elicited." When Amy learned of her imminent discharge, she showed a great deal of apprehension. The social worker reported that Amy was quite concerned with "what people will think." Attempts to reassure her seemed to help to allay her fears somewhat.

Upon her return home, Amy found that everyone she met who knew about her hospitalization was quite concerned about her welfare. Her husband had arranged to work the day shift so that he could be with her at night. She discovered that her mother and father would visit her at frequent intervals during the day, saying that they "were just driving by and wondered how things were going." Amy found it difficult to accomplish household duties, and occasionally her husband would return home and find her still dressed in her bathrobe. He said little about this but it seemed to her that at times he looked at her peculiarly when this would happen.

After several weeks her husband suggested that perhaps she would enjoy going back to her job as a waitress on a part-time basis and she agreed. Amy returned to the coffee shop and asked the manager if she could have her old part-time job back. The manager replied that he was sorry but that someone else had been hired in her absence. He suggested that perhaps she should look for a job where she "wouldn't have to deal with people so much" and offered to help her find such a job. Amy reacted to this remark with considerable emotion. She ran out of the shop in tears. The manager was distressed by her reaction and called her husband to inform him of what had happened. The husband immediately left work and began to look for her. He also called the police because, as he noted later, "I didn't know what she might do because of her condition."

Amy was found by the police standing on a bridge staring vacantly into the water below. Her clothes were disheveled and she was unresponsive when asked what she was doing there. Amy was returned home and after her parents and husband had a hurried conference, they decided to hospitalize her for her own protection. The husband called the psychiatric hospital and reported what had happened to the staff physician. He agreed that she should be hospitalized immediately.

This time, when Amy was informed of their decision, the parents and husband noted that she did not seem surprised or particularly disturbed. She agreed to the hospitalization quite passively and remarked, "I must be sick; I don't know what's wrong."

The Psychoanalytic Perspective

Amy J. is a thirty-four-year-old woman and an only child. Her early difficulties included severe anxiety and extreme defensiveness. When asked about her difficulties by her concerned parents and husband, she responded with defensive denial. She denied any problems by stating, "I'm OK, don't worry."

At the same time, Amy began to regress. Her regression was reflected in her failure to perform routine household chores and her failure to appear for work as a waitress. The regressive behavior continued, and, in addition, Amy began to have uncontrollable fits of crying.

The denial and regression may be interpreted as attempts to deal with the intense anxiety resulting from a deep-rooted id-ego conflict. Id impulses reflecting a need for dependence had come into conflict with ego motives to cope with the demands of reality in the form of her household and job obligations. Since the dependency needs appeared to be intense, it is likely that they reflect fixated needs at the oral stage of development. Fixation at the oral stage often manifests itself in an infantile need to be cared for.

When Amy's husband and parents suggested that she visit a physician, the id-ego conflict was intensified and resulted in intense anxiety and projection. She accused her parents of "trying to get rid of her." Thus, her own need to escape from the reality demands and responsibilities of her own life was projected upon her parents and husband. The intensity of her emotional reactions and her irrationality prompted the examining physician to recommend hospitalization.

Once in the hospital, she remained suspicious and distrustful. At the same time, the supportive hospital setting served the purpose of meeting Amy's dependency needs and the severity of the id-ego conflict to some degree. However, the conflict remained unresolved. Her anxiety increased again briefly when she learned of her imminent discharge from the hospital. For Amy, discharge symbolized the potential loss of support for her dependency needs and thus reactivated the basic conflict.

Nevertheless, she was discharged and soon the unresolved conflict began to reassert itself. Regression reappeared in the form of a continued inability to cope with household chores. At times her husband would find her still in her bathrobe at the end of the day.

The struggle between the ego demands to function effectively and the infantile needs of the id continued, and after several weeks she reapplied for her old job as a waitress. Naturally, she was deeply conflicted about this venture, and when she learned that her employer had no intention of rehiring her, her ego was overwhelmed and she ran out of the shop in tears. She was later found standing on a bridge in a disheveled condition.

Her remarks when found reflected the fact that her basic conflict was still repressed and completely out of awareness. Amy remarked in a bewildered tone, "I don't know what's wrong." She was subsequently rehospitalized.

Unless the basis of the fixated oral needs and resulting id-ego conflict are explored in intensive psychoanalysis, it is likely that Amy will continue to experience episodes of regression and need periodic hospitalization.

The Illness Perspective

PATIENT   Amy J.   MALE _____ FEMALE __X__

AGE   34   SINGLE _____ MARRIED __X__

DIAGNOSIS: 1. Depressive reaction, endogenous type.
               2. (Rule out schizophrenic reaction)

MEDICATION: Elavil 10 mg., t.i.d.

Amy J. is a thirty-four-year-old, well-nourished white, married female. The onset of her illness was marked by symptoms of anxiety, fear, depression, and emotional turmoil including episodic crying. Ideas of reference also became apparent early in the patient's illness. She is reported to have believed that people were "working on her mind" and that her relatives were "trying to get rid" of her.

The precipitating event associated with the acute onset of her illness was a visit to the family physician. He reported her to be agitated and irrational, and recommended hospitalization.

The symptoms displayed by the patient are characteristic of endogenous depression, but schizophrenia should be ruled out. This diagnostic impression is confirmed by the staff physician's mental status examination report, which follows.

> Patient is a 34-year-old, white, married female. At the time of admission she appeared withdrawn and depressed. Prior to admission she had been found wandering in a field by the police.
>
> Her behavior on the ward has been withdrawn and generally uncooperative. Nurses' report indicates some suspiciousness and the report of the referring physician suggests some idea of influence. Affect is somewhat flattened. Memory for remote and immediate events is not markedly impaired but she is unable to report with accuracy the events surrounding her arrest. Judgment is somewhat faulty and she insists she is just here for a rest, although she admits that she is in a psychiatric hospital. Orientation for place is intact but she is somewhat disoriented for person. She does not know the names of the ward personnel or the ward physician. Orientation for time is fair. She does know the month and the year, but is vague about the exact date and day of the week. Insight appears somewhat impaired. She does not know exactly why she is here but reports that she feels she is being watched by ward personnel. She appeared quite guarded in my interview with her but did admit that she was afraid that her relatives might be trying to get rid of her. She also said she felt as if people were "trying to read my mind and to work on it."
>
> Current *diagnostic impression is: Endogenous depression.*

The patient was discharged approximately one month after admission. Patient was readmitted as a result of a recurrence of her symptomatology. It was reported that she displayed some suicidal behavior at that time.

In general, antidepressant medication has not had the expected effects. In light of the previously reported delusions and other psychotic behavior, the likelihood of a diagnosis of schizophrenia seems greater. It is suggested that medication be changed to *thorazine, 20 mg., t.i.d.* . . .

Patient appears to be responding favorably to phenothiazines. This supports the tentative diagnosis of schizophrenia. It is recommended that she be continued on a maintenance dosage and be treated on an outpatient basis.

Current diagnostic impression: Schizophrenic reaction, chronic undifferentiated type, in partial remission.

The Learning Perspective

Amy J. is a thirty-four-year-old married woman who works part-time as a waitress. Little is known about her reinforcement history. However, the fact that she was an only child suggests that she had previously received a relatively high level of positive reinforcement in the form of attention from her parents.

Amy's principal pattern of maladaptive behavior is characterized by a general decrease in the frequency of emitted behavior. Examples of responses in her behavioral repertoire that had decreased in frequency include performing household chores, preparing meals, and reporting to work. These behaviors had previously been maintained by their effect on stimulus persons in her environment who controlled reinforcement, particularly her husband. When Amy's husband failed to praise her or to pay attention to her, her behavior no longer controlled the reinforcements in her environment. Since Amy's behavior no longer had reinforcing events contingent on it, she became helpless. This loss of control over reinforcing events in the environment led to many of the results of learned helplessness, including loss of appetite, social and sexual deficits, sleep loss, and most important, a feeling that nothing she could do would make much difference.

The stimulus properties of Amy's maladaptive behavior elicited attention, a generalized reinforcer, from her husband and her parents. The increased attention is reflected in their concern about her health and their decision to "keep an eye on her." Since much of their attention was contingent upon her episodes of crying and lowered level of responsiveness, the frequency of the maladaptive behavior increased as a result of this systematic positive reinforcement.

When it was suggested that she see a physician, Amy's response was also maladaptive. The stimulus situation involving physicians may have been associated in the past with aversive consequences. Her response suggests that this is the case, since she avoided this threatening situation by running away the night before the scheduled visit. As with most maladaptive avoidance responses, this behavior had additional aversive consequences, including arrest and incarceration. The "vicious cycle" quality of this pattern is evident in the sequence of avoidance responses followed by further negative reinforcement.

The anxiety-provoking power of the situation involving the visit to the physician remained quite strong since Amy's previous avoidance responses had provided no opportunity for extinction to occur. As a result, when she was forced to confront this stimulus situation by her husband and parents, her anxiety response and attempts to escape were intense. The resulting behavior was seen as sufficiently maladaptive by those controlling reinforcers in her life to warrant hospitalization.

It should be noted that hospitalization constituted a reinforcing event for Amy's parents and husband since it marked the termination of her aversive behavior for them.

Once hospitalized, Amy's behavior came under the control of a different set of reinforcement contingencies, those of the institution and staff. Attempts to affect her environment through emotional behavior were met with a variety of aversive consequences, including withdrawal of positive reinforcement and sedation. Amy soon learned the "patient role" and became quiet and unobtrusive.

When released from the hospital, Amy reentered her home situation where her low level of instrumental behavior again received considerable attention as well as other forms of contingent social reinforcement from her parents and husband. Predictably her "depressed" behavior again increased in frequency, as her helpless situation returned.

At this point she lost her job, and the behavior of her employer constituted yet another aversive stimulus situation. Her husband and her parents again saw her escape from the situation as maladaptive. Their decision to rehospitalize her was immediate, since this response had resulted in the termination of the aversive consequences of Amy's behavior for the parents and husband on a previous occasion.

The Social Perspective

Amy's difficulties began when her husband and parents started to notice some puzzling changes in her behavior. Her husband reported that Amy had failed to make dinner for him on several occasions and had begun to neglect her housework. Her parents reported other changes in Amy's behavior. To them she did not seem to be herself and appeared more nervous than usual. These initial norm violations on Amy's part were viewed by her husband and her parents with a minimum of concern. In fact, Amy's husband stated that it seemed to him that she had merely "forgotten" to make dinner. Her parents also minimized these early signs. From their point of view, her peculiar behavior could have been the result of "not enough sleep." In any case, Amy's norm violation was initially minimized, rationalized, or denied.

Despite the attempts of Amy's husband and parents to mini- mize her rule-breaking behavior, her behavior persisted and in fact became more difficult to ignore. Amy began to have crying fits and failed to report to work. At this point, Amy's husband talked over the problem with her parents. They agreed to become more vigilant toward Amy's behavior but continued to refrain from mentioning their concern to Amy herself. It is likely that their vigilance provided cues to Amy that something was "wrong" with her.

Amy's husband and parents were beginning to suspect that she was suffering from "mental problems." This made them decide that they had to do something about her peculiar behavior. They decided to begin by having her examined by a physician.

Shortly afterward, Amy's actions precipitated a public crisis which made it virtually impossible for her husband and parents to deny any longer that her difficulties were more serious than they had thought at first. The evening before her appointment with the physician, Amy ran away from home and was subse- quently picked up by the police. She refused to identify herself. She was wearing bedroom slippers when the police arrested her and was unable to give any coherent explanation for her behavior. The public crisis which Amy set in motion by running away from home reached a climax in the doctor's office. She burst into tears and repeated over and over again that she refused to see the doctor. At this point the physician decided that her behavior was "irrational" and that she should be sent to a psychiatric hospital for observation. Amy's husband and parents offered no objection; apparently they too were convinced that there was something mentally wrong with Amy.

The physician, as well as Amy's husband and parents, was apparently quite willing to interpret her behavior as mental illness. She behaved in ways that could be interpreted as consistent with the general stereotype of "craziness." She was agitated, extremely emotional, did not appear to be making sense, and could not be calmed down. Thus the compatibility of Amy's behavior with the deviant stereotoype made it easy to label her problem as mental illness.

Amy did not share her husband's, her parents', and the physician's view of her behavior. She said she felt "that they are trying to get rid of me," which, in a sense, they were. Thus, at this point in the case, Amy resisted defining her own problem as "mental" and continued to resist being "typecast" as a mental patient.

But in the hospital a number of events occurred that made it more difficult for Amy to resist thinking of herself as a mental patient. Her own clothes and personal belongings were taken away from her and she was given institutional clothing to replace them. She was placed in a locked ward under constant observation and was thus not considered to be responsible for her own behavior. The staff saw Amy's efforts against being identified as a mental patient simply as troublesome behavior, typical of mental patients. Finally, the staff conference that concluded with Amy's being diagnosed as "schizophrenic" officially labeled her as mentally ill.

As Amy's hospitalization continued, a variety of rewards and punishments in the psychiatric hospital setting offered additional inducement for her to accept her role as just another mental patient. When she displayed anger and resentment at being held in the hospital for an additional period of time she received heavy sedation. Similarly, when Amy's relatives had been informed of the staff's decision to keep her in the hospital, she was told that everyone felt that it was the best thing for her and that she "would be back to normal in no time"; this made it quite explicit that other people viewed her as not normal.

Eventually, the rewards and punishments operating in the institutional setting had their effect; rather than showing a variety of strong emotional reactions to her situation, Amy became quiet and withdrawn. However, when she learned that she was about to be discharged, she expressed considerable apprehension and concern with "what people will think." It is clear from this that Amy knew that mental patients were not considered ordinary persons and that once on the "outside" she would carry with her the stigma of the mentally ill.

Amy's concerns about her stigmatized identity apparently

were well justified. Although a number of people expressed concern about her welfare, she couldn't help but realize that she was treated as someone who was "different."

Her transformed social identity and stigmatized status created yet another public crisis for Amy. When she attempted to regain her old job, her ex-boss said that the job had been filled. Furthermore, he suggested that she look for a job where "she wouldn't have to deal with people so much." The implication of his statement was clear to Amy: that as an ex-mental patient she was different, somehow not quite "right," and that she now possessed a spoiled identity.

Not surprisingly, Amy reacted to her ex-boss's remark with a great deal of emotion and ran out of the shop in tears. Amy's capabilities of self-control had been impaired as she had slowly incorporated the deviant role definition. She was found on a bridge, her clothes disheveled; she looked very much the mental patient. Her outburst, of course, was viewed by others as yet another instance of her mental problem, and she reentered the vicious circle: norm violation followed by the response of others to her inappropriate behavior and deviant status, and yet another hospitalization.

At this point, Amy has settled into a career of chronic "mental illness." Despite her effort to resist her new role definition as someone with mental problems, her bewilderment and dismay at others' rejection of her led her to accept the deviant role definition as the only alternative. As she agreed to be hospitalized a second time, Amy was heard to remark, "I must be sick; I don't know what's wrong."

The Humanistic Perspective

Amy J. is a married woman in her early thirties. She is the only child of her parents who live in the same neighborhood as do Amy and her husband. As an only child, she grew up in an atmosphere in which she was the center of attention in the family. Like most parents, Amy's father and mother always "wanted the best" for her. So when she dropped out of high school at 16, they said very little about this although it was a bitter disappointment for them. They had always told her that she was "good" when she performed competently at school, but failures were greeted with disappointed silence. Slowly Amy began to value herself for what others thought she should be rather than for what she felt and wished to be. A false outer self developed, eager to obtain approval, but that denied inner fears, hopes, or desires.

Amy was eager to please others, and when she married she made a special effort to do things which would please her husband. At first, the house was always immaculate and dinner was on the table when he arrived home at night. To supplement the family income she took a part-time job as a waitress.

From time to time she was unable to meet the demands of her job and those of housewife. Although her husband said little about these lapses, Amy knew he noticed them and seemed to her to be disappointed. Slowly an incongruence developed between her concept of her self as an effective working housewife and the experience of her failures. The incongruence became even more severe when her husband and parents began to ask about her health. She knew this was their way of pointing out her failures to her.

At this point Amy's vulnerability to anxiety greatly increased and she began to react defensively to inquiries about her well-being. She denied that anything was wrong. At times, Amy herself was almost convinced by her denial. But at other times she could not convince herself that she was meeting the expectations of her husband and parents and would burst into tears. The false outer self was becoming more fragile each day.

When Amy's parents and husband suggested that she see a physician she interpreted the suggestion as a further indication of their belief that she was a helpless, ineffective person. She could no longer deny her difficulties, and the incongruence between her idea of the person she should be and the person that others saw greatly increased. This was an overwhelming experience for Amy and her behavior became disorganized. The night before her appointment she ran away from home rather than face the physician, who, it seemed to Amy would also be critical of her for her failures. When she finally did see the physician her defenses were no longer adequate to deal with the incongruity and an intense emotional scene ensued. Seeing how irrational Amy seemed, the physician recommended that she be hospitalized. Naturally, this only seemed to confirm to Amy what she had feared all along—that she was seen by others as a worthless person.

In the hospital her concept of herself began to change. Everyone seemed to be treating her as someone who could not manage herself, and she began to suspect that it was true. Nevertheless, she did not appear to be upset and after a time was released from the hospital. Back at home, her feeling of inadequacy did not make it any easier to deal with even routine household chores. Her parents also did a number of things to confirm her feelings of worthlessness. Although they said they were only "dropping by," she knew that they did not trust her to get through the day.

It was in this state of vulnerability to threat that she finally summoned the courage to get back her old job as waitress. Perhaps her husband and parents would value her more if she were working again. But her employer only confirmed her worst fears about what people thought of her. He said there was no opening and suggested that she find a job where "she wouldn't have to work with people."

Overwhelmed by his rejection, she ran away from the shop in tears. She wandered around in a disorganized state not knowing where she was going. Her husband finally found her standing on a bridge in a disheveled condition. Her remark at that time suggests that her self-concept had now changed and that she too now saw herself as an incompetent sick individual. She agreed to be rehospitalized and said, "I must be sick; I don't know what's wrong."

Perhaps Amy's crisis will be resolved in continued failure and rejection. Or, perhaps, the crisis can become an opportunity for growth and a chance to realize her potential. Others can help but in the last analysis, it is up to Amy.

Overview of the Case Histories

Now you have a clearer sense of how perspectives select and shape our description of human behavior. Clearly, each perspective emphasizes different events in the generalized case history and interprets them differently. Some perspectives focus narrowly on a few aspects of Amy's life and others ignore whole segments of her experience.

If you had tried to rewrite Amy's case history from each perspective, the results might have been a bit different from my attempt. That is to be expected. But the important point remains. You would have found yourself selecting, interpreting, and systematically omitting various events in her life depending on the perspective you applied.

In Table 9-1 each of the five perspectives is listed along with its major concepts and the events in Amy's life that are examples of the concept.

This gives us a more concrete basis for comparing the appli-

TABLE 5-1 Events in the Case of Amy J. and Concepts Used to Interpret Them in Each Perspective

PSYCHOANALYTIC		ILLNESS		LEARNING		SOCIAL		HUMANISTIC	
Concept	Event	Concept	Event	Concept	Event	Concept	Event	Concept	Event
Denial	"I'm OK"	Symptoms	Anxiety; depression; crying; delusions	Reinforcement history	Parental attention	Residual rule-breaking	Nervous behavior; failure to do housework; "forgetting"	Conditions of worth	Amy values self for what others value
Regression	Failure at work and home			Behavioral decrement	Failure at work and home				
Id impulses conflict with ego motives	Need to be cared for versus need to cope	Precipitating event	Outburst in physician's office	Loss of contingent reinforcement	Husband's failure to praise work	Rule-breaking denied	"She's not getting enough sleep"	Incongruence	Discrepancy between self-image of "good housewife" and lapses
Projection	"Trying to get rid of me"	Diagnosis	"Schizophrenia"	Learned helplessness	Social and sexual deficits; self-loss feelings of ineffectiveness	Public crisis	Episode in physician's office	Disorganized behavior	Outburst in doctor's office
Repression	"I don't know what's wrong"	Treatment	Medication; hospitalization			Deviant stereotype applied	"She must be sick"	Feelings of vulnerability produced	Others treat her as inadequate
		Chronicity	"Repeated symptomatic" behavior	Avoidance response	Running away	Stigma	Fear of what people will think; ex-boss suggests different job	Self-concept altered	"I must be sick"
				Reinforcement event	Hospitalization				
				Employer's behavior	Aversive stimulus	Incorporates deviant role definition	"I must be sick"	Life crisis as growth opportunity	Entire episode in Amy's life

cation of each perspective with the others. Still, such a comparison is a bit mechanical. The essence of each perspective is not just the interpretation of particular events, but the way it makes the account seem coherent and "whole" by itself. Each perspective transforms Amy's life into a different reality.

LEARNING MORE
Projects for the Reader

1. In the case histories you have just read, we noted that different events in Amy J.'s life were selected as relevant depending on the perspective. But noting what has been *omitted* can also be instructive. Can you tell what has been omitted in each case? What does the omission suggest to you?

2. Among the five case histories, some make Amy J. look more seriously disturbed than others. Which do you think makes her look most disturbed and which makes her look least disturbed? Do you have any opinion about why this is the case? Is there anything about the perspectives themselves that would produce this effect?

3. What treatment might be prescribed for Amy from the point of view of each perspective? What or whom specifically do you think the target of intervention would be in each case?

4. Read a full-length biography written from a particular psychological perspective. There are a number of "psychohistories" now available that you might wish to read. Erik Erikson is one such dynamically oriented biographer. Or, you might wish to read B. F. Skinner's *Walden II* as an application of the learning perspective to a whole community.

Glossary

Accessory symptoms Part of Bleuler's classification of schizophrenic symptoms, including hallucinations, paranoid ideation, grandiosity, hostility-belligerence, or resistiveness-uncooperativeness.

Actualizing tendency The tendency of the organism as a whole to develop all its potentialities in a manner that serves to maintain or enhance itself. The actualizing tendency involves both meeting biological needs and striving for autonomy from external forces. It is the only motive postulated in Rogers' system.

Acute disorder Disorder with a sudden onset and of short duration. Acute disorders are usually considered reversible.

Adaptation As contrasted with maladaptive behavior or responses, a defining characteristic of abnormal behavior. The process by which the organism responds and adjusts to the demands of the environment.

Altered state of consciousness (ASC) State of consciousness other than the normal state. Methods for achieving ASC include psychedelic drugs, meditation, yoga, hypnosis, and fasting. ASCs are seen as means to personal growth.

Anal stage A period in development, according to Freud, in which the child's character develops in a retentive or expulsive way paralleling the retaining or expelling of feces.

Anxiety As experienced by the person phenomenologically, a state of tension or uneasiness for which no known cause exists. Anxiety is likely to occur when the awareness of incongruence between the self and experience is impending.

Behaviorism A major approach to the study of abnormal behavior. Stresses observable behavior, specifiable environmental stimuli, and the acquired capability of stimuli to elicit or strengthen behavior.

Career The sequence of movements from one position to another in a social or occupational system.

Career contingency Those factors on which the individual's mobility from one social position to another depends.

Case history A clinical description of a particular person and the events that shape his or her behavior.

Cathexis The investment of an idea or an action with the special significance for the person.

Chronic disorder Disorder that is longlasting and tends to be irreversible.

Classical conditioning The process whereby an originally neutral conditioned stimulus, through continuous pairing with an unconditioned stimulus, acquires the ability to elicit a response originally given to the unconditioned stimulus.

Conditions of worth A person's view of his or her own experiences as being more or less worthy of respect. In the humanistic perspective, a predisposing factor in the development of abnormal behavior.

Community mental health A discipline aimed at prevention, early treatment, and care of psychological disorders within the community context.

Concordance Showing similar characteristics; for example, among identical twins researchers find a high degree of concordance (or similarity) in certain traits.

Confession Disclosure of past sins to significant others in one's life. Confession is a necessary but not a sufficient condition for cure in Mowrer's view.

Conflict Opposition of motives and drives.

Contingencies Two events, having a relationship usually thought of as causal, with one event following the other.

Control group In research, a group of subjects for whom the experimental conditions are not provided for purposes of comparison with the experimental group; allows experimenters to see the effects of manipulation on behavior of subjects who are part of the experimental condition.

Coverants Covert responses or operants. Included are wishes, hopes, and fantasies, now considered to be a legitimate matter of study by those who follow the learning approach.

Covert sensitization Fantasy of aversive event following undesired behavior (e.g., violent nausea following urge to smoke).

Defense The organism's response to threat. The goal of defense is to maintain the self-structure as it currently exists. Defense achieves the maintenance of the existing self-structure in the face of incongruity by distorting experience in awareness. A distortion serves to reduce the incongruity between the current state of self and the discrepant evidence of experience. Denial and distortion are forms of defense that serve the same general purpose.

Defense mechanism A reaction designed to maintain the individual's feelings of adequacy and to reduce anxiety. Defense mechanisms operate at an unconscious level and tend to distort reality. Examples are denial, projection, reaction formation, regression, and repression.

Deinstitutionalization Encouraging the placement of hospitalized mental patients back into the community. In part, this treatment policy stems from a recognition of the debilitating effects of long-term hospitalization and the negative effects of the patient role.

Denial   In Freudian theory, a defense mechanism in which the existence of conflicts or external threats are denied by the person.

Depression   An emotional state characterized by discouragement, dejection, sadness, apathy, and self-blame.

Deviance   The response of other people to the rule-breaker. Deviance is a quality of people's response to an act and not a characteristic of the act itself. *Primary deviance* and *secondary deviance* are distinguished from each other according to their origins; abnormal behavior can arise in response to being labeled, or hospitalized (secondary), or as a result of some internal (primary) cause, such as brain damage.

Deviant career   "The sequence of movements from one stigmatized position to another in the sector of the larger social system that functions to maintain social control" (Scheff, 1966, p. 39).

Diagnosis   The determination of the nature of a disease or abnormality based on symptoms displayed.

DSM *(Diagnostic and Statistical Manual of Mental Disorders)*   The standard nomenclature and reference for diagnosis in the United States published by the American Psychiatric Association.

Discrimination   The reinforcement of a response in the presence of a particular stimulus but not in the presence of other stimuli. The outcome of this procedure is that the response will occur in the presence of the stimulus associated with reinforcement and not in other situations.

Disease   Disorder characterized by symptoms, either mental or bodily, that indicate mental or physical dysfunction.

Disorder   One or more syndromes with common etiological factors.

Disorganized behavior   In Rogers' theory, an incongruence between self-concept and experience that a person is not able to cope with using defenses. The person's behavior pattern then shows a shifting between acting in terms of self-concept and in terms of discrepant experiences.

Ego   That part of the psychological structure that is usually described as the "self." It is the aspect of the personality that mediates between the needs of the id and reality.

Erogenous zones   Areas of the body that are subject to sexual excitation. Freud includes the mouth, the anus, and the genital organs.

Etiology   Causation: the systematic study of the causes of disorders.

Existentialism   A part of the humanistic movement. A philosophy that emphasizes the individual's responsibility for becoming the person one wants to be and for making free choices regarding one's own life.

Experience (as a noun)   Includes both physiological and psychological events—all that is going on in the organism at a given moment in time. These events are potentially available to awareness.

Experience (as a verb)   To receive the impact of exterior and interior events at a given moment in time. Events that are perceived at the level of consciousness are said to be experienced.

Expiation   The only effective method of self-cure. Once confession has occurred, the individual must recommit the self to society and engage in behaviors that support social norms rather than violate them.

Extinction   The removal of the reinforcer used in conditioning a response; the resulting decline in response strength.

Fixation   Occurs when aspects of the earlier development of the individual acquire a primary role in later development. Typically, fixation is thought to represent a cathexis of earlier development and earlier ways of dealing with id-ego conflicts that persist in later behavior.

Flooding   Therapeutic procedure in which intense exposure to feared situations elicits anxiety with the expectation that the anxiety will be extinguished.

Free-floating anxiety   A neurotic anxiety in which the person seems always apprehensive that something dreadful will happen to him or her.

Functional analysis   A method used by behaviorists to search for the stimulus that was responsible for an observed response.

Generalization   A failure of discrimination. A response reinforced in the presence of a particular stimulus may also occur to stimuli that are similar to the original stimulus, even though the response was never reinforced in their presence.

Gestalt therapy   A therapeutic approach to expanding awareness and maximizing human potential. The basic injunctions include being centered in the present, observing rather than analyzing, and attempting to relive and identify with past events or experiences (e.g., through psychodrama).

Guilt   A normal emotion that results from an actual or objective transgression or sin. Guilt is often referred to as "real guilt" to distinguish it from the Freudian concept of guilt, which refers to guilty feelings concerning emotions or thoughts rather than actions.

Human potential movement   A portion of the humanistic movement emphasizing personal growth.

Humanistic perspective   A view of abnormal behavior that emphasizes personal growth and emphasis on the whole person. Includes self-theories, some elements of existentialism, and some elements of phenomenology.

Hypnosis   A mental state in which a person is knowingly brought into a trance through suggestion. Afterward the person may not recall what occurred under hypnosis.

Id   The reservoir of instinctual drives in the psychological structure of the individual. It is the most primitive and most inaccessible structure of the personality.

Ideal self   The ideal self is the concept of that self which the individual would most like to have, the self-concept upon which is placed the highest value.

Illness perspective   A view of abnormal behavior in which the language and concepts of physical medicine are used as a model to describe deviant behavior.

Impression management   Means of influencing others' views of oneself in order to pursue one's own goals. For example, some research shows that hospitalized mental patients may be capable of displaying behavior to the treatment staff that will gain them either discharge or further treatment.

Incongruence   A discrepancy or conflict that the organism experiences. The discrepancy is between the self as the individual perceives it and the actual experience of the organism. For example, one may perceive oneself as having one set of characteristics, but an accurate symbolization of one's experience would indicate a different set of characteristics. A state of incongruence in the organism may be characterized as internal confusion or tension.

Infectious disease   Disease in which a microorganism such as a virus attacks the body through a particular organ or system of organs. An example is general paresis, a behavior disorder associated with syphilis of the brain.

Instrumental conditioning   Process of development of behavior in which the organism must emit the response before reinforcement can occur. Therefore, the response is *instrumental* in receiving reinforcement.

Introspection   The study of internal or psychological private events, usually through examination of one's own experience.

Labeling   Acknowledgment in some public way of a person's role. Once labeled (e.g., as "ex-mental patient"), a person is subject to many contingencies of that role, according to the social perspective adherents.

Learned helplessness   Occurs when there is no relationship between the efforts of the organism to receive reinforcement and the outcomes of those efforts. Helplessness that arises from environmental circumstances.

Learning   Acquired functional relationships (contingencies) among stimuli, responses, and reinforcers. Both classical and operant conditioning arrangements are said to result in learning.

Learning perspective   A view of abnormal behavior that describes both a formulation of abnormal behavior as well as a relatively well-defined program of treatment based upon the principles of learning theory.

Learning theory   A set of principles used to describe the acquisition of new behavior. The two mainstreams of thought in learning theory rely on (1) the principles of classical conditioning, or (2) the principles of operant conditioning. These two approaches overlap and complement each other.

Libido   The instinctual drives of the id. The energy of the sexual drive.

Maintaining cause   A cause of mental illness that serves to reinforce abnormal behavior and thus maintains it over time (e.g., poor conditions in a mental hospital).

Maladaptive behavior   According to the learning perspective, abnormal behavior. Its characteristics are (1) being inappropriate in the eyes of those who control the reinforcements for the person, and (2) leading to a decrease in the amount of positive reinforcement given the abnormally behaving person.

Media stereotypes   Reinforcement by the mass media of traditional pre-conceptions (e.g., mental disorder). Advocates of the social perspective note that the media generally portray fictional rather than realistic accounts of mental disorder and reaffirm traditional views of insanity.

Medical model   A system describing abnormal behavior based on its analogy to physical medicine.

Metaphor   System for describing new concepts or unfamiliar patterns through implied comparison; a process of thought.

Modeling   A learning mechanism involving the observation and imitation of others. Advocates of the learning perspective believe it is one mechanism by which abnormal behavior develops.

Moral anxiety   In Freudian theory, the result of conflict between the id impulses and the superego. A person feeling moral anxiety will often feel intense shame or guilt.

Moral perspective   A view of abnormal behavior that opposes Freudian theory. In this view anxiety is the result of guilt, and neurotic individuals are considered to be under- rather than oversocialized. Proponents of this view emphasize personal responsibility for behavior.

Need hierarchy   A listing of human needs set out by Maslow, a proponent of the humanistic perspective, who posits that basic human needs are listed at the bottom, while those less basic to human existence occupy higher levels. The higher needs function only when lower needs have been satisfied.

Neurosis   A psychological disorder involving anxiety, hysteria, depression, obsessions and compulsions. It is a nonpsychotic disorder in which the person retains contact with reality.

Neurotic anxiety   According to the psychoanalytic view, the ego is aroused by its perception of the possibility of being overwhelmed by the instincts of the id. Free-floating anxiety, phobia, and panic reactions are all forms of neurotic anxiety.

Norepinephrine   A hormone in the brain and elsewhere in the body that plays a role in the transmission of nerve impulses.

Norms   The agreed-upon rules of conduct or demeanor of the group.

Norm violator   One who disturbs or disrupts the agreed-upon rules of the group within a particular social environment.

Normal science   A period in the history of science in which one view dominates and directs the way in which we see the world. During such times nearly all practitioners of the science engage in research, with a strong commitment to a particular conceptual scheme.

Nosology   The classification of diseases.

Oedipus complex   In general, a sexual attraction to the parent of the opposite sex, and anger or hostility toward the parent of the same sex. Shown in children during the fourth or fifth year of their development, this phenomenon was considered by Freud to be a crucial determinant of the person's later attitudes toward the opposite sex and toward people in authority.

Operant conditioning   Operant conditioning involves the strengthening of an operant response (one which is emitted rather than elicited) by the presentation of a reinforcing stimulus if, and only if, the operant response occurs.

Oral stage In Freudian theory, a stage in the first year of life, in which the child gratifies libidinal needs through putting things into the mouth and later biting.

Paradigm clash The conflict or clash between the prevailing view of normal science and a new, emerging conceptual scheme. Often the new paradigm produces a shift in the problems available for scientific investigation and transforms the ways in which the scientist sees the world.

Penis envy The Freudian idea that girls act in a way that indicates their wish to be like and to have the power of their brothers or male counterparts. Such power is symbolized in the male's penis.

Perceptual defense The use of defense mechanisms, such as repression or denial, to distort the perception of threatening material.

Phallic stage In Freudian theory, a developmental stage in which the genital organs become a source of satisfaction to the child. During this stage the Oedipal complex develops.

Phenomenology An approach that emphasizes the individual's understanding of his or her own world as the person understands it.

Phenothiazines A class of major tranquilizers having specific effects on the brain chemistry of schizophrenics.

Phobia A strong, irrational fear of particular objects or situations (e.g., fear for certain harmless animals or heights).

Pleasure principle In Freudian theory, the demand that an instinctual need be gratified at once. The principle that guides the id.

Positive regard The perception of a self-experience in another person, which leads to favorable or pleasant experiences for that perceiver. When this occurs, the perceiver is said to be experiencing positive regard for that individual. The need for positive regard is learned early in childhood.

Precipitating cause A cause of psychological disorder that serves as a "trigger" for the disorder. A precipitating life event could be a sudden loss of a loved one, a disaster, a major failure in one's life, or a sudden physiological change.

Predisposing cause An event or condition that occurs long before any abnormal behavior is observed, yet may predispose a person to later difficulties.

Primary process Usually refers to modes of thinking that are primitive, illogical, and perceptually vivid. Primary process may also refer to drive energy that is mobile and can be displaced onto other objects.

Prognosis Statement concerning the likely course and outcome of a disorder.

Projection Defense mechanism by which id impulses are attributed to some object or person in the external world.

Psychoanalysis Process of psychological investigation and treatment developed by Freud. Relies heavily upon the study of the early history and development of the person.

Reaction formation   The mechanism by which an instinctual impulse is hidden from awareness by its opposite. Often distinguishable from a real impulse by its exaggerated form.

Reality principle   Means by which ego balances the person's pursuit of gratification with the demands of external reality.

Regression   Retreat to an earlier stage of development in behavior to allow the id impulses expression at a level not possible at higher levels of development.

Reinforcement   The process by which response strength (i.e., the probability of a response) is changed as a result of either classical conditioning or operant conditioning.

Reinforcer   Any event following a response that changes the strength of that response.

Remission   Recovery or improvement in the course of mental illness.

Repression   One of the fundamental defense mechanisms. Repression removes psychologically painful ideas from the individual's awareness. Dangerous desires or intolerable memories are kept out of consciousness by this mechanism as well.

Residual rule-breaking   Norm violations that do not fall into an explicit rule category but which may result in others labeling the rule violator as "mentally ill."

Response   Any behavioral event whose strength can be manipulated by changing antecedent stimuli or consequent events.

Response independence   Occurs when an animal or person cannot predict or control important outcomes and is said to be helpless. The state of no relationship between responses and reinforcement.

Response strength   Basic dependent variable in learning theory. Can be inferred in verbal behavior from such variables as pitch, speed, rapidity of emission, and immediate repetition.

Role concept   Behavior expected of an individual in a particular social situation. A role may be conceived of as the product of the individual's behavior and of social forces operating in the transaction between the individual and his or her audience.

Rule-breaking   Behavior that clearly violates agreed-upon rules of the group. Examples are crime, perversion, drunkenness, or bad manners.

Secondary process   In Freudian thinking, usually refers to thinking that is logical or rational. It is also used to refer to drive or drive energy that is bound or cathected to specific objects or ideas.

Self-actualization   Important theme of the humanistic movement. A process described by Maslow and others in which one develops the ability to perceive reality efficiently, be detached and objective, be interested in one's fellow human beings, and discriminate between means and ends. Self-actualized people are creative, have a sense of humor, and are able to resist the forces of the culture in which they live.

Self-concept   In the humanistic perspective, the person's self-experience that then develops into the perceptual object the person experiences as "me" or "I."

Self-experience The self-experience is the "raw material" from which the self-concept is formed. This includes any experiences the individual has that he identifies as involving the "me," "I," or "self."

Sex-role stereotypes Fixed ideas accepted within a culture of what role should be carried out by members of one sex or the other. Notions of appropriate behavior for female and male children that are culture bound.

Sexism Favoritism shown to one sex or the other.

Sin In Mowrer's view, behavior that violates social norms. In general, behavior thought to be deviant or abnormal is considered sinful.

Social perspective A view of abnormal behavior that emphasizes the role of society in judging whether mental illness exists. This perspective looks to context and social reactions rather than symptoms in isolation.

Social role A pattern of behavior associated with a distinctive social position (e.g., father, teacher, employer, or patient).

Socialization Process by which an individual learns the rules of his or her culture. Encompasses behavioral, cognitive, and affective learning.

Sociopathy State of being in opposition to the customary rules of society. Mowrer argues that the sociopath has not internalized the norms and values of society enough to feel any guilt concerning his or her own misconduct.

Specific etiology That causal condition which is necessary but not sufficient for an illness to occur; it does not by itself produce the illness.

Spontaneous remission Recovery without or with minimal treatment from a mental illness.

Status A socially acknowledged position in a group.

Stigma A stigmatized person is one with a discrediting identity. Persons who have been labeled as "mentally ill" or as "ex-mental patients" are usually said to be stigmatized.

Stimulus Any objectively defined situation or event that is the occasion for an organism's response.

Superego That structure of the personality that is concerned with ethical and moral feelings and attitudes. The superego is usually identified with the "conscience."

Symptom A physical or behavioral manifestation of illness.

Syndrome Patterns or constellations of symptoms that are typical of a disorder.

Systemic disease Disease in which some organ or organ system breaks down or fails because it already possesses some inherited defect or weakness. The organ or organ system is predisposed to break down and may do so if subjected to prolonged stress.

Therapy The application of various treatment techniques either to affect symptoms or to affect etiological factors.

Third force A third approach to the study of abnormal behavior, presenting an alternative to behaviorism and psychoanalysis. This "third force" comprises three distinct viewpoints: self-theories, some elements of existentialism, and some of phenomenology.

Threat The state that exists when the individual actually perceives incongruence between the self and experience.

Total institutions Goffman's description of an environment (e.g., prisons and mental hospitals) in which all aspects of the individuals' lives occur in the same place and under the same authority; where each phase is carried out in the company of others who are being treated alike and doing the same things; and where all activities are tightly scheduled by a body above the general population as part of a single plan that is designed to fulfill the institution's aims.

Transactional view In the social perspective, the emphasis on interpersonal aspects of labeling processes and the role of the labeled person in perpetuating his or her "sick" role.

Traumatic disease A disease produced by some external or environmental event or agent. An example is serious physical damage produced by poisoning or skull fracture.

Unconditional positive regard Positive regard experienced toward an individual irrespective of that individual's values or behavior. As Rogers (1959) puts it; "If self-experiences of another are perceived by me in such a way that no self-experience can be discriminated as more or less worthy of positive regard than any other, then I am experiencing unconditional positive regard for this individual" (p. 208).

Unconscious The portion of the psychological structure of the individual where repressed or forgotten memories or desires reside. These memories or desires are not directly available to consciousness but can be made available through psychoanalysis or hypnosis.

Vulnerability Vulnerability refers to the potential for psychological disorganization that exists because of the incongruence between the self and experience. Thus an individual is vulnerable to anxiety when incongruence exists but is not yet perceived in awareness.

Wish fulfillment In psychoanalytic theory, when immediate gratification of a wish or drive is impossible, the memory traces of the individual are activated and an image of the desired object may be produced to gratify the need for tension reduction.

Withdrawal A retreat from physical, emotional, or intellectual experience. Can be exhibited as a generalized fear of people, seclusiveness, or mutism.

References

Akiskal, H. S., & McKinney, W. T., Jr. Depressive disorders: Toward a unified hypothesis, *Science*, 1973, *182*, 20–29.

Allport, G. W. *Becoming: Basic considerations for a psychology of personality.* New Haven: Yale University Press, 1955.

American Psychiatric Association. *Diagnostic and statistical manual of mental disorders (DSM-II)* (2d ed.). Washington: American Psychiatric Association, 1968.

Anonymous. Phenomenology in perspective: Is there schizophrenia? *Schizophrenia Bulletin*, 1970, *2*, 11–14.

Ausubel, D. P. Personality disorder *is* disease. *American Psychologist*, 1961, *16*, 69–74.

Back, K. Policy enthusiasms for untested theories and the role of quantitative evidence: Labeling and mental illness. In N. J. Demerath, O. Larsen, & K. S. Schuessler (Eds.), *Social policy and sociology*. New York: Academic Press, 1975, 135–147.

Bandura, A., & Rosenthal, T. L. Vicarious classical conditioning as a function of arousal level. *Journal of Personality and Social Psychology*, 1966, *3*, 54–62.

Barber, T. X. *LSD, marihuana, yoga, and hypnosis.* Chicago: Aldine, 1970.

Barber, T. X., et al. (Eds.) *Biofeedback and self-control: A reader.* Chicago: Aldine-Atherton, 1971.

Barber, T. X., Spanos, N. P., & Chaves, J. F. *Hypnosis, imagining, and human potentialities.* Elmsford, N.Y.: Pergamon, 1974.

Bardwick, J. M. *Psychology of women.* New York: Harper & Row, 1971.

Bardwick, J. M. (Ed.) *Readings on the psychology of women.* New York: Harper & Row, 1972.

Becker, H. S. *The other side: Perspectives on deviance.* New York: Free Press, 1963.

Becker, H. S. Outsiders: Studies in the sociology of deviance. New York: Free Press, 1964.

Bem, S. L., & Bem, D. J. Training the woman to know her place: The power of a non-conscious ideology. In M. H. Garskoff (Ed.), Roles women play: Readings towards women's liberation. Belmont, Ca.: Brooks/Cole, 1971.

Bernard, J. The future of marriage. New York: World, 1972.

Berne, E. Games people play. New York: Grove Press, 1964.

Bittner, E. Police discretion in emergency apprehension of mentally ill persons. Social Problems, 1967, 14, 278–292.

Blaney, P. H. Contemporary theories of depression: Critique and comparison. Journal of Abnormal Psychology, 1977, 86, 203–223.

Blashfield, R. K. Evaluation of the DSM II classification of schizophrenia as a nomenclature. Journal of Abnormal Psychology, 1973, 82, 282–289.

Blashfield, R. K., & Draguns, J. G. Evaluative criteria for psychiatric classification. Journal of Abnormal Psychology, 1976, 85, 140–150.

Blum, G. S., & Miller, D. R. Exploring the psychoanalytic theory of the "oral character." Journal of Personality, 1952, 20, 287–304.

Boring, E. G. When is human behavior predetermined? Scientific Monthly, 1957, 84, 189–196.

Braginsky, B. M., Braginsky, D. D., & Ring, K. Methods of madness: The mental hospital as a last resort. New York: Holt, Rinehart and Winston, 1969.

Braginsky, B. M., Grosse, M., & Ring, K. Controlling outcomes through impression management: An experimental study of the manipulative tactics of mental patients. Journal of Consulting Psychology, 1966, 30, 295–300.

Breger, L., & McGaugh, J. L. Critique and reformulation of "learning-theory" approaches to psychotherapy and neuroses. Psychological Bulletin, 1965, 5, 338–358.

Buchwald, A. M., & Young, R. D. Some comments on the foundations of behavior therapy. In C. M. Franks (Ed.), Behavior therapy: Appraisal and status. New York: McGraw-Hill, 1969.

Buckley, W. A methodological note. In T. J. Scheff, Being mentally ill: A sociological theory. Chicago: Aldine, 1966, pp. 201–205.

Bugental, J. R. T. The search for authenticity: An existential–analytic approach to psychotherapy. New York: Holt, Rinehart and Winston, 1965.

Buss, A. H. Psychopathology. New York: Wiley, 1966.

Cameron, N. Personality development and psychopathology: A dynamic approach. Boston: Houghton Mifflin, 1963.

Cassirer, E. Language and myth. New York: Dover, 1946.

Cattell, R. B. The description of personality. I. Foundations as trait measurement. *Psychological Review,* 1940, *50,* 559–594.

Cautela, J. R. Covert conditioning. In A. Jacobs & L. B. Sachs (Eds.), *The psychology of private events: Perspective on covert response systems.* New York: Academic Press, 1971. Pp. 109–130.

Chapanis, A. Men, machines and models. *American Psychologist,* 1961, *16,* 113–131.

Chesler, P. *Women and madness.* New York: Doubleday, 1972.

Chomsky, N. Review of B. F. Skinner, *Verbal behavior. Language,* 1959, *35,* 26–58.

Chun, K., & Sarbin, T. R. An empirical study of "metaphor-to-myth transformation." *Philosophical Psychology,* 1970, *4,* 16–21.

Clausen, J. A., & Yarrow, M. R. Paths to the mental hospital. *Journal of Social Issues,* 1955, *11* (4), 25–32.

Cohen, S. *Drugs of hallucination.* London: Paladin, 1970.

Cumming, J., & Cumming, E. *Closed ranks: An experiment in mental health education.* Cambridge: Harvard University Press, 1957.

Dabrowski, K. In J. Aronson (Ed.), *Positive distintegration.* Boston: Little Brown, 1964.

Davidson, H. Dr. Whatsisname. *Mental Hospitals,* 1958, *9,* 8.

Denner, B., & Price, R. H. (Eds.) *Community mental health: Social action and reaction.* New York: Holt, Rinehart and Winston, 1973.

Diefendorf, A. R. *Clinical psychiatry.* New York: Macmillan, 1921.

Dodds, E. R. *The Greeks and the irrational.* Berkeley, Ca.: University of California Press, 1951.

Dodds, E. R. *Pagan and Christian in an age of anxiety.* New York: Cambridge University Press, 1965.

Dollard, J., & Miller, N. E. *Personality and psychotherapy.* New York: McGraw-Hill, 1950.

Eastman, C. Behavioral formulations of depression. *Psychological Review,* 1976, *83,* 277–291.

Ellis, A. Should some people be labeled mentally ill? *Journal of Consulting Psychology,* 1967, *31,* 435–446.

Eriksen, C. W. Perceptual defense as a function of unacceptable needs. *Journal of Abnormal and Social Psychology,* 1951, *46,* 557–564. (a)

Eriksen, C. W. Some implications for TAT interpretation arising from need and perception experiments. *Journal of Personality,* 1951, *19,* 283–288. (b)

Eriksen, C. W. Defense against ego-threat in memory and perception. *Journal of Abnormal and Social Psychology,* 1952, *27,* 430–435.

Eriksen, C. W. Discrimination and learning without awareness: A methodological survey and evaluation. *Psychological Review,* 1960, *67,* 279–300.

Eriksen, C. W. Perception and personality. In J. M. Wepman & R. W. Heine (Eds.), *Concepts of personality.* Chicago: Aldine, 1963.

Erikson, E. H. *Ghandi's truth.* New York: Norton, 1969.

Eysenck, H. J. Classification and the problem of diagnosis. In H. J. Eysenck (Ed.), *Handbook of abnormal psychology.* London: Pitman, 1960. (a)

Eysenck, H. J. Learning theory and behaviour therapy. In H. J. Eysenck (Ed.), *Behavior therapy and the neuroses.* London: Pergamon, 1960. (b)

Eysenck, H. J., and Rachman, S. *The causes and cures of neurosis.* London: Routledge and Kegan Paul, 1965.

Fenichel, O. *The psychoanalytic theory of neurosis.* New York: Norton, 1945.

Ferster, C. B. A functional analysis of depression. *American Psychologist,* 1973, *28,* 857–870.

Freud, S. (1894) The neuropsychoses of defense. In J. Strachey (Ed.), *The standard edition of the complete psychological works,* Vol. 3. London: Hogarth, 1962.

Freud, S. (1901) Psychopathology of everyday life. *Standard edition,* Vol. 6. London: Hogarth, 1960.

Freud, S. (1911) Formulations on the two principles of mental functioning. In *Collected papers of Sigmund Freud,* Vol. IV. London: Hogarth, 1949.

Freud, S. (1923) The ego and the id. *Standard edition,* Vol. 19. London: Hogarth, 1961.

Freud, S. (1926a) *The problem of anxiety.* New York: Norton, 1936.

Freud, S. (1926b) Inhibitions, symptoms, and anxiety. *Standard edition,* Vol. 20. London: Hogarth, 1953, pp. 77–175.

Freud, S. (1930) Civilization and its discontents. *Standard edition,* Vol. 21. London: Hogarth, 1961.

Freud, S. (1933) *New introductory lectures on psychoanalysis.* New York: Norton, 1933.

Freud, S. (1940) *An outline of psychoanalysis.* New York: Norton, 1949.

Fromm, E. *Escape from freedom.* New York: Holt, Rinehart and Winston, 1941.

Goffman, E. The moral career of the mental patient. *Psychiatry: Journal for the Study of Interpersonal Processes,* 1959, *22,* 123–131.

Goffman, E. *Asylums: Essays on the social situation of mental patients and other inmates.* Garden City, N.Y.: Anchor, 1961.

Goffman, E. *Behavior in public places: Notes on the social organization of gatherings.* New York: Free Press, 1963. (a)

Goffman, E. *Stigma: Notes on the management of spoiled identity.* Englewood Cliffs, N.J.: Prentice-Hall, 1963. (b)

Goldman, A. R., Bohr, R. H., & Steinberg, T. A. On posing as mental patients: Reminiscences and recommendations. *Professional Psychology,* 1970, *1,* 427–434.

Goldstein, K. *The organism.* New York: American, 1939.

Goldstein, M. J., Judd, L. L., Rodnick, E. H., & LaPolla, A. Psychophysiological and behavioral effects of phenothiazine administration as a function of premorbid status. *Journal of Psychiatric Research,* 1969, *6,* 271–287.

Gordon, J. S. Who is mad? Who is sane? R. D. Laing: In search of a new psychiatry. *The Atlantic,* January, 1971, 50–66.

Gove, W. R. (Ed.) *The labeling of deviance: Evaluating a perspective.* Beverly Hills, Calif.: Sage, 1975.

Grier, W. H., & Cobb, P. M. *Black rage.* New York: Basic Books, 1968.

Gruenberg, E. M. Foreword. In *DSM-II.* Washington: American Psychiatric Association, 1968.

Hall, C. S. *A primer of Freudian psychology.* New York: New American Library, 1954.

Hall, C. S., & Lindzey, G. The relevance of Freudian psychology and related viewpoints for the social sciences. In G. Lindzey & E. Aronson (Eds.), *Handbook of social psychology,* Vol. 1. Cambridge: Addison-Wesley, 1968.

Hanson, N. R. *Patterns of discovery.* New York: Cambridge University Press, 1965..

Hartmann, H. Psychoanalysis as a scientific theory. In S. Hood (Ed.), *Psychoanalysis, scientific method, and philosophy.* New York: New York University Press, 1959.

Haughton, E., & Ayllon, T. Production and elimination of symptomatic behavior. In L. Ullmann & L. Krasner (Eds.), *Case studies in behavior modification.* New York: Holt, Rinehart and Winston, 1965, pp. 94–98.

Heller, J. *Catch-22.* New York: Simon & Schuster, 1961.

Hilgard, E. R. Psychoanalysis: Experimental studies. In D. L. Sills (Ed.), *International encyclopedia of the social sciences,* Vol. 13. New York: Macmillan, 1968.

Hoffman, A. *Revolution for the hell of it.* New York: Dial, 1968.

Holzman, P. S. *Psychoanalysis and psychopathology.* New York: McGraw-Hill, 1970.

Homme, L. E. Perspectives in psychology, XXIV: Control of coverants, the operants of the mind. *Psychological Record,* 1965, *15,* 501–511.

Hook, S. Science and mythology in psychoanalysis. In S. Hook (Ed.), *Psychoanalysis, scientific method, and philosophy.* New York: New York University Press, 1959.

Horney, K. *Neurosis and human growth.* New York: Norton, 1950.

Howes, D., & Solomon, R. L. A note on McGinnies' emotionality and perceptual defense. *Psychological Review,* 1950, *57,* 229–234.

Hughes, E. C. Dilemmas and contradictions of status. *American Journal of Sociology,* 1945, *1,* 353–359.

John Hancock Mutual Life Insurance Company. *The Mind.* Pamphlet, 1954, p. 15.

Jones, E. *The life and work of Sigmund Freud.* New York: Basic Books, Vol. 1, 1953; Vol. 2, 1955; Vol. 3, 1957.

Kallman, F. J. *Heredity in mental health and disorder.* New York: Norton, 1953.

Kanfer, F. H., & Phillips, J. S. *Learning foundations of behavior therapy.* New York: Wiley, 1970.

Kelly, G. A. *A theory of personality: The psychology of personal constructs.* New York: Norton, 1963.

Kety, S. Biochemical theories of schizophrenia. *Science,* 1959, *129,* 1590–1596.

Kisker, G. W. *The disorganized personality.* New York: McGraw-Hill, 1964.

Kittrie, N. N. *The right to be different: Deviance and enforced therapy.* Baltimore: Penguin Books, 1973.

Kramer, M. Introduction: The historical background of ICD-8 (International Classification of Diseases-8). In *DSM-II,* Washington: American Psychiatric Association, 1968.

Kuhn, T. S. *The structure of scientific revolutions.* Chicago: University of Chicago Press, 1962.

Lachman, R. The model in theory construction. *Psychological Review,* 1960, *67,* 113–129.

Laing, R. D. *The divided self.* London: Tavistock, 1959.

Laing, R. D. *The politics of experience.* New York: Ballantine, 1967.

Lamy, R. E. Social consequences of mental illness. *Journal of Consulting Psychology,* 1966, *30,* 450–455.

Langer, E. J., & Abelson, R. P. A patient by any other name . . .: Clinician group differences in labeling bias. *Journal of Consulting and Clinical Psychology,* 1974, *42,* 4–9.

Lehrman, N. S. Precision in psychoanalysis. *American Journal of Psychiatry,* 1960, *116,* 1097–1103.

Lemert, E. M. *Social pathology: A systematic approach to the theory of sociopathic behavior.* New York: McGraw-Hill, 1951.

Leo, J. Psychoanalysis reaches a crossroad. *New York Times,* Aug. 4, 1968, pp. 1, 56.

Levy, L. *Psychological interpretation.* New York: Holt, Rinehart and Winston, 1963.

Lewinsohn, P. M. A behavioral approach to depression. In R. J. Friedman & M. M. Katz (Eds.), *The psychology of depression: Contemporary theory and research.* Washington, D.C.: V. H. Winston, 1974. (a)

Lewinsohn, P. M. Clinical and theoretical aspects of depression. In K. S. Calhoun, H. E. Adams, & K. M. Mitchell (Eds.), *Innovative treatment methods in psychopathology.* New York: Wiley, 1974. (b)

Luborsky, L. A psychoanalytic research on momentary forgetting during free association. *Bulletin of the Philadelphia Association for Psychoanalysis,* 1964, *14,* 119–137.

Luborsky, L. Momentary forgetting during psychotherapy and psychoanalysis: A theory and research method. In R. R. Holt (Ed.), *Motives and thought: Contributions to a psychoanalytic theory of behavior.* New York: International Universities Press, 1967.

Luborsky, L. New directions in research on neurotic and psychosomatic symptoms. *American Scientist,* 1970, *58,* 661–668.

Maher, B. A. *Principles of psychopathology.* New York: McGraw-Hill, 1966.

Mandler, G., & Kessen, W. *The language of psychology.* New York: Wiley, 1959.

Marcuse, H. *Eros and civilization.* Boston: Beacon Press, 1955.

Marcuse, H. *One dimensional man.* Boston: Beacon Press, 1964.

Marzolf, S. S. The disease concept in psychology. *Psychological Review,* 1947, *54,* 211–221.

Maslow, A. H. *Motivation and personality.* New York: Harper & Row, 1954.

Maslow, A. H. Deficiency motivation and growth motivation. In M. R. Jones (Ed.), *Nebraska symposium on motivation.* Lincoln: University of Nebraska Press, 1955, pp. 1–30.

May, R. *Psychology and the human dilemma.* Princeton, N.J.: Van Nostrand, 1967.

May, R. *Existential psychology* (2d ed.). New York: Random, 1969.

McGinnies, E. Emotionality and perceptual defense. *Psychological Review,* 1949, *56,* 244–251.

Mechanic, D. Some factors in identifying and defining mental illness. *Mental Hygiene,* 1962, *46,* 66–74.

Meehl, P. E. Schizotaxia, schizotypy, schizophrenia. *American Psychologist,* 1962, *17,* 827–838.

Meehl, P. E. Some ruminations on the validation of clinical procedures. In E. Megargee (Ed.), *Research in clinical assessment.* New York: Harper & Row, 1966.

Mehrabian, A. *An analysis of personality theories.* Englewood Cliffs, N.J.: Prentice-Hall, 1968.

Meichenbaum, D. H., & Cameron, R. The clinical potential and pitfalls of modifying what clients say to themselves. In M. J. Mahoney & C. E. Thoresen, *Self-control: Power to the person.* Monterey, Ca., 1974.

Mendel, W. M., & Rapport, S. Determinants of the decision for psychiatric hospitalization. *Archives of General Psychiatry,* 1969, *20,* 321–328.

Menninger, K. *The vital balance.* New York: Viking, 1965.

Miller, D., & Dawson, W. H. Effect of stigma on re-employment of ex-mental patients. *Mental Hygiene,* 1965, *49,* 281–287.

Miller, D., & Schwartz, M. County Lunacy Commission Hearings: Some observations of commitments to a state mental hospital. *Social Problems,* 1966, *14,* 26–35.

Milton, O., & Wahler, R. G. Perspectives and trends. In O. Milton & R. G. Wahler (Eds.), *Behavior disorders: Perspectives and trends* (2d ed.). New York: Lippincott, 1969.

Moore, R. *Nils Bohr: The man, his science, and the world they changed.* New York: Knopf, 1966.

Mowrer, O. H. *The crisis in psychiatry and religion.* Princeton, N.J.: Van Nostrand, 1961.

Mowrer, O. H. Freudianism, behavior therapy, and "self-disclosure." *Behavioral Research and Therapy,* 1964, *1,* 321–337. (a)

Mowrer, O. H. *The new group therapy.* Princeton, N.J.: Van Nostrand, 1964. (b)

Mowrer, O. H. Learning theory and behavior therapy. In B. Wolman (Ed.), *Handbook of clinical psychology.* New York: McGraw-Hill, 1965.

Mowrer, O. H. The basis of psychopathology: Malconditioning or misbehavior? *Journal of National Association of Women Deans and Counselors,* 1966, *29,* 51–58. (a)

Mowrer, O. H. Abnormal reactions or actions? (An autobiographical answer). In J. A. Vernon (Ed.), *Introduction to psychology: A self-selection textbook.* Dubuque, Iowa: Wm. Brown, 1966. (b)

Munroe, R. L. *Schools of psychoanalytic thought.* New York: Holt, Rinehart and Winston, 1955.

Nagel, E. Methodological issues in psychoanalytic theory. In S. Hook (Ed.), *Psychoanalysis, scientific method, and philosophy*. New York: New York University Press, 1959.

Naranjo, C. Present centeredness in Gestalt therapy. In R. Ornstein (Ed.), *The nature of human consciousness*. San Francisco: Freeman, 1973.

National Association for Mental Health. *Facts about mental illness, fact sheet*. 1963.

National Association for Mental Health. *Some things you should know about mental and emotional illness*. Leaflet (no date).

Nunnally, J. C., Jr. *Popular conceptions of mental health*. New York: Holt, Rinehart and Winston, 1961.

Ornstein, R. (Ed.) *The nature of human consciousness*. San Francisco: Freeman, 1973.

Pelletier, K. R., & Garfield, C. *Consciousness: East and West*. New York: Harper & Row, 1976.

Perls, F. *Gestalt therapy verbatim*. Lafayette, Ca.: Real People Press, 1969.

Perry, J. W. Reconstitutive process in the psychopathology of the self. *Annals of the New York Academy of Sciences*, 1962, *96*, 853–876.

Phillips, D. L. Rejection: A possible consequence of seeking help for mental disorders. *American Sociological Review*, 1963, *28*, 963–972.

Price, R. H. Signal-detection methods in personality and perception. *Psychological Bulletin*, 1966, *66*, 55–62.

Price, R. H. Psychological deficit vs. impression management in schizophrenic word association performance. *Journal of Abnormal Psychology*, 1972, *79*, 132–137.

Price, R. H. The case for impression management in schizophrenia: Another look. In R. H. Price & B. Denner (Eds.), *The making of a mental patient*. New York: Holt, Rinehart and Winston, 1973.

Price, R. H. & Denner, B. (Eds.) The making of a mental patient. New York: Holt, Rinehart and Winston, 1973.

Rachman, S. Spontaneous remission and latent learning. *Behaviour Research and Therapy*, 1963, *1*, 133–137.

Rapaport, D., & Gill, M. M. The points of view and assumptions of metapsychology. In Merton M. Gill (Ed.), *Collected papers of David Rapaport*. New York: Basic Books, 1967.

Reich, T., Clayton, P. J., & Winokur, G. Family history studies: V. The genetics of mania. *American Journal of Psychiatry*, 1969, *125*, 64–75.

Rice, J. K., & Rice, D. G. Implications of the women's liberation movement for psychotherapy. *American Journal of Psychiatry,* 1973, *130,* 191–196.

Rogers, C. R. A theory of therapy, personality, and interpersonal relationships, as developed in the client-centered framework. In S. Koch (Ed.), *Psychology: A study of a science.* Vol. 3. New York: McGraw-Hill, 1959, pp. 194–235.

Rogers, C. R. *On becoming a person.* Boston: Houghton Mifflin, 1961.

Rogers, C. R., & Skinner, B. F. Some issues concerning the control of human behavior: A symposium. *Science,* 1956, *124,* 1057–1066.

Rosenhan, D. L. Madness: In the eye of the beholder. (Review of T. J. Scheff, *Being mentally ill.*) *Contemporary Psychology,* 1968, *13,* 360–361.

Rosenhan, D. L. On being sane in insane places. *Science,* 1973, *179,* 250–258.

Rosenhan, D. L. The contextual nature of psychiatric diagnosis. *Journal of Abnormal Psychology,* 1975, *84,* 462–474.

Rosenthal, D. *Genetic theory and abnormal behavior.* New York: McGraw-Hill, 1970.

Ryan, W. *Blaming the victim.* New York: Random House, 1971.

Salter, A. *The case against psychoanalysis.* New York: Citadel, 1963.

Sarason, I. G., & Ganzer, V. J. Concerning the medical model. *American Psychologist,* 1968, *23,* 507–510.

Sarbin, T. R. On the futility of the proposition that some people be labeled "mentally ill." *Journal of Consulting Psychology,* 1967, *31,* 447–453.

Sarbin, T. R. The transformation of social identity: A new metaphor for the helping professions. In L. Roberts, N. Greenfield, & N. Miller (Eds.), *Comprehensive mental health: The challenge of evaluation.* Madison, Wis.: University of Wisconsin Press, 1968.

Sarbin, T. R. Schizophrenic thinking: A role-theoretical analysis. *Journal of Personality,* 1969, *37,* 190–206.

Sarbin, T. Foreword. In D. Braginsky & D. D. Braginsky (Eds.), *Mainstream psychology: A critique.* New York: Holt, Rinehart and Winston, 1974.

Sarnoff, I., & Corwin, S. M. Castration anxiety and the fear of death. *Journal of Personality,* 1959, *27,* 374–385.

Scheff, T. J. Decision rules, types of error, and their consequences in medical diagnosis. *Behavioral Science,* 1963, *7,* 97–108.

Scheff, T. J. *Being mentally ill: A sociological theory.* Chicago: Aldine, 1966.

Scheff, T. J. (Ed.) *Mental illness and social processes.* New York: Harper & Row, 1967.

Scheff, T. J. (Ed.) *Labeling madness.* Englewood Cliffs, N.J.: Prentice-Hall, 1975.

Schon, D. A. *Displacement of concepts.* London: Tavistock, 1963.

Schroder, D., & Erlich, D. Rejection by mental health professionals: A possible consequence of not seeking appropriate help for emotional disorders. *Journal of Health and Social Behavior,* 1968, *9,* 222–232.

Schwartz, C. G. Perspective on deviance: Wives' definitions of their husbands' mental illness. *Psychiatry,* 1957, *20,* 275–291.

Sears, R. R., Maccoby, E. E., & Levin, H. *Patterns of child rearing.* Evanston, Ill.: Row, Peterson, 1957.

Seligman, M. E. P. *Helplessness: On depression, development, and death.* San Francisco: Freeman, 1975.

Seward, G. H., & Williamson, R. C. (Eds.) *Sex roles in changing society.* New York: Random House, 1970.

Shapiro, D. *Neurotic styles.* New York: Basic Books, 1965.

Sherfey, M. J. *The nature and evolution of female sexuality.* New York: Random House, 1972.

Silverman, J. When schizophrenia helps. *Psychology Today,* 1970, *4,* 62–65.

Skinner, B. F. *The behavior of organisms.* New York: Appleton, 1938.

Skinner, B. F. *Walden Two.* New York: Macmillan, 1948.

Skinner, B. F. *Science and human behavior.* New York: Macmillan, 1953.

Skinner, B. F. *Verbal behavior.* New York: Appleton, 1957.

Skinner, B. F. *Beyond freedom and dignity.* New York: Knopf, 1971.

Smith, K., Pumphrey, M. W., & Hall, J. C. The "last straw": The decisive incident resulting in the request for hospitalization in 100 schizophrenic patients. *American Journal of Psychiatry,* 1963, *120,* 228–233.

Snow, C. P. *Two cultures.* Cambridge, England: Cambridge University Press, 1969.

Snyder, S. H. *Madness and the brain.* New York: McGraw-Hill, 1975.

Spitzer, R. L. On pseudoscience in science, logic in remission, and psychiatric diagnosis: A critique of Rosenhan's "On being sane in insane places." *Journal of Abnormal Psychology,* 1975, *84,* 442–452.

Spitzer, S. P., & Denzin, N. K. *The mental patient: Studies in the sociology of deviance.* New York: McGraw-Hill, 1968.

Stampfl, T. G., & Levis, D. J. Essentials of implosive therapy: A learning-theory-based psychodynamic behavior therapy. *Journal of Abnormal Psychology,* 1967, *72,* 496–503.

Stern, E. *Mental illness: A guide for the family.* National Association for Mental Health, 1957, p. 1.

Stoller, R. J. Symbiosis anxiety and the development of masculinity. *Archives of General Psychiatry,* 1974, *30,* 164.

Sutich, A. J., & Vich, M. A. (Eds.) *Readings in humanistic psychology.* New York: Free Press, 1969.

Szasz, T. S. The myth of mental illness. *American Psychologist,* 1960, *15,* 113–118.

Szasz, T. S. *The myth of mental illness.* New York: Hoeber-Harper, 1961.

Szasz, T. S. *The myth of mental illness.* New York: Dell, 1967.

Szasz, T. S. *Schizophrenia: The sacred symbol of psychiatry.* New York: Basic Books, 1976.

Tart, C. T. States of consciousness and state-specific sciences. *Science,* 1972, *176,* 1203–1210.

Tart, C. T. *States of consciousness.* New York: Dutton, 1975.

Temerlin, M. K. Suggestion effects in psychiatric diagnosis. *Journal of Nervous and Mental Disease,* 1968, *147,* 349–353.

Tennessee Department of Mental Health. *Mind Over Matter,* Vol. 7, No. 4, 1962.

Thoresen, C. E., & Mahoney, M. J. *Behavioral self-control.* New York: Holt, Rinehart and Winston, 1974.

Torrey, E. F. *The death of psychiatry.* New York: Penguin Books, 1975.

Toulmin, S. *Foresight and understanding.* Bloomington, Ind.: Indiana University Press, 1961.

Turbayne, C. M. *The myth of metaphor.* New Haven: Yale University Press, 1962.

Ullmann, L. P., & Krasner, L. *Case studies in behavior modification.* New York: Holt, Rinehart and Winston, 1965.

Ullmann, L. P., & Krasner, L. *A psychological approach to abnormal behavior.* Englewood Cliffs, N. J.: Prentice-Hall, 1969.

Watson, J. B. Psychology as the behaviorist views it. *Psychological Review,* 1913, *20,* 158–177.

Watson, J. B., & Rayner, R. Conditioned emotional reactions. *Journal of Experimental Psychology,* 1920, *3,* 1–14.

Weiss, J. M., Glazer, H., & Pohorecky, L. Coping behavior and neurochemical changes in rats. Paper presented at the Kittay Scientific Foundation Conference, New York, March 1974. (a)

Weiss, J. M., Glazer, H., & Pohorecky, L. Neurotransmitters and helplessness: A chemical bridge to depression. *Psychology Today,* 1974, *8*(7), 58–65. (b)

Wenger, D. L., & Fletcher, C. R. The effect of legal counsel on admissions to a state mental hospital: A confrontation of professions. *Journal of Health and Social Behavior,* 1969, *10,* 66–72.

Wiest, W. M. Some recent criticisms of behaviorism and learning theory with special reference to Breger and McGaugh and to Chomsky. *Psychological Bulletin,* 1967, *67,* 214–225.

Wolfer, J. A. Concerning the concern over the medical model. *American Psychologist,* 1969, *24,* 606–607.

Wolpe, J. *Psychotherapy by reciprocal inhibition.* Stanford, Ca.: Stanford University Press, 1958.

Wolpe, J., & Rachman, S. Psychoanalytic "evidence": A critique based on Freud's case of Little Hans. *Journal of Nervous and Mental Diseases,* 1960, *130,* 135–148.

Yager, J. What happens when nothing you do matters? *Contemporary Psychology,* 1975, *20,* 921–922.

Yates, A. J. Symptoms and symptom substitution. *Psychological Review,* 1958, *65,* 371–374.

Yarrow, M. R., Schwartz, C. G., Murphy, H. S., & Deasy, L. C. The psychological meaning of mental illness in the family. *Journal of Social Issues,* 1955, *11,* 12–24.

Zeitlyn, B. B. The therapeutic community: Fact or fantasy? *International Journal of Psychiatry,* 1969, *7,* 195–200.

NAME index

subject index